Julius Caesar

Julius Caesar

Michael Grant

BARNES
&NOBLE
B O O K S
N E W   Y O R K

To Patrick and Antony Grant

1997 Barnes & Noble Books

ISBN 0-88029-752-2

Printed and bound in the United States of America

97 98 99 00 01 M 9 8 7 6 5 4 3

QF

Contents

List of Maps

Acknowledgments

I owe acknowledgments to the following for quotations: J. V. Cunningham, *New Mexico Quarterly Review* and The Swallow Press (Decimus Laberius), G. Highet, Routledge and Kegan Paul Ltd and Barnes and Noble Inc (O. Kiefer, *Sexual Life in Ancient Rome*, Lucan); J. Wight Duff, Ernest Benn Ltd and Barnes and Noble Inc (*A Literary History of Rome in the Silver Age*, Lucan); R. Graves and Penguin Books (*Suetonius: The Twelve Caesars*); P. Whigham and Penguin Books (*The Poems of Catullus*); Penguin Books (*Cicero: Selected Works*, ed. M. Grant).

MICHAEL GRANT

Table of Dates

BC 100   Birth of Caesar.

87   Nomination to priesthood of Jupiter.

84   Marriage to Cornelia.

80   Attachment to governor of Asia. Visit to Bithynia. Wins Civic Crown.

78   Attachment to governor of Cilicia.

77, 76   Speeches for prosecutions.

c. 76   Birth of daughter Julia.

75   Capture by pirates. Study at Rhodes.

73   Member of board of priests.

c. 72   Military service at Rome.

69   Funeral speeches for widow of Marius and for Cornelia.

69–68   Quaestor in Further Spain.

67   Marriage to Pompeia.

67–66   Speech or speeches in favour of Pompey's commands. Association with Crassus. Curator of the Appian Way.

65   *Curule aedile.*

63   Chief priest. Speech against death-penalty for supporters of Catiline.

62   Praetor. Divorce of Pompeia.

61–60   Governor of Further Spain.

60   First Triumvirate.

59   Consul. Marriage to Calpurnia. Marriage of Julia to
       Pompey.

58   Governor of Cisalpine Gaul, Narbonese Gaul and
       Illyricum. Campaigns against Helvetii and Ariovistus.
       Clodius tribune at Rome.

57   Campaign against Belgae (Nervii).

56   Triumvirate renewed at Luca. Campaign against Veneti.

55   Campaign against Usipetes and Tencteri. Crossing of
       Rhine. First expedition to Britain.

54   Second expedition to Britain. Disaster at Atuatuca. Death
       of Julia.

53   Campaign against Eburones. Crassus killed after disaster
       at Carrhae.

52   Pompey sole consul. Great Revolt of Vercingetorix
       defeated at Alesia.

51   Siege of Uxellodunum. End of Gallic War.

50   Curio tribune at Rome.

49   Civil War begins. Caesar occupies Italy. Battle of Ilerda.
       Nearer Spain won. Surrender of Massilia. First
       dictatorship of Caesar.

48   Pompey defeats Caesar at Dyrrhachium but is defeated at
       Pharsalus and murdered by Egyptians. Caesar's
       Alexandrian War.

47   Alexandrian War ends. Pharnaces defeated at Zela.

46   Sons of Pompey defeated at Thapsus (north Africa).
       Caesar dictator for ten years.

45   Sons of Pompey defeated at Munda (southern Spain).

44   Caesar perpetual dictator (February), murdered (March).

Foreword

A hundred years ago, Gaius Julius Caesar was variously described as the greatest man of action who has ever lived, the greatest man the earth has ever produced, and even as 'the entire and perfect man'. In an age like our own which has seen too much of men of action, enthusiasm on this particular score may have become somewhat muted. But it still remains impossible to think of anyone who has ever united a more spectacular and varied collection of talents.

He was an astute politician, a masterly propagandist and showman, a clever and effective administrator, an exceptionally gifted writer, a man of great and wide learning and taste, and a military genius who moved with terrifying speed and exercised magnetic authority over his troops. He possessed extraordinary personal charm, and was so successful with women that his ancient biographers often attributed to him the morals of the farmyard. But this was not wholly accurate, since there was a calculating element in his sex life that applied even to the famous affair with Cleopatra.

Indeed, shrewdness was an element that appeared in almost everything he did, except on the relatively few occasions—more frequent during his hurried last years of power—when impatience got the better of him. The calculations were very often concerned with money. His life could be seen as one continual exercise in the raising of funds.

He did not get much of a chance to massacre the British, but the campaigns in Gaul were filled with appalling and sickening brutalities, involving slaughter on a gigantic scale. This too was calculated, though it is questionable whether it effectively served its purpose of intimidation. At all events, in the civil wars that followed, an attempt was at last made to replace cruelty by clemency. This was again a deliberate policy, since now the enemies were no longer 'barbarians', whose slaughter (whatever humane current philosophies might say) was only objected to by eccentrics, but the fellow-Romans whose favour Caesar spent all his life in seeking.

In the end, he wooed them—or at least wooed the members of the governing class in vain, since he became the autocrat whom they could no longer endure. The pinnacle was reached by gradual stages, each leading inexorably to the next. Circumstances drove him from minor illegalities to major ones, and before long nothing could save him from eventual retribution except a despotism which would place him for ever beyond his enemies' reach.

The aristocratic Roman Republic, which had achieved such great things in the past, was staggering into dissolution. Summing up the whole past in his own person, Caesar forecast and foreshadowed the future by sweeping away the ruins and establishing the one-man rule which was afterwards perpetuated by the long succession of Roman emperors: the rulers who never stopped calling themselves 'Caesar', with Kaisers and Czars to come.

Among Julius Caesar's array of gifts was a startling capacity to work his will upon others. The governing groups which Caesar overcame and superseded were proud, brutal and dishonest, a strange mixture of legalism and violence, and Caesar was often as vicious as the worst of them. The time for romanticising his political autocracy is past. But our own changes of attitude seem to make it all the more excusable to add yet one more to the many attempts to weigh up against one another the extremes of good and bad which converged within this single man. For the effects of what he did reached immensely far and are with us still.

The Roman people had recently established throughout the Mediterranean area an imperial unity such as had never existed before and has never appeared again. And it was largely through his aggressions, atrocities and genocides that this multi-racial state became not only Mediterranean but continental as well, the ancestor of what we know as Europe. It seems unfair and disconcerting that the man who achieved all this should also have been a cultural figure of the first magnitude.

The later Republic possessed not only an unprecedentedly lavish material civilisation but a superb literary culture, by no means purely imitative of its masters in Greece. In this world Caesar could hold his own beside Cicero, Catullus and Lucretius. No one else, except perhaps Winston Churchill, has ever approached his achievement of writing so brilliantly about world events that had been dominated by himself.

I am very grateful to my wife for all her help with this book. I also want to thank Mr. Michael Raeburn, Mr. Alan Kendall and Miss Susan Phillpott of Messrs Weidenfeld and Nicolson for producing the original volume, and Mr. John J. Kelly for this new edition.

Julius Caesar

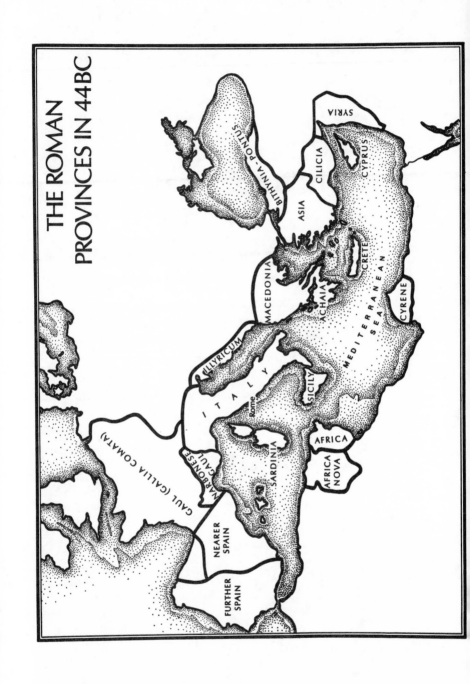

THE ROMAN
PROVINCES IN 44BC

FURTHER
SPAIN

NEARER
SPAIN

GAUL (GALLIA COMATA)

NARBONESE
GAUL

SARDINIA

ITALY

Rome

SICILY

AFRICA
NOVA

AFRICA

ILLYRICUM

MACEDONIA

ACHAIA

CRETE

MEDITERRANEAN
SEA

CYRENE

BITHYNIA-PONTUS

ASIA

CILICIA

SYRIA

CYPRUS

CHAPTER ONE

Rome and the Young Caesar

*T*he modest house where Caesar was born, in the noisy, teeming quarter of the Subura, was only a short distance from the Forum, the centre of Roman public life.

The principal officials of the state were the two consuls, elected to serve for a single year. To hold this office was the supreme honour available to a citizen, and for centuries the public life of Rome had been directed by the inner circle of men whose ancestors had included consuls. 'Nobility' meant this consular ancestry, and the nobles, although often both versatile and able, were among the toughest and greediest potentates the civilised world had ever seen. The leading families, exploiting their traditional flair for government and power politics, dominated the elections and the financial and foreign affairs of Rome. Their methods included bribery, lavish popular entertainments, ruthless marriage alliances, and armies of hangers-on who could be seen crowding round the great men in their homes and the Forum every day. There was an intimate, far-reaching system of mutual dependence between the patrons and their clients, who could also provide the strong-arm methods which their bosses, dangerously combining Mediterranean temperament and Prussian drive, often needed to combat the violence and treachery that surrounded them.

The senate was the place where they chiefly exercised their power, and within the senate immense authority rested with the inmost nucleus of ex-consuls. These 'consulars' might dispute among themselves; but they generally stood firm against outsiders. They and the other nobles tended, with notable exceptions, to be conservatives, 'good men' as they called themselves, bent on upholding the status quo, private property, and the prestige of their own senate, which, although its decrees were technically only advice and not law, basked in the radiance of a potent antique tradition.

Its decrees possessed this advisory character because the lawgiving body was the assembly of the Roman people, which also elected the principal officials of the state. Yet this was very far removed from a representative democracy. A good many Italians, the majority of them belonging to cities with full Roman status, officially possessed the vote. But only a fraction of them ever had the physical opportunity to exercise the right to use it; besides, a cumbersome system of group voting lent itself to every possible abuse. These abuses were directed by the nobles. The Romans were a legalistic people, and elections had to take place in due form, but in the final years of the Republic they were distorted and corrupted by the same formidable cabals that controlled the workings of the senate.

During the third and second centuries BC this crazy, creaking structure had conquered huge areas around the Mediterranean Sea. At the time when Caesar was born, the empire consisted of Italy (which at that time roughly extended to the Apennines), its annex of Cisalpine Gaul (north Italy), and the provinces of Sicily, Sardinia-Corsica, Narbonese Gaul (southern France), Nearer and Further Spain, Macedonia and Achaia (Greece), Illyricum (the coast of Yugoslavia, sometimes attached to Macedonia and sometimes to Cisalpine Gaul), Cilicia (a ring of coastguard stations in southeastern Anatolia), and the pre-eminently wealthy provinces of Africa (Tunisia) and Asia (western Anatolia). The acquisition of these two outstanding dominions in 146 and 133 BC destroyed the old character of Rome as extended city-state or an Italian federation. But very few of the metropolitan politicians felt any responsibility for empire. The provinces were lucrative perquisites in the unceasing, engrossing struggles for power at Rome, and it was useful to mobilise provincials as allies in those struggles.

For a long time political parties did not exist. By means of ferocious feuds and grim bargaining the nobles gathered to their support whatever social and economic groups they could, operating in conflicting, shifting gangs which expanded and disintegrated round energetic men. Yet in the later Republic these groups were tentatively approaching a merger stage in which two main tendencies were represented. Although it is often difficult to detect consistent principles, one of these trends was pro-senatorial, conservative and often reactionary, and the other favoured the method of appealing over the heads of the senate to the assembly of the people. Politicians inclined to adopt this latter technique were consequently called the people's men (*populares*), though their 'popular' interest was not in democracy but in getting their own way. Meaningless slogans and credibility gaps featured on both sides, but they were phrased in different terms.

The rough division between the groups of nobles favouring these types of approach first became apparent in the 130s and 120s BC when two young nobles, Tiberius and Gaius Gracchus, failed to secure senatorial support for their land reforms and went straight to the assembly instead. Both brothers met their deaths in riots, and a century of political violence had begun. The changing times assumed sinister significance in another way when Marius, a man of middle-class Italian origins who had risen to military glory in spite of senatorial opposition, hastened the development of Roman professional armies, which soon began to look to their generals rather than the state for their rewards.

In 90–89 an unprecedented civil war broke out when many communities in Italy—those that did not possess full Roman privileges and the vote—rebelled against their continued exclusion, which they blamed on short-sighted diehards. Rome, though not defeated in the war, had to concede their request, but there followed prolonged and bloodthirsty civil wars between the anti-conservative, 'popular' Marius, supported and succeeded by Cinna, and the patrician Sulla—who, after his two enemies were dead, won a decisive victory over their followers. Sulla assumed the ancient emergency office of dictator, and held it, not for the normal duration of six months, but for more than a year. Then he abdicated. But before taking this step, he tried to revive the shattered senatorial system by a host of measures which artificially safeguarded conservative control.

The first idea that came to the young Caesar's parents about his career, when he was thirteen, was based on ancient religious traditions that were strong in the Julian family. These inspired them to form the plan that he should occupy the priesthood of the supreme Roman deity, Jupiter. This post possessed great social distinction, retaining vestiges of the remotest antiquity. Yet in retrospect Caesar's appointment would have been a strange twist of destiny, since the office was hedged around with a mass of extraordinary, archaic taboos. They are a treasure-house for modern anthropologists, but at the time they meant that the holder of the priesthood was limited to a single wife as long as he lived (which would not have suited Caesar, or other leading Romans either), and that he could scarcely engage in any public life at all—he must not only do no work, but must see no work done! However, Caesar's inauguration had to wait until he was older and meanwhile his life was not uneventful.

When he was fifteen, his father died at Pisa. He had served as praetor, the second most important post after the consuls, and had achieved the governorship of Asia, but had never been elected as a consul. Since, however, he had consuls among his ancestors, the family was noble. But it was more than this, for it also belonged to that select list of particularly blue-blooded clans which were known as patrician. There are various interpretations of the cognomen *Caesar*: perhaps an early member of the family had been cut out of the womb (*caesus*) (the term 'Caesarian section' arises from the legend that this is how Julius Caesar was born). Like a number of similar houses, the Julii had declined and lost contact with the main centres of power, since they lacked the huge funds necessary for grand careers, which therefore went to the wealthy non-patrician (plebeian) families instead. Caesar's two sisters both made respectable though not brilliant marriages, but in his own case it now proved possible to play the family's strongest card. This was the fact that the sister of Caesar's father had married the outstanding man of her day, the farouche and terrifying Marius, who, although politically a child and a bloodthirsty child at that, achieved immense fame as a military genius. Marius was now dead, but his supporter and successor, Cinna, retained the link with the Julian house. Caesar was already married, or possibly only engaged, to a girl called Cossutia, whose family, although rich, was of no great political or social importance. But the wife of the priest of Jupiter had to be a patrician, which Cossutia was not; and divorces for political reasons, almost always initiated by the man, were extremely frequent. Accordingly, the young man now married Cinna's own daughter Cornelia (84). Cinna's motive was evidently to forge a friendship with the house of Caesar's mother, Aurelia, whose three male cousins, the Aurelius Cottas, were liberal nobles of unusual calibre who could be relied upon to oppose Cinna's arch-enemy, Sulla.

This favourable prospect deteriorated sharply when Cinna was almost at once assassinated; and then two years later Sulla became dictator at Rome (81). His condition for Caesar's continued welfare was that he should divorce Cinna's daughter and marry a wife who was politically acceptable to himself. This was a sign of goodwill, and contemporaries such as Pompey who had received the same request were complying. Yet Caesar rejected the overture. Did he do this because he loved Cornelia? Since he was a young bridegroom this may have been at least part of his motive. But it is not possible to think of any other political disadvantage, throughout his whole life, that he ever incurred for the love of a woman. Yet was his refusal of the offer really so disadvantageous? Caesar, at nineteen, must already have possessed some of his later political discernment, and he may have calculated that Sulla would not last and that the other side, in the long run, could be a better investment.

If so, this was a considerable risk to take with the frighteningly savage dictator, and it only narrowly paid off. Caesar was deprived of his wife's dowry and the prospect of her future legacies, and found himself debarred from the priesthood of Jupiter to which he had been nominated. Moreover, he thought it wise to disappear into hiding until his mother's family and the influential priestly college of the Vestal Virgins, who tended the hallowed sacred fire, intervened on his behalf. Sulla let the matter drop, but Caesar had to undergo the paralysing experience of a personal interview with him. The glaring and blotchy-faced dictator commented unfavourably on the young man's appearance, for he was altogether too eccentric in his clothes, affecting a loose belt round his waist, and fringed sleeves reaching to the wrist. He also behaved rather fussily about his coiffure, and liked to have superfluous hair plucked out. He was a fairly tall, though rather slight, youth, with a clear complexion and lively dark eyes.

It seemed highly advisable to get him out of Sulla's sight, and so it was arranged that he should sail off to western Anatolia to join the staff of the governor of Asia. There, as a senator's son, he was given a fairly responsible mission to Bithynia, a state to the north of the province that had ostensibly remained independent but was in fact a client of Rome. His duty there was to collect and bring back some ships that were required for the tail-end of a war against Rome's notorious enemy, Mithridates of Pontus. King Nicomedes IV of Bithynia, a cultured but murderous Greco-Asiatic with a long record of not always very willing collaboration with Rome, was deeply impressed by Caesar's charms, and apparently entered upon a homosexual relationship with him. Or so gossips and political enemies continued to say, with many coarse variations, for the next thirty years and more. In any event, when a visiting Roman business mission came to dinner with the monarch, they found Caesar among a group of effeminate young men who were playing the part of royal cup-bearers. Caesar evidently enjoyed his visit, because soon after he had left he found an excuse to go back to Bithynia again; and even much later in his life he spoke up in various causes affecting its royal house. Young Roman nobles habitually went to bed with men as well as girls, and probably the king was a dominant influence on Caesar's early life, and helped to give him a more cosmopolitan outlook than most Romans of his class possessed.

His next activity was of a very different nature, for in a minor military operation at Mytilene (Lesbos) he won the oak-wreath or Civic Crown. That was an extremely distinguished decoration, but at this epoch it was sometimes awarded for frivolous reasons, and we do not know what Caesar did to earn it: but quite possibly he performed some act of gallantry. He then moved on to south-eastern Anatolia (Cilicia), in order to serve for a brief period on the staff of a governor who was conducting operations against pirates infesting the area. But there Caesar heard that Sulla was dead, and he decided to return immediately to Rome (78). When, however, a certain Marcus Lepidus led a movement against Sulla's conservative reforms, no doubt seeking to attract supporters for the 'popular' Marian line, Caesar, for all his allegiance to Marius, rightly made up his mind that the agitation was premature and doomed to failure, and refused to have anything to do with it.

Instead he embarked on a normal activity for young men in their twenties, the launching of prosecutions in the law-courts. The entire education of an upper-class Roman boy centred upon public life and oratory, and Caesar had been well educated by a former slave, Antonius Gnipho, a mild and easy man unconcerned with remuneration, whose training at Alexandria and Rome had made him a master of Greek and Latin rhetoric. Caesar wrote

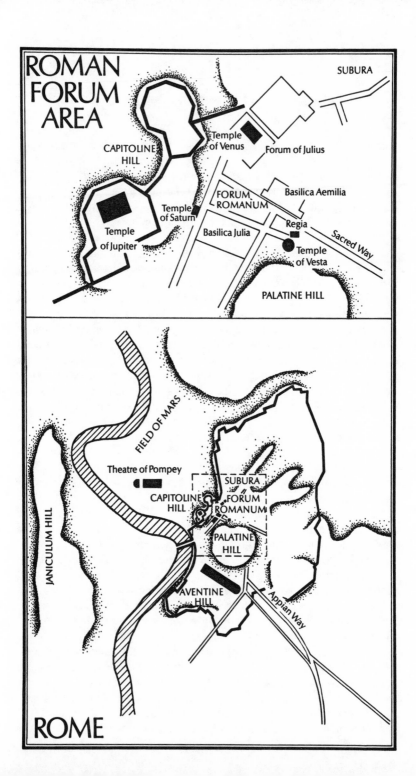

ROMAN FORUM AREA

SUBURA

CAPITOLINE HILL

Temple of Venus

Forum of Julius

Temple of Jupiter

Temple of Saturn

FORUM ROMANUM

Basilica Aemilia

Basilica Julia

Regia

Temple of Vesta

Sacred Way

PALATINE HILL

FIELD OF MARS

Theatre of Pompey

JANICULUM HILL

SUBURA

CAPITOLINE HILL

FORUM ROMANUM

PALATINE HILL

AVENTINE HILL

Appian Way

ROME

verses and he also developed a highly effective style of public speaking, using a pure, plain language and a somewhat high-pitched delivery accompanied by vigorous gesticulation.

These accusations undertaken by political aspirants tended to fasten on former provincial governors, whose conduct, indeed, all too often made them vulnerable to charges of extortion or embezzlement or even treason. The ulterior purpose of such prosecutions was to avenge personal wrongs or eliminate rivals, and they provided a favourite way for pushing young men to make themselves known and advance their fortunes. In 67, for example, the accuser of Marcus Cotta, a cousin of Caesar's mother, was rewarded with the convicted man's consular honours though he was only a tribune. That was the sort of thing that Caesar was aiming at when he charged a senior nobleman, Cnaeus Dolabella, with extortion from the Macedonians he had governed (77). But the move was useful for two other reasons as well. It was calculated to make the prosecutor provincial friends, who would be bound to be useful in the future; and it indicted a man known for his support of Sulla against Caesar's uncle, Marius. Dolabella, who retorted with unkind comments about his accuser's relations with the king of Bithynia, was acquitted. But Caesar published his speech, and it enhanced his reputation. So did a second prosecution in the following year, directed against a particularly notorious agent of Sulla, Gaius Antonius Hybrida, who had mercilessly plundered the Greeks. The enquiry, conducted by a praetor, came to nothing, but Caesar, who had again spoken well, made some more provincial friends.

He had not done badly, in a minor way, but his public speaking could still do with improvement, and he therefore announced his intention of going to study on the island of Rhodes. His professor there was to be the famous Greek rhetorician Apollonius Molon, whose lectures had already been attended by Cicero, six years Caesar's senior and the outstanding young orator of the day. On the way Caesar found time to deal with affairs in Bithynia, where his friend Nicomedes had just died; Rome, in accordance with his will, was annexing the country so that there were profits to be had. Off the coast of Anatolia he was kidnapped by the pirates of whose threats to Mediterranean security and trade he already had some experience. When they demanded a heavy ransom he compelled the local communities to raise the sum, and then, on his own private initiative, turned on the pirates and captured a substantial number of them. Having failed to arrange for their execution by the governor of Asia, who may have benefited from their activities, he himself, without any authority, had them crucified. He then intervened, again on his own account, against Mithridates of Pontus, with whom war had just broken out for the third time owing to his rejection of Rome's annexation of his Bithynian neighbours. Caesar's two years in the east concluded with a brief period of attachment to a Roman official who was attempting to deal with the pirate menace. The willowy and affected youth of a short time ago had become, at the age of twenty-six, a hardened seafarer who had crossed to Anatolia four times in the past seven years. He had also become an adventurous skirmisher capable of decisions that seemed astonishingly independent of his seniors.

He returned to Rome in 73, on hearing of the death of his mother's cousin, Gaius Cotta, whose seat on the board of priests he now managed to obtain for himself. These priests (*pontifices*) were all nobles, mostly men of considerable grandeur, and since official acts had to be accompanied by religious observances, membership of the board was a political advantage. Caesar's prosecution of noble ex-governors a few years previously does not seem to have made their peers condemn him as an opponent of the régime which Sulla had bolstered up in their favour. Yet now he again showed his hostility to that system by keenly supporting a move to rescind an important part of Sulla's fabric. This related to the tribunes of the people, whose ancient office traditionally enabled them to veto proposals made by officials of any rank. A tribune's doors were never locked, and any member of the people could appeal to him by day or night against any alleged public injustice. However, these ancient ombudsmen had long been brought under control by the senate, until the Gracchi resuscitated their powers in order to attack conservative obstruction. However, the two young men had both died violent deaths, and so in 100 did Saturninus, who had schemes for giving the tribunes almost dictatorial authority. Sulla, intent on re-establishing senatorial control, had decided to reduce the tribunate to complete impotence, restricting its executive and judicial powers, severely limiting its right of veto, and above all enacting that its occupants would be permanently disqualified from other offices. Two years before his death Gaius Cotta, a skillful negotiator, had the last provision rescinded—the first legal and accepted retreat from Sulla's constitution—and two years later Caesar himself supported a move to revive the other rights that the tribunes had lost. In 70 the process was completed. Meanwhile, Caesar had been occupied in a short spell of official military service, a prerequisite for a political career. When it was over he spoke in favour of a measure granting an amnesty to anti-Sullans who were living in banishment. In this speech, the first he ever delivered before the assembly, Caesar stressed his particular obligation to strive towards the recall of his wife's brother, who was one of the exiles concerned. At about the same time, perhaps, he made a speech defending an Italian who had been a victim of Sulla's proscriptions.

The Marian, anti-conservative trend of this young politician soon became even clearer. For when his aunt, who was the widow of Marius himself, died in 69, it was Caesar who delivered the oration at her public funeral. Moreover, in contravention of an order by Sulla, effigies of Marius and his son were carried in the procession. Caesar characteristically combined this affront to the conservatives by recalling that he could outbid them all in pedigree, for his address also emphasised two immensely grandiose family traditions, the first claiming that the Julii were descended from the goddess Venus herself, and the second asserting that the genealogy of the dead woman's mother went back to a Roman king of legendary antiquity, Ancus Marcius. Immediately afterwards, Caesar reverted to the 'popular', Marian link again when another member of his family died. This was his own wife Cornelia, who had borne him a daughter Julia, probably the only child he ever had. Women who died so young were not usually accorded public obituary speeches, but Caesar honoured her in this way, and his moving words made a strong impression. He cannot have failed to exploit the occasion by including laudatory references to her father Cinna, the ally and associate of Marius.

At this time Caesar had just been appointed to the junior position of quaestor. Since the time of Sulla there were twenty holders of these posts, which like others of greater seniority were elected annually; the office, tenable at the age of thirty, carried with it admission to the senate. At home, quaestors were custodians of the state treasury, and abroad they assisted provincial governors. Caesar did not obtain one of the more distinguished metropolitan appointments, but was assigned to the governorship of Further Spain. In this considerably Romanised area, based on the Guadalquivir valley, his main duty was to administer justice. In tasks of that kind a young politician could find many opportunities to create debts of gratitude useful for his future public life. Caesar also learnt much about an outstanding figure of the previous decade, Sertorius, who had revolted from the conservatives at Rome and kept the Marian cause alive in Spain until only four years previously. He had a powerful imagination and magnetic personality, and rare gifts of military leadership and of sudden disconcerting activity which may well have awakened a response in Caesar's heart.

Nevertheless, he was anxious to return to the hub of the Roman world—so anxious that, having barely served his year, he left the province before the governor himself. On his return journey Caesar stopped in Cisalpine Gaul, the area that is now north Italy but did not at that time form part of the homeland, having first been a sort of indeterminate annex to the peninsula and then for the past twenty years a Roman province. Its cities south of the river Po had Roman citizen rights like those which the whole of Italy itself now enjoyed, but to the north of the river only two townships, Aquileia and Cremona, were in possession of this privilege. The rest of the Transpadane area had stopped at the intermediate status of Latin rights, which meant that only the municipal officials and councillors were Roman

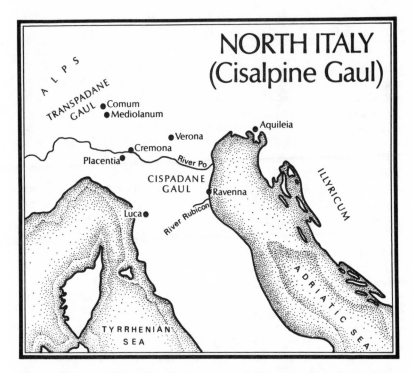

NORTH ITALY (Cisalpine Gaul)

ALPS

TRANSPADANE GAUL

Comum
Mediolanum

Verona

Aquileia

Cremona

Placentia

River Po

CISPADANE GAUL

Ravenna

ILLYRICUM

Luca

River Rubicon

ADRIATIC SEA

TYRRHENIAN SEA

citizens. This inequality caused resentment, since the region, for all its extraordinary mixture of races, was highly Romanised, populous and wealthy. Accordingly, Roman politicians vied with one another for the credit of securing it full rights, and Caesar, too, on his way back from Spain, exploited the unrest in the hope of securing grateful clients in this vital area. Indeed he agitated so vigorously that two legions destined for the east were held back in Italy by the government, which thus bestowed a considerable compliment upon his rising nuisance-value.

When Caesar returned to Rome he married a woman called Pompeia: her dowry was needed because political promotion without money was impossible. She was scarcely related, if at all, to Caesar's older contemporary, Pompey, but her grandfathers had been Sulla and a consul who was one of his followers. Caesar, although supporting Marian causes, still found it convenient to have a foot in the other camp. Pompeia's feelings are not recorded, but if gossip spoke correctly (and it is so unanimous that we must assume, allowing for exaggeration, that it did) Caesar was, even for his time and place, a husband of quite exceptional infidelity. Whatever the truth about his homosexual past, he now pursued an extraordinary number of liaisons with women. His lifelong mistress and friend was Servilia, a rapacious, ambitious patrician at the centre of a great family network of political intrigue. Caesar's mistresses served him as invaluable sources of information and instruments for advancement. It was said that he had affairs with the wives both of

Pompey and Crassus. Whether this was true or not, the existence of the story shows how much trouble he took to be friendly with the women of the two most important politicians in Rome—during the next seven years his role remained strictly subordinate to theirs.

CHAPTER TWO

Under the Shadow of Pompey and Crassus

*P*ompey, six years older than Caesar, had so far had an infinitely more brilliant career. He inherited great personal power and a tradition of violence from his father, a cruel, avaricious, treacherous consul who built up a feudal following in his native Picenum (Marche) and served Sulla as one of his principal generals. Pompey's own youth showed precocious disregard for tradition and human life. As a major commander already in his mid-twenties, he was difficult for even Sulla to deal with, and after the dictator's death he suppressed first the Marian rebellion of Sertorius in Spain, and then the Italian slave-revolt of Spartacus (71).

On becoming consul with Crassus in the following year, at an age well below the statutory limit, he revealed his contempt for the conservative heritage of Sulla by sponsoring the restoration of tribunes' rights which had been initiated by Caesar's kinsman, Gaius Cotta. Then this prodigy was offered the chance of seeking even more sensational laurels. His opportunity was the scandalous disruption of the Mediterranean by pirates, who, operating in collusion with Rome's enemy Mithridates, not only kidnapped Roman officials of exalted birth such as Caesar, but held the whole empire to ransom. Already eight years earlier Gaius Cotta had been obliged to apologise to the people of Rome for the shortage of food owing to their lootings; and since then they had sacked the Aegean commercial centre of Delos, and had even dared to raid the coasts of Italy right up to Ostia at the mouth of the Tiber itself. The tribune Aulus Gabinius, who came from Picenum like Pompey, now proposed that in order to enable the menace to be dealt with once and for all a far-reaching command should be conferred on his compatriot. Since it became clear that the senators were far too suspicious of Pompey's radical or even possibly autocratic intentions ever to agree, Gabinius reverted to the very essence of 'popular' Marian politics by ignoring the senate altogether and placing the bill directly before the assembly of the people.

There every senator who spoke attacked the proposal violently, except Caesar, who made himself highly conspicuous by enthusiastically taking the opposite line. Not only was the measure a sensible one, but it also provided a chance to hit out at the conservatives who had done well out of Sulla. Besides, one of the numerous women with whom Caesar maintained intimate relations was Gabinius' wife. Most important of all, Pompey was the man to help his career, which might well, later on, need special quasi-imperial commands of just the same sort. Caesar's action was also a bid for the support of the knights, those powerful financiers and businessmen outside the senate, men like Cicero's correspondent Atticus—who preferred secret power and solid profit to public office. These knights by definition possessed a minimum capital of twenty thousand pounds, and had become a strong independent force in the successive crises that were racking the state from the second century BC onwards. The interests of the two classes often blurred and overlapped, but Gaius Gracchus had perpetuated the friction by enacting that knights should supersede senators on the lucrative and influential jury panels of the courts. Sulla, on behalf of the nobles, reserved this decision, but in 70, with the support of Pompey and Crassus, Lucius Cotta (Gaius' brother) had given them back a substantial share—one-third of the membership of the panels; in effect, two-thirds, since another third went to a class resembling the knights but possessing a lower property qualification. (The remaining third stayed with the senators.) Now these financiers, who wanted safe maritime trading, disagreed with the senate, and supported the move by Gabinius and Caesar to give Pompey the appointment.

The bill was passed, and after he had dealt with the pirates in a lightning three-month campaign Pompey received an even more important commission to deal with Mithridates of Pontus, who remained wholly unconquered after more than twenty years, and was still spreading ruin to Roman security and commerce throughout the whole of vital Anatolia. The conservatives bitterly opposed the appointment, since it meant the eclipse of their own nominee, Lucullus, whose initial successes had petered out in mutinies. But Cicero, who boasted no consuls as ancestors but had made his name in a sensational case against a noble governor four years earlier, spoke successfully in favour of this new command; and Caesar may well have spoken for it too. The law was certain to be passed, and it was better to gain Pompey's favour than to offend him.

Besides, it would be convenient to have him out of the way for a few years, for Caesar found it awkward that Pompey was so unfriendly with Crassus, the other principal statesman of the day. They had co-operated as joint consuls in 70, but Crassus continued to resent the way in which Pompey, first in Sulla's Italian campaign and then in the slave war, had contrived to get the credit for operations of which he himself had borne the principal burden. Also, Caesar needed to keep in with Crassus, who at this stage was far richer than Pompey. Crassus was a courteous, affable, crafty man, whose political ambitions were hampered by defective qualities of leadership, which he sought to make up for by money. His financial flair was enormous. Although a law forbade senators to take part in commercial enterprises, they were allowed to lend money and invest capital in land, and by such means and others Crassus' fortune rose from £350,000 to over £10,000,000; he maintained that nobody should be called leader who could not maintain an army on his income. There were many stories about his astute speculations. When properties were burning down, he bought them up cheap and then put out the fires. When he was accused of seducing a Vestal Virgin, all he was really doing, during their long tête-à-têtes, was to try and buy land from her at less than the proper price. Politically, he belonged to the middle of the road. He found husbands of superb pedigree for his daughters; and yet, against the interests of the nobles, he was ready to help Pompey restore the tribunes and favoured the knights on whom he depended for his financial operations. Now Pompey was away, and Crassus' intentions, though always concealed beneath a mysterious smoke-screen, seem to have been directed towards the further building up of his own power without overtly breaking with Pompey, who might be needed when he eventually came back.

Crassus made a fine art of working through others, and he was prepared to invest huge sums in order to further the career of a promising, ambitious, youngish politician who needed such help and could help him in return. Caesar was all of these things: and he was also desperately impoverished. The cost of public life was at this time prohibitive. Political costs had become astronomical, grand houses had to be maintained, and the population of Rome must be entertained with big shows. Everything had become more and more competitive and expensive, and the unavoidable outlays of bribery were varied and vast. The only hope of recovery was to gain office at Rome and pass from there to a provincial governorship, which even if it only lasted for a year brought gigantic opportunities of legal, quasi-legal or wholly illegal gain. The risks of prosecution were great, but they could be dealt with when the time came, if necessary by disbursing a portion of the loot. Meanwhile the current dangers of poverty were more pressing, for poverty necessitated the borrowing of money, and the laws regulating repayment were, as in every ancient society, ruinously harsh.

Caesar had started with modest means which needed to be multiplied many times over before a really successful public career became even conceivable. He was also remarkably extravagant, partly because he liked to be, and partly because it was not wise to look hard pressed. He was a passionate art collector, and enjoyed buying attractive slaves. As early as the seventies he had built himself an expensive country mansion on Lake Nemi, but then, discontented with the house, he had at once had it pulled down again. By the end of that decade it was rumoured that he was seriously in debt; and now since five more years had passed—and the pickings of a quaestorship in Spain were small—the sum had probably become a good deal larger. And yet this was the time when funds were really needed, because it had become imperative, if any of his ambitions were to be realised, to pursue official promotion at home.

So Caesar spent the next few years as Crassus' pensioner. In response for good services, the financier rode his agents on a very loose rein. Caesar found it possible to become curator of the Appian Way, the road from Rome to Capua, which he restored at his own or rather Crassus' expense, thus earning valuable obligations of gratitude from municipalities along the road. Then, in 65, he became curule aedile. This metropolitan post was concerned with the prosaic supervision of public order and buildings, but its importance lay in opportunities to win popularity by organising theatrical and gladiatorial games and beast hunts. Caesar, with Crassus' help, was able to supplement the statutory twenty-two days of these entertainments by a highly spectacular series of gladiatorial duels in honour of his long-dead father. The senate, alarmed, hastily decreed a limitation in the numbers of gladiators who could be employed, but even so Caesar's three hundred and twenty pairs of combatants, decked out in silver, were easily a record. He had revealed an important aspect of his personality—his unusual talents as a showman and self-advertiser. He completely stole the thunder from the ill-tempered and protesting conservative, Bibulus, who was his fellow-aedile and had added his own contribution to Crassus' funds. These distasteful displays won Caesar a great many votes in the years that lay ahead. In order to point the moral, he carried people's minds back to the funeral demonstrations of four years earlier by arranging that the trophies of Marius' victories, which Sulla had removed, should be re-erected in the Forum. But the respected leader of the right wing, Catulus, was far from pleased. He could scarcely be expected to be, since Marius had murdered his father; and he himself felt a marked distaste for Caesar's new patron, Crassus. As for Caesar, Catulus remarked that the period in which he had been undermining the Republic in secrecy had come to an end—he was now quite openly bringing up siege machines for its destruction. In return, Catulus became one of the two men whom Caesar disliked more than anyone else throughout his life (the other was to be Cato).

Crassus also launched, with Caesar's help, a number of political balloons that achieved no immediate success. For example, he showed sympathy with the Transpadanes' grievances which Caesar had begun to exploit a few years previously. He also made a tentative move to get his hands upon the wealth of the quasi-independent state of Egypt, which had ostensibly been left to Rome by one of its kings sixteen years earlier, but had not actually been annexed. Perhaps he intended to use Caesar for this move. In any case, conservative opposition, now supported by Cicero who was hoping for a consulship, ensured that the idea came to nothing. Crassus and Caesar also saw opportunities in a far-reaching land-law brought forward by a tribune named Rullus in December 64. Again Cicero blocked action, but Caesar had noted for further reference Rullus' scheme to appoint an all-powerful commission which would distribute among rural districts some of the city's vast proletariat of impoverished, parasitic idlers. Cicero liked to represent such issues as dismal defeats for Crassus and Caesar; but it was not expected that everything would succeed the first time, and the proposals had gained them friends, caused disarray among their enemies, and prepared the way for action later on. Nor did these apparent set-backs hinder Caesar's climb up the political ladder. On the contrary, his progress now continued with a good deal more speed than before.

In the early months of 63 he scored the greatest success he had achieved during the thirty-seven years of his not yet very distinguished life. For he was now elected to the vacant office of chief priest of the Roman state—*pontifex maximus*, the title that survived paganism to become the appellation of the Popes. This chief priesthood, which was reserved for nobles, constituted a special sort of post, tenable not for a year like the other major offices of state, but for life, and bestowed not on a pair or group of colleagues, but on a single man. Its occupant, although in no way debarred from holding other appointments, was the head of the state clergy and possessed authority to decide questions of sacred law. Since, at Rome, these were so closely intermingled with politics, the chief priesthood was a considerable factor in political success and a channel of patronage.

The startling feature of Caesar's appointment was that he easily defeated two other candidates of far greater seniority. One of them was the governor under whom Caesar had served in Cilicia fifteen years ago, and the other was the outstanding conservative, Catulus, who had sharply criticised Caesar's honours to Marius two years earlier. Both these men owed all their early advancement to Sulla, so that the election of Caesar was a striking success for his Marian affiliations. But, as on earlier occasions, he combined this 'popular' cause with a snobbish appeal based on the antiquity of his house. None of his rivals could boast the distinct advantage of an ancestor who had held the same office, and Caesar repeated or invented the story that his remote and mythical forebear Iulus, the founder of the Julian house, had been chief priest of Rome's parent city, Alba Longa. Such a fiction would not be treated with undue scepticism by the Romans of the day, among whom ancient patriotic tales were strongly in fashion; and no doubt the fable played a part in Caesar's victory. He recaptured the office for a patrician from the plebeian nobility for the first time for nearly seventy years.

Chief priests were rather curiously appointed, by a vote of seventeen out of thirty-five electoral groups (tribes) of the assembly. Caesar's financial inducements to the potential voters outbid Catulus, who attempted to bribe him to withdraw and thus imprudently disclosed how far he could afford to go. Caesar's investment in his candidature, no doubt mainly provided by Crassus, was so heavy that on leaving his home for the election he warned his mother not to expect him back at all unless he won, since if he lost he would be forced to leave the country. His gamble was a rash one, since even success would scarcely rescue his finances, whereas failure would have been catastrophic. However, he emerged as the winner. Victory meant a change of abode, since he now moved from his family home in the cramped Subura into the official residence. This imposing house, in which he continued to live for the rest of his life, adjoined the chief priest's office and archives (Regia), and was linked with the sacred precinct of Vesta which was tended by the Vestal Virgins.

Caesar disbelieved totally in religion, but keenly carried on his family's expertise in its rituals and traditions, and, as his myth of Iulus suggests, fully shared the contemporary interest in primitive national religious institutions, which was to culminate during the next generation in the patriotic epic of Virgil. Moreover, like other Romans and Greeks before him, he was thoroughly alive to the possibilities of exploiting the state cults for political purposes. The idea of Marx that religion was an opiate for the masses was nothing new: the politicians of Rome were glad to use it for the purpose.

Caesar very soon displayed his antiquarian virtuosity in another field, when he staged an elaborate legal charade against an old man called Rabirius. As long ago as the year of Caesar's birth, Rabirius had been allegedly implicated in the murder of the unpleasant anti-conservative politician, Saturninus. Public attention to the matter was now revived, because the riot in which Saturninus was killed had been encouraged by an emergency decree of the senate. These decrees, which were a controversial feature of the later second century BC, merely instructed state officials to take 'whatever measures were necessary' to preserve the state, urging them to strengthen their determination and not to neglect their business. Their actual legal powers, then, were not increased by such a decree; and yet the result could be that men were killed without the trial and appeal to the people to which, as citizens, they were entitled. The fate of Saturninus was ancient history, but politicians of the 'popular' persuasion felt it useful to demonstrate the hysterical abuse which such decrees could bring about, in the hope of preventing their revival as a weapon of conservative power. And so Rabirius was now prosecuted for this long-past offence. His capable accuser, the tribune Titus Labienus, was already suspected of having arranged legal adjustments which had facilitated Caesar's candidature for the chief priesthood. In the case of Rabirius, the lot which appointed the two judges fell by a suspicious coincidence upon Caesar and one of his relations, who proceeded to dig out of the files an archaic high-treason procedure with gruesome penalties. The case, defended by Cicero, went from senate to assembly, where the hearing was suddenly terminated by the flying of a flag on the Janiculum hill, which by a tradition obsolete for many centuries signified that an Etruscan invader was approaching!

Probably the clue to this masquerade lay in the origins of Labienus. He came from Picenum and was a firm partisan of Pompey, who had inherited many supporters in the area. This warning demonstration against the conservatives, then, seems to have been directed by the absent Pompey, with the co-operation of Caesar and Labienus. But they were not interested in having the old Rabirius actually executed, and the flag was hauled up with the collusion of the responsible official, the city praetor, Metellus Celer—'seashore and void and airy waste', Cicero called him—who had likewise been an officer of Pompey in the east. Ever since 120 BC the dominant pressure group in the senate had been provided by the immensely powerful, prolific and wealthy family of the Caecilii Metelli, not patrician but plebeian, yet the strongest of all the noble houses. By intermarriage and other means they had raised up first Sulla and then Pompey, thus showing that they were more concerned with opportunist alliances, however risky, than with truly supporting the precarious Republican fabric of the state.

In the case of Rabirius, then, Caesar was working with Pompey, feeling he had to keep in with the man whose eastern conquests, now approaching their completion, made him far the greatest figure in the state. But he and Caesar's other senior partner, Crassus, got on so badly with one another that Caesar was relieved to win a little more independence by securing election for 62 to a praetorship. The annual holders of this office were eight in number, and served as judges in various lawcourts. But more important was the entitlement of every praetor, after his year of office, to be appointed as governor of a province, with all the consequent opportunities for profit. In his praetorship, therefore, and in the governorship that would follow, Caesar saw perhaps the only chance of paying off his debts and becoming a power in his own right, independent of Pompey who overshadowed everything from the east, and of Crassus who was dominant at Rome.

Such an increase in independence was especially desirable because a major internal political crisis was now brewing in the capital—and it was one which severely tested Caesar's diplomatic gifts. This was the conspiracy of Catiline, a ruinously debt-ridden patrician of dangerously unstable character but considerable magnetic charm, to which aristocratic women and youths were as susceptible as proletarians. His record as Sulla's agent was murky, his governorship of Africa disgraceful enough to have warranted prosecution; and his name had been associated with an alleged plot to murder the consuls of 65 and replace them by a shady pair who had been unseated for excessive bribery. What part, if any, Catiline played in this incident is obscure. Pompey may have had something to do with it, because one of the unseated consuls was his brother-in-law, but rumours that Crassus and Caesar were involved can be discarded since Crassus did not want to start a massacre, which would have been fatal to owners of property. Yet they lent their backing to the further legitimate career of Catiline, seeing him not yet as a revolutionary but as another indebted and pliable henchman. Accordingly, in 64 Catiline had been acquitted, by a court presided over by Caesar, of atrocities during the Sullan epoch which Caesar, according to his record, should have deplored. Crassus and Caesar also seem to have supported him for the consulship of the following year. But Catiline, who had been rejected as a candidate two years earlier owing to his impending prosecution, was defeated at the polls. The successful candidates were Gaius Antonius Hybrida, a deplorable nobleman whom Caesar had attacked thirteen years earlier, and the rapidly rising Cicero. Although 'new men' like him, without any consuls among their ancestors, notoriously found it difficult to gain consulships, the conservatives decided he was preferable to Catiline, whose attitude to their traditions, despite his blue blood and Sullan record, must have begun to inspire alarm. After this rebuff to Catiline, Crassus and Caesar ceased to support him since he now revealed an embittered revolutionary programme far removed from Crassus' plutocratic aims.

Such a programme was tempting for desperate men, since the general flash-point was low, and grievances abounded. The Gracchi had been rightly disturbed by the disastrous situation of the Italian land, its farmers decimated by war and industrialisation, its peasant industries eclipsed in Etruria and the south by capitalist, slave-run pastures and plantations, many of them encroaching on what should properly have been public land. These were the conditions in which many Italians, further embittered by their failure to obtain the full privileges of Roman citizenship, had embarked on their terrible national rising, the Social War of 90–89. Caesar's kinsman, Lucius Julius Caesar, had initiated legislation offering Roman citizenship to all Latin (half-privileged) and other communities which had not revolted; and later another law filled in the gaps. In theory, a man could now remain a loyal townsman of his own municipality and yet also be a member of the great sovereign state. Rome was not merged in Italy, but Italians were absorbed in the citizen body of Rome. Yet in practice the position still remained far less satisfactory. This

was largely because, for the remainder of the eighties and worst of all under
Sulla, one civil war after another plunged the peninsula into a succession of
massacres, proscriptions, expropriations, and imposed settlements of
ex-soldiers. These ruinous events caused fearful losses almost everywhere,
especially in Etruria and central Italy. Into Rome, too, infiltrated a perilous
influx of destitute and potentially violent men, including, as time went on,
many settlers who had failed to make good, because ex-soldiers often made
bad farmers, and their damaged property or depleted soil made it impossible
to compete with slave labour and provincial grain. Discontent was acute
throughout Italy, and ready to exploit this misery were bankrupt, unscrupulous aristocrats at Rome, none of them more desperate or dangerous than
Catiline, smarting as he was under repeated frustrations.

And so he embarked on a plan to overthrow the government by violence.
When Crassus got wind of it, he and Caesar abandoned Catiline, if indeed
they had not done so already; and they even passed on information about
the plot to the consul Cicero. What they reported was probably not news to
him, since he had been kept well informed through the mistress of one of
the conspirators. But the gesture demonstrated the two men's break with
Catiline, although Caesar's conservative enemies, notably Catulus, cited his
heavy debts as evidence in the opposite direction, and Crassus angrily charged
Cicero with fabricating rumours that he, too, was involved in the conspiracy.
The successive phases of the melodrama are revealed in the incomparable,
richly coloured, written adaptations of Cicero's speeches that have handed
down to us his orgy of self-praise for suppressing the conspiracy. Finally, the
senate passed an emergency decree directed against Catiline. He fled to
Etruria to prepare for a march on Rome, whilst in the capital five of his principal supporters were arrested and consigned to the private custody of leading
senators: their guilt was beyond a doubt, since letters incriminating them
had been seized from a visiting delegation of Gauls. The prisoners, whose
custodians included Caesar and Crassus, were men of high rank, with senators
among their number. What on earth was to be done with them?

Now followed the famous meeting of the senate on 5 December 63, at
which Caesar took a prominent part in the discussions about their future.
Crassus found it less embarrassing to stay away: but Caesar as praetor-elect
could not.

The consul-elect, Silanus, on whom the constitution imposed the disagreeable duty of opening the debate, proposed that the imprisoned men,
and four others who had not been caught, should be executed. Not a word
of disagreement came from the fourteen ex-consuls present. Then it was
Caesar's turn to speak. If he supported the death penalty he would be backing
just the sort of dubiously legal conservative measure, based on an emergency
senatorial decree, which his action against Rabirius earlier in the year had

been intended to prevent. He would also be letting down his former associate Catiline, whom many still supported as a preferable alternative to the old guard. In addition, he would be causing the deaths of men who included a relation of his own by marriage and a kinsman of Pompey's supporter, Gabinius. To defend the rebels, on the other hand, was out of the question. This was a critical dilemma of his career, and the speech he delivered, of which we have an apparently accurate record from the Roman historian Sallust, was a masterpiece of skill. While utterly dissociating himself from what the defendants had done, he equally deplored the capital penalty, and proposed instead that the conspirators should be imprisoned for life in Italian country-towns, and their property confiscated; and that any proposal for their release, at whatever future time, should be regarded as high treason. Caesar revealed his special talent for putting his opponents in the wrong by a display of sweet reasonableness. Deprecating emotional decisions, he expressed doubt whether a sufficient emergency to justify extreme measures still existed, since the men were, after all, in confinement. In any case, so dreadful and unprecedented a fate as execution would attract too much notice and would look like an act prompted by emotional vindictiveness.

But Caesar's judicious words also contained a heavily implied threat. People, he said, are apt to forget the crime and remember the punishment: and the responsibility of senators who had taken the lives of fellow-citizens would not be forgotten. And in any case, he added (giving a rare glimpse of his own philosophical views) Epicurus had been right in saying that perpetual imprisonment—the penalty he was suggesting—is a worse punishment than death, since beyond the grave there is no life and therefore no suffering at all. Caesar particularly addressed himself to the consul-elect, Silanus, who had first proposed that the prisoners should be executed. Silanus' wife, Servilia, had been Caesar's mistress for years, and had just sent her lover an affectionate letter which reached him while he was actually delivering his speech. Silanus now pretended that his earlier words had been misunderstood: he had not meant to speak in favour of execution at all. In fact, he had come round to Caesar's view; and many other senators did the same.

Cicero, as chairman, made a cautious and rather equivocal speech, hoping to induce the senators to take collective responsibility for execution. And then, in far stronger support of the same view, came a decisive intervention by a member of the senate who was a good deal more youthful than those who generally swayed its decisions, the thirty-two-year-old Cato. This young tribune-elect was as obstinate and formidable as his great-grandfather, Cato the Censor; and his antique Roman, Stoic inflexibility was to become a legend. An alcoholic, but otherwise austere, self-righteous, ferocious and fearless, Cato relentlessly defended his own aristocratic caste, but scourged the undeserving rich and hated financiers. He despised the poor so much that he could step down from his principles to bribe them; his view of Rome was a narrow one which excluded Italians and demanded an old-fashioned city-state. Although his obstructionism was often short-sighted, he was crafty enough to stand at the centre of a complicated system of family alliances. This, as Catulus aged and the Metelli flagged, gave him the virtual leadership of the conservatives, who included no one more conservative than himself. Cato was tough enough to give up his wife to another man, and then take her back when her second husband had died and left her money. But he deplored Caesar's relations with Servilia, who was his step-sister, and he was furious when Caesar received the letter from her during the debate. Above all, he loathed Caesar's politics; and Caesar reciprocated by lavishing upon this lofty self-advertiser a furious hatred such as he never felt for anyone else except Cato's predecessor as leader of the diehards, Catulus.

On the present occasion, Cato lashed out abusively against Caesar's ostensibly moderate proposal, declaring that he had deliberately confused the issue and was, moreover, himself implicated in Catiline's plot. He also violently attacked his own brother-in-law, Silanus, for his feeble change of mind, and the conclusion he came to was that the conspirators would remain dangerous for as long as they lived, and must therefore be put to death. It was paradoxical, in the light of later events, to find Caesar speaking for constitutional correctness and Cato for expediency; nor was persuasiveness usually one of Cato's merits. But in this historic debate he carried the day, and the plotters were immediately executed. As Caesar left the senate he, too, nearly met his death, at the hands of Cicero's bodyguard of knights, young men of the propertied class threatened by Catiline. But among the poor, who had nothing to lose by a revolution, Caesar had increased his popularity by seeking, though in vain, to moderate the verdict.

The first days of his praetorship in 62 were turbulent. On the very first day of the new year he delivered a virulent attack on Catulus. The elder statesman had agreed with Cato that Caesar was involved in the plot, and now Caesar struck back by charging that the restoration of the Temple of Jupiter on the Capitoline hill, which had been entrusted to the old man sixteen years ago and still remained incomplete, was corruptly and criminally delayed. At the same time Caesar sought to create a breach between the right wing and Pompey, whose return home was now imminent, by suggesting that the latter should be given the task instead of Catulus.

He also expressed agreement with Metellus Nepos of the great Caecilian clan, who had launched his year as tribune by strongly suggesting that Pompey, who was related to him by marriage, should bring back his army in order to restore order in Italy. This idea, with its frighteningly dictatorial implications, had probably emanated from Pompey's followers rather than

himself. Crassus would have been united with the nobles in hating it to come
to anything. But Caesar knew there was no danger of this, and so he
applauded Metellus' proposal, once again with the intention of detaching
Pompey from the conservative cause. In opposing the measure Cato, tribune
though he now was, nearly lost his life in the worst riots at Rome for many
years. Caesar was blamed for these disorders by the senate, which suspended
both him and Metellus from their functions and indicated its underlying fears
by declaring that any critics of the Catilinarian executions would be enemies
of the state. However, when large crowds, including Catilinarian sympathisers, demanded Caesar's reinstatement, the senate, reassured by his
statesmanlike handling of the demonstrators, took the opportunity to concur.

A positive step to outbid the dangerous popularity of Caesar and Pompey
was now taken by Cato, who persuaded the senate to authorise the monthly
distribution of one and a quarter bushels of wheat to 320,000 Roman appli-
cants at less than half the market price. This arrangement resumed on a much
larger scale a practice which had existed earlier but was terminated by Sulla.
Since the fourth century BC the Mediterranean world had accepted the idea
that governments must ensure cheap and adequate food, and Cato was not
giving something away for nothing; though, for all his high principles, he
was obviously opening the door to hated 'popular' politicians who would outbid him by doing just that.

This measure was approved under the shadow of Catiline, who had
resorted to open warfare against the state and still held out in the Apennines.
But soon afterwards he was cornered and killed at Pistoria (Pistoia). The successful general was Marcus Petreius; Cicero's colleague Gaius Antonius
Hybrida, deeply involved with Catiline, proved unable to take command
against him owing to a diplomatic attack of gout. Now that Catiline was gone,
the conservatives felt encouraged to launch a more thoroughgoing purge of
his supporters at Rome. Although Caesar as praetor was immune from trial,
a notorious informer named Lucius Vettius denounced him to the commissioner in charge of the investigation. But Caesar had Vettius beaten up and
imprisoned and his furniture smashed, and arrested the commissioner for
allowing such a case against a senior official to be heard in his court. He also
appealed to Cicero to confirm that he had, in fact, passed on information
against the plotters to the authorities; and Cicero felt obliged to testify that
this was so. He had borrowed heavily from Crassus for the purchase of a new
house, and this was part of the interest he had to pay—although in a memorandum which was not published until after his death he expressed the belief
that both Crassus and Caesar were, in fact, involved in the conspiracy.

At the end of the year Caesar was involved in an incident which casts a gro-
tesque light upon Roman political, social and religious life. The Good

Goddess (*Bona Dea*) was a deity worshipped exclusively by women. Every December her rites were celebrated in the house of a senior official, and now they were due to take place in the home of Caesar, praetor and chief priest. The ritual included numerous peculiar features of immemorial antiquity. Wine, for example, was brought in for the women, because it was handed down that the Good Goddess had been made drunk by her father; but it was euphemistically called milk, and its jar was described as a honeypot. Whether or not, as rumour believed, the women drank a good deal too much on these occasions, the strictest of all the many taboos with which the rites were hedged around was that no man must be present. Even paintings and mosaics showing men or male animals were veiled for the occasion.

On the morning after the celebration of 62, the noble households of Rome were horrified to learn that a male had managed to gate-crash the ceremony disguised in a woman's clothes. A slave-girl had penetrated the deception, and at once reported the atrocity to Caesar's mother, Aurelia, who, before throwing the intruder out, identified him (so she said) as the smartest and most dissolute character in Rome, a man in his middle thirties called Publius Clodius Pulcher. It was at once stated and assumed that his purpose in engaging in this masquerade was to make love to Caesar's wife, Pompeia. Her husband promptly divorced her, calmly evading the question of her culpability but uttering an epigram of which the gist was that members of his family—the high priest's household—must be free not only of guilt but even of mere suspicion. There are several versions of the statement, the most famous being Plutarch's, 'Caesar's wife must be above suspicion'. Whatever his actual words were, they may have implied a bitter reference to the current insinuations about his own Catilinarian past. But the fact that he used the occasion to secure a divorce suggests he felt that Pompeia, who had not produced a child, was expendable. And in any case the ridiculous role of a cuckold, which he was said to inflict so liberally on others, was not one which he welcomed for himself.

Had Clodius really been there? Aurelia, who usually 'never let her out of her sight', could well have invented the story to frame the young woman. On the other hand an affair in such improbable, difficult and blasphemous circumstances was just the sort of sick joke that might have appealed to Clodius. An elaborate case of sacrilege was prepared against him, largely in the hope of further embarrassing Caesar. A violent exchange of abuse developed between Clodius and the leading conservatives, who threw in, for good measure, the additional accusation that he was guilty of incest with every one of his three sisters. Cicero associated himself with these attacks. His wife thought that he, too, was excessively interested in the most notorious of these girls (who broke the heart of the poet Catullus), but in any case Cicero was deeply wounded by the news that Clodius had sneered about his consulship.

Accordingly he now proceeded to demolish the defendant's alibi for the night of the alleged adventure, thus making a dangerous and lasting enemy. Caesar, on the other hand, after playing a preliminary part as chairman of the board of priests, caused great surprise by refusing to offer any testimony against Clodius. Honour had been satisfied; and Caesar, not to speak of his patron Crassus, knew a useful and totally unscrupulous political ally when he saw one. The result of the trial was an acquittal for Clodius. Cicero called the judges a dirtier crowd than you could meet in any gambling saloon, and claimed that Crassus, to get Clodius off, had bribed them with money, women, and introductions to upper-class youths.

This was a major scandal, but it was still a small storm compared to the really significant event of the month. For many eyes at Rome were anxiously turned to Brundusium (Brindisi), where Pompey now landed from the east, bringing with him nearly forty thousand devoted soldiers. His achievements were colossal and unprecedented. He had put an end to Mithridates, Rome's malignant foe for a quarter of a century, and had annexed his huge kingdom in northern Anatolia. He had also taken over Syria, the wealthy nucleus and remnant of the historic Hellenistic realm of the Seleucid successors of Alexander; and he had captured Jerusalem. Conservatives could say Pompey only reaped the victories of his aristocratic predecessor, Lucullus, and it is true that his laurels were earned somewhat cheaply, with the easy preponderance of strength which he always liked to achieve before military action. Yet he could claim to have conquered 1,538 towns or fortresses and 12,178,000 human beings. Thirty-nine new cities owed their foundations to him, and he had carried the arms of Rome to the Caucasus, the Sea of Azov and the Red Sea. The climax of a Roman general's victory was the Triumph he returned to celebrate in the capital; and Pompey's Triumph, commemorating victories over no less than fifteen nations and parading 324 captured and hostage princes and their sons, presented an imposing magnificence beyond the dreams of all previous commanders. Pompey paid twenty-four million pounds into the treasury, and his conquests and loot raised the annual revenue of Rome by no less than seventy per cent, from ten to seventeen millions. Greek cities pronounced him the 'warden of earth and sea'. At his winter quarters twelve kings had simultaneously paid him court. He could boast that whole countries and their rulers had been enrolled as his obedient clients. With the aid of financial agents, among whom the banker Cluvius was pre-eminent, Pompey's holdings of mortgage bonds made him more than patron of the east: he was almost literally its owner. The sums which came to him personally from its monarchs rose far above any precedent in Roman history. He had attained gigantic wealth—he could easily, by now, have bought up Crassus himself. So Caesar, without breaking with Crassus, took the initiative in proposing the honours which Rome showered upon Pompey.

CHAPTER THREE

The Three-headed Monster

Caesar had bowed to the superior strength of Pompey by backing his political interests at Rome. But now he could try and repair his own solvency by departing for the provincial governorship to which his service as praetor entitled him. It would not be unwelcome to absent himself for a while from the capital, where he was so completely eclipsed by the returning conqueror. Moreover, there was a special reason why it was better not to stay at home. While Pompey had been in the east, Caesar was believed to have had a love affair with his wife Mucia. Although she had borne Pompey three children, one of his first acts on his return was to divorce her. He offered no reason, but allegedly threw off a learned but interpretable remark about Aegisthus who had become the lover of Clytemnestra while her husband Agamemnon was away at Troy. So it had become time for Caesar to go elsewhere for a while.

The allocation of provinces had given him Further Spain. At first he found it hard to get away, since moneylenders from whom he had borrowed proceeded to demand securities, under threat of arrest and seizure of his baggage. It was said that his obligations amounted to five million pounds, and that Crassus, still investing in his future, now advanced him nearly a fifth of that sum, enough to satisfy the most pressing of his creditors. Then Caesar was able to make his departure, and he did so as quickly as possible, even before his appointment had been confirmed by formal senatorial decree. His pretext was the urgency of military operations against bandits infesting the mountains of Lusitania (Portugal and western Spain). For a governor was not only the chief justice and principal civilian administrator of his province, but its commander-in-chief as well.

After a journey of three weeks Caesar reached Corduba (Cordova), the provincial capital. Finding that the bandits refused to settle in the plains, he enlisted new troops against them and conducted a vigorous offensive between the Tagus and the Douro, consolidating this area as part of the province. Then he sailed from Gades (Cadiz) up to Brigantium (Betanzos) at the north-western extremity of the peninsula, launching Roman soldiers for the first time upon the waters of the Atlantic. Somehow Caesar wrung a vast amount of money out of these operations. His political enemies claimed he had plundered unresisting towns and accepted excessive gifts; and yet he avoided gaining too much of a bad name at Rome. This was largely because he was able to send the capital a very large sum, including 'voluntary' contributions by Spanish cities. In consequence he was voted a Triumph. But he also found it possible to enrich his soldiers, who hailed him as their victorious general (*imperator*). Above all, however, he obtained a great deal of money for himself, and this went a considerable way towards paying the debts which had weighed so heavily upon him. Such personal enrichment, if conducted with a certain amount of circumspection, was legitimate, because a governor not only received official allowances far in excess of his expenditure, but when distributing the booty from military operations to the treasury and his troops he was held to be entitled to provide for himself as well.

And yet accusations that Caesar neglected all civil business in favour of war and gain were not quite justified, because in the short time that remained to him in Spain he made a practical attempt to tackle a serious local situation. This related to debts, a problem with which he was only too well acquainted. The populations of Spain were financially crippled by wars and uneven economic advances, and indebtedness had reached enormous proportions. The present legal position was that creditors were actually permitted to seize the whole of their debtors' income. Caesar modified this to two-thirds of the income. That still sounds severe to us, but it was milder than what people were used to. The reform gave the governor many grateful clients who would be useful in the future, and it foreshadowed Caesar's later legislation on a much larger scale at Rome itself.

But in other and more significant respects, too, his governorship was a turning point in his career. Not only did it rescue him from bankruptcy, but it changed his entire way of life. This first experience of leading troops into battle, in the country where the inspiring Sertorius, friend of his uncle Marius, had fought before him, was a revelation. For, although a small enough affair in itself, it showed him what he did best: and what he best liked to do.

Nevertheless, this newly discovered métier had to wait. Further progress in his career, at its present stage, could only be made possible by returning to Rome. And this presented certain complications. Like any other successful Roman politician, Caesar aimed at the consulship his ancestors had achieved, the climax of all normal ambitions. It was also a point of honour to seek this office in 'his year', that is to say the first possible year when he was eligible. According to ordinary practice that was the year in which a man reached the

SPAIN

Brigantium · Pyrenees Mountains · Osca · Ilerda · Tarraco · TARRACONENSIS · River Douro · River Ebro · River Tagus · ATLANTIC OCEAN · LUSITANIA · Corduba · River Guadalquivir · Hispalis · Ategua · Munda · Gades · BAETICA · Carthago Nova · Balearic Is · MEDITERRANEAN SEA · MAURETANIA

age of forty-three; but in the case of a patrician an advantage of two years was permitted. This meant that, having been born on 13 July 100, Caesar could already be consul in 59, and could stand for the office, therefore, in July of the previous year.

However, the consulship was not enough for him. He also wanted the Triumph which his large dispatches of funds from Spain had secured for him. A commander voted a Triumph must not enter the city before the celebration had taken place. On the other hand, a recent law enacted that every candidate for the consulship must appear at the capital in person, and hand in his name on a fixed day about a month before the July elections. Prompt though Caesar had been in quitting Spain in 60, he did not reach Rome until about June, and this presented him with an impossibly tight timetable. It would not have been entirely unprecedented for the senate to authorise a candidate to stand for the consulship *in absentia*, and Caesar requested this exemption for himself. But Cato talked out the whole of the last day on which the matter could be discussed, so that no permission was given. Perhaps he invented the institution of the filibuster: certainly he slammed the door upon all hopes of the Republic and Caesar ever again co-operating in harmony. Cicero wrote to his friend Atticus, the recipient of so many of his fascinating letters, that he had hopes of making Caesar, 'who has the wind in his sails just now,' a better citizen. But the prospect, if any existed, of Caesar settling down as a good conservative was quite eliminated by Cato's action.

What is more, the senate seems to have allowed itself a further ungracious gesture. At this time the provinces that consuls went out to govern after their year of office—provinces which were, of course, more important than those of praetors—had to be earmarked before the names of the incumbents were known, that is to say before the elections to the consulships took place. On this occasion, however, the senate anticipated that Caesar would be elected, and wanted to snub him and curtail his power; and so they earmarked for the consuls of 59 a province defined as 'forests and cattle-runs'. This may have been an area of south-eastern Italy, normally supervised by one of the comparatively humble quaestors. In any case it was a ludicrously trivial assignment for a consul. Perhaps it was argued that the disordered situation of Italy could justify such an appointment, or, alternatively, that it was merely a token allocation to enable more worthy provinces to be voted at a later date in accordance with future developments in the frontier areas. But the allotment of this minor forestry commission still looks like a deliberate conservative insult to Caesar.

Meanwhile Caesar, since he could not have both Triumph and consulate, renounced the former and stood for the latter, to which he was duly elected. His colleague was Bibulus, the determined reactionary who had already been reluctantly yoked with Caesar as aedile and then again as praetor. In order to become consul, Bibulus had climbed down from his principles and offered Caesar money in exchange for electoral support. But Caesar refused. He had already half ruined Bibulus to pay for their election as aediles, and was not sure the man had enough money left to be of any use; he also knew how much Bibulus disliked him. However, his own funds were still insufficient to make him consul. A little earlier, he would have gone to Crassus for assistance, but this time, as far as we know, he did not. The reason, probably, was a difference of opinion about Pompey. His overwhelming victories in the east must have been hard for the jealous Crassus to tolerate with equanimity, whereas Caesar, less strongly placed, still felt it imperative to lend the conqueror his support. Accordingly, his loan came this time not from Crassus, but from a third candidate for the consulship, the wealthy Lucceius. However, Lucceius himself failed to get in, since all the conservatives, including Cato, united in a massive operation of bribery which secured the second place for Bibulus.

The prospect of having such a colleague was a melancholy one for Caesar, and it gave added urgency to an important plan on which he was now working. This was nothing less than a scheme to bring the two most important men in Rome together with himself in order that the three of them might now combine to suppress this traditionalist Republican faction which was so determined to frustrate their ambitions. The time was ripe because the conservatives had snubbed not only Caesar but, what was much more serious, Pompey also, and, for good measure, Crassus as well. Pompey's estrangement from the nobles, already foreshadowed by their dislike of his military successes, had been accelerated by his divorce of Mucia, for her half-brothers, Metellus Celer and Metellus Nepos, belonged to the most powerful clan in Rome. Mucia had helped her husband Pompey and her reputed lover Caesar to secure the support of Celer in the Rabirius case of 63, and it was no doubt also partly because of her that Nepos, again working with Caesar, had supported Pompey's interests when the latter was on his way home. But after the divorce Celer, having stifled his resentment long enough to get a consulship, soon ceased to favour him, and in due course Nepos cooled off as well. Pompey's alliance with the great Caecilii Metelli, which had lasted with ups and downs for fifteen years, was for the present at an end.

At this time Pompey, who enjoyed being married and during his life married five times for politics, was casting around for another suitable wife. His first idea was to re-establish his position with the conservatives. His eye turned towards Cato's nieces, and he proposed himself as the husband of one, and his younger son as husband of the other. Cato, however, turned the proposal down, observing that he was not to be caught through women; though the ladies of his family are said to have regretted his decision—until Pompey's too visible bribery of voters in his garden made them feel that Cato was right. But the worst rebuff of all came when Pompey, who had acted with highhanded independence in regulating eastern affairs, failed to persuade the senate to ratify his acts and pass the land-law providing for his unprecedentedly victorious troops. Celer was now against him, and so, naturally, was Cato— and by the summer of 60 Pompey felt obliged to allow the land bill to be dropped.

The conservative classes had moved away from him, fearing he might try to become dictator. But they were wrong, for when he returned to Italy Pompey had dutifully disbanded his army, clearly demonstrating that he wanted to stay within the rules. He was tortuous, ungenerous, selfish and insincere. Eight times during his life he changed his party allegiance. But he was genuinely interested in decent government, and what he wanted for himself was not supreme power but applause. He shied from the consequences to which his ambition might lead. Pompey was not the man to shock Republicans by repeating Sulla's march on Rome: what he would really have liked was the admiration of every noble in the place. And now, at forty-six, when his constructive life was finished, when his resolution was faltering, when his failure to learn political procedures during his meteoric early life was proving a handicap, he was cruelly rejected by the reactionary forces which he would have liked to lead.

Crassus too, his longstanding resentments intensified by Pompey's victories, zealously joined in the suppression of the land-law. And yet Crassus had something in common with Pompey, for he, too, was now humiliated by the diehards. The question at issue was a financial one. The knights enjoying Crassus' special protection were patrons of great companies which bought from the government the right to farm taxes in Rome's wealthiest province, Asia. Now, finding they had overbid—in other words, that they had miscalculated in their bargain with the government—they asked for the contract to be reversed, and for a new one, greatly reducing their liability, to be established instead. Crassus backed them. Cicero knew it was an outrageous suggestion, but attached great importance to co-operation between senate and knights, and so accorded them his support. Cato, however, killed the proposal, offering highly offensive comments about the ethics of these financiers who were so often at daggers drawn with his fellow-nobles in the provinces. The conservatives were evidently ready to go to any length and cost to thwart men who seemed likely to threaten the predominance of their cliques. But this time they had over-reached themselves. Indeed, by following the inflexible initiative of Cato, they had brought about the downfall of all that they most wanted to preserve.

During this momentous year Pompey and Crassus sank their differences, and united with Caesar—spurned like themselves by the forces of tradition—to form the private but all-powerful and dictatorial understanding known as the First Triumvirate. Caesar was still much the least influential of the three, but he was by far the most capable negotiator, and his Marian interests attracted people who suspected Pompey, the Sullan general, and Crassus, the Sullan profiteer. Moreover, it was he who accomplished the formidable task of bringing the other two together. Probably he and Pompey had already reached a limited agreement before the elections (of July 60) which secured him the consulship for the following year. The enlistment of Crassus may not have come until later, since, if it had already been achieved before that time, Caesar would scarcely have needed to turn elsewhere for campaigning funds. At all events by the end of the year the full tripartite agreement was complete, though it still remained a secret for the time being.

Caesar's plans to reconcile the others were communicated to Cicero by Lucius Cornelius Balbus, who played a prominent part in the agreement, as in most of the major events for many years to come. One of the most important, gifted and colourful members of Caesar's staff, he originated from Gades (Cadiz), and his ancestors no doubt included members of the Semitic (Phoenician) people who were the founders of that city. Balbus had started his public life as a dependant of Pompey during the latter's Spanish campaigns against Sertorius in the seventies, when he rendered the services which won him Roman citizenship. A youth of exceptional good looks as well as literary and philosophical talents, he had been befriended by Pompey's Greek agent and historian, the wealthy Theophanes of Mytilene, who adopted him at about the time of this First Triumvirate and later left him his entire fortune. But Balbus' most important friendship was with Caesar, whose close connections with the principal men of Gades, during his two terms of office in Spain, had included the acquisition of this invaluable organiser, string-puller and go-between.

It was very useful, at the present juncture, that Balbus was close to Pompey as well as Caesar; and he was now instructed by the latter to make the triumvirate look more respectable by the addition of Cicero, whose seniority and incomparable eloquence would be significant assets, vain and vacillating though he was. And so in about December of 60 Balbus visited the orator. His exceptional diplomatic gifts nearly proved persuasive; but not quite. Cicero was full of bitterness. He felt indignant enough with the conservatives, whose uncompromising rebuffs to Pompey, Crassus and Caesar seemed to him to have wrecked the national unity which he over-optimistically claimed to have established during the Catilinarian melodrama. But his irritation with the three potentates themselves was even greater. Crassus had admittedly seemed to praise Cicero's consulship, but he was strongly suspected of complicity with Catiline, and he had ruined Cicero's attempt to prosecute Clodius for sacrilege. As for Pompey, Cicero had behaved with gross lack of tact by sending him an immense document suggesting that his own handling of Catiline was on a par, to put it mildly, with the eastern conqueror's achievements. The recipient, of course, had reacted coldly, and Cicero's usual admiration of Pompey, or rather of an ideal Pompey who never really existed, was temporarily in abeyance.

As for his attitude to Caesar, the final versions of Cicero's Catilinarian speeches were full of feline politeness, for they were published when Caesar was expected to become consul. But Cicero could never get over a deep-rooted distaste for the man. He claimed to have been the first person to realise what Caesar was really like, 'and to have feared him as one might fear the smiling surface of the sea'. The orator's spiteful judgments of people and situations continually changed, but he always supported the Republican form of government, however unattainable its revival had really become, and in a few critical turning-points of his life he resisted pressure and lived up to his ideal. This was one of them. He refused to join the unholy alliance, whatever the penalties—and they proved to be heavy.

During the next ten years the triumvirate remained the controlling factor in Roman politics. This was not, as it has sometimes been called, a defeat for democracy. The dispute was not between senatorial government and democracy, which had never existed in Rome and never would, but between a haughty, reactionary, corrupt oligarchy and an equally ruthless tyranny conducted by three individuals. Now the latter cause had won. Later on, Cato and others after him saw this as the moment that made disaster to the conservative cause inevitable. It was not the later enmity between Pompey and Caesar, but their present sinister understandings, which caused the clanking institutions of the Roman Republic to grind to a halt.

When the ill-assorted pair, Caesar and Bibulus, took office at the turn of the year, one of Caesar's first actions was to present a law to redistribute the rural land of Italy. The beneficiaries were to include the metropolitan poor, who could come under an obligation to their patrons, but chiefly they were to be ex-soldiers, including particularly Pompey's veterans whose provision had been blocked in the previous year. This initial measure earmarked the not very large remaining public lands of Italy, with the exception only of Campania, south-east of Rome, where such domains were particularly extensive and important. The bill also arranged for the purchase of additional private estates in small parcels, provided that their previous owners were willing to sell; and it was guaranteed that prices should be not less than market value. A land commission was to be set up, consisting of twenty men guided by an inner executive committee of five. Although the law was bound to be controversial, the powers of the commission were far less sweeping than those projected in the abortive bill sponsored by Crassus and Caesar four years earlier, and in general the proposals were moderate and judicious. So was the manner of their presentation, since Caesar did not by-pass the senate but, before bringing the measure before the assembly, correctly submitted it to the senators for comment. But this outwardly conciliatory policy, as Caesar no doubt foresaw, met only with obstruction, led by Cato who saw the whole move as a lethal plot in which it was hard to say whether revolutionaries or their natural enemies the financiers were the more active; and he felt that a consul who promoted an inflammable proposal of the kind traditionally associated with mere tribunes was dangerously misusing his office. Caesar, whose customary façade of superficial calm Cato sometimes managed to penetrate, made the rare mistake of losing patience, and put a stop to Cato's filibustering by having him hauled off to prison. This decision he rapidly rescinded. But the occasion retained an ominous significance for another reason. The senate had lost the last chance in its history to act as a sensible and constructive governing body.

Inevitably, Caesar next took the bill to the assembly. There it was vetoed by three tribunes, but their intervention was illegally disregarded and they got hurt. Caesar's fellow consul Bibulus likewise tried to block the proceedings, but now the forces of the triumvirate were dramatically unmasked. To the general amazement, not only Pompey but Crassus spoke in favour of the proposal. Moreover, soldiers Caesar had borrowed from Pompey actually burst into the assembly; although unwilling to use violence himself, he was prepared to place it in the hands of his ally. Someone emptied a basket of excrement over Bibulus' head, and his emblems of office were smashed. With part of the opposition incapacitated by such means and the remainder paralysed by the unsuspected new alliance, the law was passed. But the manifest impropriety of the proceedings was to hang like a load round Caesar's neck for years to come, since the Romans, though sometimes violent, paradoxically remained legalistic at heart. He took what precautions he could by adding a new clause compelling senators and candidates for official posts to swear an oath that they would abide by the measure. The senate was by now so thoroughly intimidated that it gave way to this coercion: even Cato, yielding to Cicero's plea, compromised with his conscience in order to save his skin. And so the land commission got to work. Its members included a specialist on pigs, and other farming experts such as the encyclopaedic Varro who wrote a treatise on the subject. But among the commissioners, too, were Pompey and a brother-in-law of Caesar.

Bibulus now adopted tactics which bear no relation to modern politics but could be held to possess a certain weird ingenious validity in the terms of the historic, indeed prehistoric, procedures of the Roman constitution and religion. The antique sacred right of the auspices was based on the theory that the gods had means to let the people know whether a certain act was in accordance with their will. Caesar believed no such thing, and it is doubtful whether most of his educated contemporaries were very much more credulous. But the practice was revered and patriotic, and besides, as Cicero noted, it had sometimes proved a convenient means of putting an end to subversive meetings. Indeed, no official function could even be started until the presiding consul or praetor had watched the sky to make sure there was no flash of lightning or other adverse sign. If such a thing were seen, the whole proceedings had to be cancelled. Indeed, they were even immobilised by a mere announcement by an official or one of the augurs (priests who specialised in these natural phenomena) that he was studying the heavens.

Bibulus now announced that this was precisely what he was going to do. He openly admitted that his intention was to prevent meetings of the assembly from taking place at all, so that legislation would become impossible. Caesar totally disregarded everything his colleague said, and continued to convene assemblies and senates as he wished. It is conceivable that he was technically justified in taking this action: to decide whether or not Bibulus' unprecedented use or abuse of the auspices was actually legal set even the highly expert Roman religious jurists a pretty problem. Nonetheless, on the top of his unconstitutional behaviour over the agrarian law, Caesar's boldness in disregarding the state religion lost him esteem with the more ritualistic sort of Roman. Bibulus also endeavoured, by a similar act of obstruction, to put Caesar even more in the wrong over senate meetings. It was a rule that a consul could not summon the senate without the consent of his colleague; and henceforward no such consent was to be forthcoming. Indeed, during the last eight months of his consular year Bibulus did not budge from his own home. From there he distributed abroad a series of virulently scurrilous 'edicts' directed against the politics and sexual morals of his fellow consul. These broadsheets, which showed a certain coarse wit, attracted so much attention that there were traffic jams at the street corners where they were posted up. Critics of the triumvirs, encouraged by their growing unpopularity, called Pompey king and Caesar queen. Bibulus, embroidering still further on an ancient but never forgotten scandal, stated in one of his pamphlets that the queen of Bithynia, who had once wanted to go to bed with the king, now had the ambition to become a king herself.

Meanwhile Caesar, ignoring the charges of illegality, continued to pass measures in the interests of all three triumvirs. Crassus' financiers of Asia received the remission of contractual obligations that they had asked for, to the lavish extent of 33 per cent. Caesar accompanied the concessions with a warning that this must not happen again. Yet he himself possessed a direct interest in the tax-farmers' operations, and made a large sum out of the adjustment. Pompey's eastern settlement was also ratified.

But now it seemed advisable both to him and to Caesar that their collaboration, based on a fortuitous, temporary convergence of interests, should be cemented by a marriage tie which might make the alliance less precarious. Pompey, having divorced Mucia and subsequently failed to secure Cato's niece in her place, was in need of a wife; and if Caesar had helped to break up Pompey's former marriage, it now seemed the least he could do to provide his own daughter instead. This young woman, Julia, had nearly become unavailable because she was promised to a relation of Caesar's favourite mistress, Servilia. Now, however, Caesar had to break it to Servilia that the girl was going to marry Pompey instead. Servilia cannot have been pleased by the change of plan, especially as Pompey had murdered her first husband; and it may have been to soften the blow that Caesar reputedly gave her a pearl worth three thousand pounds. In any case during April Pompey, aged forty-seven, married the seventeen-year-old Julia. Curiously enough the marriage was the greatest success, and Pompey, who was reported by the prostitute Flora to be perfectly capable of unbending with women, took his youthful wife for repeated seaside holidays. Cicero believed that the proposal for the union came from Pompey, who needed Caesar's political skill. Caesar was glad to accept, since his illegal and dubiously legal acts, performed on behalf of his own interests and those of his fellow-triumvirs, had made him liable to all manner of future retribution unless he retained Pompey's firm support.

The new situation was reflected in a change of protocol. It was customary, at senate meetings, for a consul to call on officials in the same order throughout the year, and hitherto Caesar had started with Crassus. But from now on, whatever Crassus might feel, he called upon Pompey first.

At the same time Caesar himself, unwed since the scandal of the Good Goddess, likewise married again. His choice fell on Calpurnia, whose father, Lucius Piso, a literary man of swarthy complexion, hairy cheeks, bad teeth and a crooked expression, was needed as a docile candidate for the consulship of the following year, to balance Pompey's nominee, Gabinius. Cato complained that it was intolerable for the Roman nation to be treated like a marriage bureau. Nor can he have been any better pleased when Caesar's efforts in this direction made inroads into his own house, since his garrulous father-in-law, Lucius Marcius Philippus, took Caesar's niece as his wife and became a benevolent neutral who was no longer of any use to Cato.

Fortified by these matrimonial arrangements, Caesar moved into even more vigorous action with his second agrarian law. The first does not seem to have produced the desired results; probably speculators had got hold of the land due for distribution and were demanding excessively high prices. Accordingly, the state-owned territories in central and northern Campania, which had been omitted before, were called in for redistribution. This was the last cultivable land that still remained public property. Much of the region was on lease to tenants, many of them wealthy men, and the regular income which this brought into the treasury was the basis of the national budget. Now, in May, these estates were redistributed among twenty thousand of Pompey's veterans and Caesar's civilian clients, preference being given, it was said, to large families. The compensation methods seem to have been much harsher than those applied earlier in the year, since many smallholders were turned adrift or saddled with large rents as sub-tenants. Cato objected to the law to the best of his ability. But he was more than once beaten up and pushed off the platform.

Caesar's massive programme also included an excellent law designed to prevent provincial governors from fleecing their subjects—excellent, that is to say, as far as it went, for implementation was difficult, and sanctions were directed only against governors and not against the financiers who behaved just as badly. Another bill provided for the publication of all acts of the assembly and decrees of the senate. These had hitherto only been published on a few special occasions, and the new measure was a beneficial, if tardy, attempt to educate public opinion. But it was also intended as a weapon against the nobles, whose obstruction of popular laws would now be common knowledge.

So far, during the historic consulship of 59, Caesar had done more for his fellow triumvirs than for himself. It is true that he had benefited by the remission of the Asian tax-contracts and the planting of supporters in Campania and elsewhere. But he wanted a great deal more profit than that. There was probably nothing in the rumour that he took three thousand pounds weight of gold from the treasury and replaced it by gilded bronze, for this would have caused too much of a scandal to be practicable, but Caesar and Pompey both got their hands on another gold-mine. This was the kingdom of Egypt which, although retaining only a shadow of its former independence, possessed gigantic wealth, far in excess even of the riches of Asia and Syria which had in turn transformed the finances of the Roman state. A king of Egypt had, in a will of dubious but possible authenticity, expressed the desire to leave his country to Rome (80 BC), and subsequently Crassus had been interested in taking up the bequest. But that had come to nothing, and now Caesar and Pompey agreed to induce the Roman senate and assembly to recognise the present king Ptolemy XII (known as the Oboe Player) in return for a fabulous fee—which even he found difficulty in raising by himself, being obliged to borrow for the purpose from a Roman financier, Rabirius Postumus.

This was an immense windfall. But it did not lessen Caesar's determination, which every Roman consul shared, to be given a first-class province to provide glory and loot when his term of office was over—certainly not the mere forests and cattle runs which had apparently been allotted to the consuls of this year, before the triumvirate had got into its stride. For this purpose Caesar called upon one of his most valued agents, Publius Vatinius, a cheerful, popular, intrepid vulgarian of dreadful appearance, with swellings all over his face and neck. Caesar had arranged the appointment of Vatinius as tribune, and it was he who had secured the confirmation of Pompey's acts and the tax-remission wanted by Crassus—and had consequently been rewarded by Caesar with the company's booming shares. When the tribune wanted to break into Bibulus' house and haul him off to prison, this excessive enthusiasm had been checked by his patron. But two months later, in May, Vatinius did what was chiefly required of him by guiding through the assembly, without consulting the senate at all, a law allotting Caesar his province. This was to comprise Cisalpine Gaul (north Italy) and Illyricum, not for the usual one year or two, but for five, during which time he was entitled to nominate his own subordinate commanders.

Caesar's opponents declared the law invalid because Bibulus was watching the omens. But Caesar, with a momentary lapse from the suavity of speech which usually accompanied even his most savage blows, descended instead to the level of abuse set by Bibulus and shouted in the senate that he had got what he wanted for all their moaning, and from now on he would mount on top of their heads. Someone crudely replied that this was scarcely a possible position for a woman to assume, but Caesar, entering into the spirit of this twenty-year-old joke, retorted that the Amazons and Semiramis, queen of Syria, had not done so badly in spite of their sex.

Out of the fourteen legions which formed the standing armies of Rome's eight provinces, three were allotted to Caesar; they were stationed at Aquileia at the head of the Adriatic. It was arranged that most of the others should be in the hands of Pompey's partisans. Cisalpine Gaul, a prosperous, populous territory providing an unequalled, not too distant field for recruitment, was an enormous asset to Caesar, while Pompey, too, was happy that his ally should have this province, because he himself might need troops to threaten the capital; and he would be able to trust the Cisalpine communities since his father had helped to enfranchise them. Caesar was also authorised, by a supplementary law of Vatinius, to strengthen one of the towns in the area, Novum Comum (Como), by new settlers, and he duly proceeded to plant five thousand colonists in the place. Strictly speaking the town, like almost all others across the Po, still only possessed the half-way Latin status, in which only officials and council members became Roman citizens, but Caesar with dubious legality treated them as Roman citizens and Novum Comum as a wholly Roman citizen community; indeed, he tacitly attributed the same status to all the other Transpadane municipalities as well. Caesar's enemies, who in any case declared his whole legislation illegal because Bibulus was watching the heavens, refused to accept his measures. But this course of action was convenient to Caesar since it enabled him to maintain a nucleus of grateful dependants, who could, moreover, be temporarily imported into Rome from time to time to help his candidates win their elections. Besides, only Roman citizens could properly be recruited as legionaries, and he was able to say that the two new legions which he now began to mobilise consisted, ostensibly at least, of men of the appropriate status. This assumption encouraged the recruits, who were further stimulated by the thought that, when they retired, Caesar would see to it that they were treated as full citizens and duly rewarded with grants of land.

The second part of the province allotted to Caesar, Illyricum, comprised the eastern coastal strip of the Adriatic. Like Cisalpine Gaul, the region was conveniently close to Italy. It might also provide a chance of improving on a long list of inconclusive successes by previous generals against border tribes, which were in easy reach of the garrison at Aquileia. Moreover, here were already signs, to the north and east of the area, that a quarrel might well be picked with the large barbarian empire of King Burebistas of Dacia. Caesar may have seen wide opportunities of victory, profit and prestige in a possible extension of Roman arms to the Carnic Alps and River Save or even the Danube, to which, in fact, the frontier was taken a generation later.

This initial allocation of provinces to Caesar did not extend across the western Alps to Narbonese Gaul, the productive and advanced southern portion of

France extending between the Cévennes and the Mediterranean coast. An appeal against local tribes made by Rome's ally, the Greek port of Massilia (Marseille), had led to the annexation of this land in 121 BC, and during more recent years it had gradually been organised as a province and exploited by Roman businessmen. Upheavals beyond its northern boundaries, which offered considerable possibilities to an ambitious Roman general, had caused the senate to make a special allocation of the two Gauls, Narbonese as well as Cisalpine, to the consuls of 60, this being an indication that the territories in question were regarded as the most critical regions of the empire at the time. One of these consuls, Pompey's nominee, Afranius, gave way to Caesar in the Cisalpine area, but his colleague, Metellus Celer, had fallen out with Pompey and was eager to win laurels of his own in Narbonese Gaul. However, his departure for the province was delayed, and then, before he could leave Rome, he died.

This was the stroke of luck which gave Caesar the opportunity to add the region to his governorship, with enormous repercussions upon the subsequent history of the world. After the death of Celer, or even when he first became seriously ill, the triumvir had lost no time in setting his father-in-law Piso and son-in-law Pompey to work to induce the senate and assembly respectively to divert the unexpectedly vacant province to the command that had been allotted to himself. Meanwhile, Caesar vocally objected to a thanksgiving another general was celebrating for victories in this Narbonese area, his purpose being to show that military operations were far from concluded; and to emphasise the same point, Vatinius and others conspicuously kept away from the ceremony, preferring instead to attend a private funeral, dressed in their working clothes in order to show that this was no time for celebrations and holidays. Nevertheless the preparations for allocating the territory to Caesar were evidently not complete by the time of Vatinius' law granting him the other areas, since Narbonese Gaul was not included in these. But afterwards, probably in June, Pompey proposed in the senate that Caesar's province should be enlarged by this addition, together with a legion. Although the conferment was to be on an annual, renewable basis instead of the five-year tenure of the other areas, and the union of both Gauls under a single governor was not a complete novelty, Cato declared that 'the senate was itself placing the tyrant in its citadel'. However, the senators gave way—making a virtue of necessity, since rejection of the bill would only have meant that it would have been transferred at once to the assembly and passed there. Some members may also have consoled themselves with the thought that the job would at least keep Caesar from meddling at Rome. Indeed, if invaders really threatened the Gallic frontier, as seemed to be the case, they might even put an end to him altogether.

An attempt to do just this, by assassination, had perhaps already been made by a slave, no doubt acting on the instigation of others: the date is uncertain, but the incident may well have taken place in 59. In July of the same year there was another mysterious plot. Its central figure was the murky informer Vettius who, three years earlier, had tried to incriminate Caesar in the Catilinarian conspiracy. This time Vettius, under interrogation, claimed that a group of conservatives were planning to murder Pompey. To please Caesar, Vettius then amended the list of names he had given, so as to leave out the young Brutus who was the son of the triumvir's mistress, Servilia; the adjustment was the occasion of a typical barbed witticism from Cicero, who commented that a *night* had intervened between the two statements— and that during this interval there had been a nocturnal appeal. Next, Vettius mysteriously died in prison, perhaps at the hands of Vatinius, and no doubt without any objection from Caesar. The original scandal may have amused him as a means of discrediting the conservatives, until someone persuaded Vettius to include the name of Servilia's son. Then he was amused no longer, and Vettius became expendable.

But the incident scarcely contributed to the equanimity of Pompey, who felt very upset by the bitter and critical atmosphere, and publicly expressed apologetic embarrassment about the strong-arm methods that were being used. But Caesar was cleverly keeping himself in the background, so that when Cicero, for example, alluded sneeringly to government by an oriental potentate his reference was to Pompey. Meanwhile, the pronouncements of Bibulus were busy sowing suspicions that while Pompey was in the east he had been double-crossed by Caesar. The opposition's campaign was not going badly. Even if the triumvirs were not quite so desperately unpopular as Cicero hopefully assured his friends, they were the targets for hostile demonstrations in the theatre, and Bibulus managed to get the consular elections postponed until the autumn, though, when they finally occurred, the triumvirate duly contrived to get its nominees Piso and Gabinius elected.

And so Caesar's all-too-eventful consulship drew to an end. It had been responsible for certain beneficial measures. But, above all, it had spun many threads which could be picked up later to his own personal advantage; for such was always Caesar's way. Although, as Cato complained, he was not a mere tribune but a consul, his tenure of office had followed the popular revolutionary method of the Gracchi, because he ignored the senate and carried most of his business direct through the assembly. The senators, it was true, had been totally intransigent. But Caesar, for his part, indulged freely in violence. His earliest enactments were illegal because they had ignored tribunician vetoes; the rest were of dubious legality because they had paid no attention to the omens. It could be said, on the other side, first that neither tribunes nor omens had ever been intended for total, negative obstruction of this kind. Furthermore, the senate had undermined its own stand, first by swearing to the agrarian law, though this was admittedly done under compulsion, and then, more voluntarily, by voting him the Narbonese province. Nevertheless, the irregularities of the year, actual and alleged, meant that henceforward he would continually be liable to prosecution for high treason at every moment in which he was not covered by the immunity of a public office.

This situation became apparent immediately after the end of his consulship. For during the very first days of 58 two of the new praetors at once invited the senate to pronounce all the acts of his tenure null and void. One of these men was Lucius Domitius Ahenobarbus. His enemies described this strongly reactionary conservative as untrustworthy, bloodthirsty and cowardly, 'with every member of his body marked by some vice or crime', and his subsequent record certainly showed him to be stupid and unusually arrogant even for a Roman diehard noble. Yet this man (the great-great-grandfather of the emperor Nero) was able to command a princely inheritance comprising whole armies of farmers and metropolitan clients. He had no reason to love Pompey, who as a young man had murdered his brother. Furthermore, he cherished a special distaste for Caesar, partly because of their irreconcilable politics but especially because his own father had acquired very many dependants in Narbonese Gaul, and he himself could hardly wait to go there and become its governor. The second praetor who denounced Caesar to the senate was Gaius Memmius. That Lucretius should have dedicated to him his marvellous poem *On the Nature of the Universe* is a sign of his literary distinction. But the poetry Memmius himself wrote was erotic, as befitted a man who shared Venus as patron goddess with Caesar; and like him he displayed a powerful taste for adultery, even sending a professor to convey indecent proposals to Caesar's daughter who had married Pompey. At the same time Memmius' homosexual tendencies were vigorous—if the details offered by the poet Catullus can be believed. But Catullus was biased, since he had served on Memmius' staff and had made nothing out of it. The loot no doubt all went to Memmius himself, who later got into trouble for the extreme corruption of his public as well as his private life.

    This curious pair of officials launched a three-day debate during which, whatever Memmius' own habits, the old moral smears were brought up against Caesar again, and were combined with more telling charges about his consulship and particularly the agrarian laws. Unfortunately, Caesar's three speeches in reply, which he soon afterwards published, have not survived. The debate remained inconclusive. But, without awaiting a verdict, Caesar decided it was wiser to move just outside Rome, since once there, even before reaching his actual province, he was already entitled to assume his governorship and thus become immune to prosecution. During the three months he now spent in the neighbourhood of the city, he failed to save one of his subordinates from charges in Rome, but found it possible to arrange for the vetoing of a tribune's request that he himself should appear in court. He also managed, by the threat implied in his soldiery outside the gates, to induce the remaining tribunes to rule that no attempt should be made to deviate, to his disadvantage, from the rule that men absent on official business were exempt from hostile legal action.

Incidents such as these made it clear to Caesar that, for as long as he was going to be away in Gaul, it would be essential that as many Roman functionaries as possible should be on his pay-roll. It would also be convenient, since he himself was not going to be in the capital, for his most influential critics likewise to be removed from the scene. With this in mind, he enlisted to represent him in Rome a henchman beside whom Vatinius seemed a shy violet. This was Clodius. Caesar had already cast a surprisingly tolerant eye on the man even when he had allegedly pursued an affair with Caesar's wife in Caesar's home. Clodius was a brilliant, precocious, fluent and beautiful delinquent, exploiting or destroying without scruple the influential husbands of his sisters, one of whom, the spectacular Clodia whom Catullus so miserably loved, was the most notorious nymphomaniac in Rome. It seems not impossible that her brother's political aims left room for a genuine, rare sympathy towards the unprivileged. But what he enjoyed most of all was the disruption of authority, and his activities in this direction possessed a freelance, wayward, maverick quality of their own. Nevertheless, Caesar, probably with financial support from his fellow triumvirs, decided he could retain a sufficient degree of control over Clodius' behaviour, and planned to use him in order that the conservatives should be kept so busy and harassed that they had no time to intrigue against himself. He had become aware that his new agent possessed an unusual talent for snarling up the workings of the constitution, and he noted particularly his special gift for organised intimidation and violence. Lightly disguised as members of professional guilds, Clodius' thugs swarmed everywhere in a city which still possessed no regular force of police.

The triumvirs therefore decided to back Clodius for a tribunate in 58. There was, it is true, a legal problem, because tribunes, being the traditional defenders of the people's rights, had to be plebeians, whereas the candidate who was now being proposed was a member of the great patrician family of the Claudii. The difficulty was overcome by the characteristic Roman institution of adoption—in this case adoption by a plebeian. Adoption was frequent, and scientifically applied to political ends; men often said they had *two* fathers, a real one and an adoptive one. The act could also take place at any age, although Clodius, to whom an anti-establishment joke of this kind appealed, shocked many people by being adopted by a young man of nineteen—the same age as his own son! The correct procedure was elaborate and complex. Yet now the adoption of Clodius was hurried through in time for the elections, with Caesar as chief priest in the chair, and Pompey, who was an augur, searching the sky in vain for any sign of divine unwillingness. Clodius did not bother to conform with the usual custom of taking on his adoptive parent's family name, but instead affected the spelling of his own name with an 'o', to distinguish his new popular affiliations from the patrician Claudian clan.

The tribunate of Clodius got off to a brisk start. First he put a stop to Bibulus' farewell speech by the simple means of clapping a hand over his mouth. Then he trumped Cato's law approving the public sale of cheap corn by a measure providing for its distribution without any charge. This sensational bid for public support ate up more than half Pompey's total eastern gains, and one-fifth of the entire income of the state. Next Clodius did his duty to the triumvirate by getting both Cicero and Cato out of the way. His demand for Cicero's exile was based on the allegedly illegal execution of the Catilinarians during his consulship just over four years earlier, though it was also not unconnected with Cicero's destruction of Clodius' alibi in the Good Goddess case, vengeance being regarded as a natural, respectable right. The triumvirs all behaved evasively. Pompey and Caesar said they had told Clodius he must not act against the orator. But, if so, this was merely for form's sake. Only recently Cicero had blurted out a public criticism of Caesar, who certainly did not want to leave him in Rome raking up the events of the previous year. However, he also tried to soften the blow, or make it look more respectable, by successively offering Cicero a series of jobs abroad—on a diplomatic mission to Egypt, then on his own staff in Gaul, and finally, on the commission which was redistributing land. But Cicero refused all these lucrative suggestions. Pompey misleadingly told him Clodius would do him no harm, and then dishonestly advised him to stay and fight it out, insinuating that Caesar's advice to go away was not inspired by friendly motives. But when Cicero called for another interview, he sneaked out of the back door. Crassus was no more helpful. And so in March 58 Cicero went into exile in the Balkans, spending sixteen months in the gloomiest and most articulately deplored experience of his life.

Cato, surprisingly enough, was easier to get out of the way. He was requested to go and organise the annexation of Cyprus from the brother of the king of Egypt, and preferred this patriotic mission, designed to increase Roman revenue, to the prospect of staying among Clodius' hooligans. Caesar was pleased to have him outside Rome, and Clodius was happy to inflict him on the Cypriot monarch, against whom he harboured a grudge for having sent too small a ransom when Clodius had once been kidnapped by pirates. The king committed suicide at the prospect of dealing with Cato, whose subsequent settlement, though the accounts were lost on his way back to Rome two years later, was said to have shown characteristic inflexibility.

CHAPTER FOUR

Atrocities Against Gauls and Germans

Confident that all conservative opposition at Rome would be paralysed by Clodius' gangs, Caesar set out northwards for the Gallic War which was destined to occupy the next eight years of his life. We are better informed about it than about any other military operations of the whole of antiquity, because we have seven books of Caesar's own *Commentaries on the Gallic War (De Bello Gallico)*. This is the only contemporary narrative of a major Roman foreign war that has come down to us—and it is written by the principal protagonist. As the greatest of Roman historians, Theodor Mommsen, declared, 'the enormous differences between these Commentaries and everything else that is called Roman history cannot be adequately realised.'

No wonder also that the work was commended to students of war by practical authorities of the calibre of Turenne, Napoleon and Wellington. The *Commentaries* (as it is a little unfair to expect schoolboys to appreciate) are written in a masterly style, a pure, unrhetorical 'Attic' diction, lucid and compact, made up of words that are simple and unerringly chosen. The Latin word *Commentary* means memorandum or notebook, or at most something between 'official log' and 'historical commentary'—a general's dispatch embellished with speeches and a spare sufficiency of background; a possible model, which Caesar may have had in mind, was provided by the Greek politician Aratus of Sicyon (271–213 BC), who left his memoirs.

Yet Caesar's book is, in fact, highly original, since he was consciously creating his own genre and a new style, unafraid of comparison or contrast with the mighty literary names of the past. And he was taking sides, as Roman writers often liked to do, in a historiographical battle inherited from Athenians of four and five centuries ago. For Caesar was, by implication, declaring himself a supporter of the practical, personal, first-hand, factually verified method of Thucydides'—himself a man of action—against the ornate, rhetorical didacticism of historians influenced by the professor Isocrates, whose approach was just now coming into fashion at Rome. Later, Livy became the principal exponent of this more flowery school, but already

Cicero had a leaning towards its dramatic rotundity—a fact which perhaps explains his suggestion that Caesar's work is not an end-product but raw material, though he does add that its pleasing, clear and correct brevity would be hard indeed to improve upon. Caesar's officer, Hirtius, who had the daunting task of rounding off the work with a final eighth book, emphasised not only the articulate excellence of Caesar's style, but the ease and speed with which he wrote. This swift movement communicates a telling urgency to the whole story, and it is best to read the *Commentaries* with the same rapidity: even to the modern age, which is not very interested in pure narrative, Caesar's deeds, stirring and horrible alike, speak for themselves as freshly as when they were written down. Comment is restricted, except in order to make some forcible point. Praise and blame, too, are pared to a minimum, and so is information about people; and yet the down-to-earth, brutal tale is shot with occasional unexpected personal touches and sudden flashes which raise it to formidable literary heights.

Pollio, himself author of an important contemporary history that is now lost, remarked that Caesar sometimes copied the reports of his subordinate commanders too faithfully, a fault he would have corrected in a revised edition. Pollio, who served under Caesar, added that his memory was sometimes at fault. That is hardly surprising, but Pollio goes on to suggest there were also deliberate distortions: which raises the whole question of the reliability of the *Commentaries*. As in this post-Freudian, post-Hitlerian world we know only too well, no history can be free of the biases of its author, unconscious and conscious alike. These dangers are accentuated when the writer was himself one of the leading actors on the stage, and our reservations should not, of course, be lulled by the seeming objective impersonality with which Caesar writes of himself in the third person.

His book had an eye on posterity, but it was mainly written for his own generation—the Roman governing class of politicians from whom, throughout these long years in Gaul, he never took his eyes. He went into the war already surrounded by a storm of criticism, and as the hostilities proceeded he incurred a great deal more. The major purpose of the *Commentaries* was to provide a counterblast. It would, no doubt, have been over-optimistic to expect to silence his most ferocious opponents, but there was a good chance of winning over the floating voters. For their benefit, Caesar displayed yet again his masterly talent for putting his opponents in the wrong, indicating the patriotic correctitude, indeed inevitability, of all his actions, and their absolute conformity with the mandate entrusted to him by the government of Rome. The way to demonstrate all this was not by lying. An occasional distortion or exaggeration might pass muster, but downright lies could all too easily be caught out; because, after all, Caesar was by no means the only Roman who wrote home, and eventually returned home, from the Gallic campaigns.

The speeches inserted in the *Commentaries*, it is true, are nothing like word-for-word reports. Nor indeed, as anyone who has tried to address gatherings out of doors can confirm, could they have been delivered to the large throngs of soldiers who were often supposed to be their audiences. Yet this method of narration was not an attempt to draw wool over anyone's eyes, but a convention, which readers of the day would understand, for painting in backgrounds and motivations. Moreover, these orations sometimes put into the mouths even of Caesar's most determined enemies as convincing arguments as any barrister could have devised: for the story would not have been complete without this explanation of the other side. Of specific self-criticism, not unnaturally, there is little or no trace. This is not a conspicuous feature in the memoirs of any general, and it is scarcely likely to be prominent in a work specifically designed to justify Caesar politically to the people who mattered at home. Good propaganda, directed to such a purpose, is attentive to selection and window-dressing—and the *Commentaries* are among the most potent propaganda ever written.

This persuasive element seems particularly strong in the initial sections, which relate to a time when it was most pressingly needed; and it would seem that this portion of the work, and each of the annual reports that follow, was completed at the end of the year with which it deals. When the various books were published is another problem. Perhaps they were seen by leading people year by year as they were written, in order to win support in successive crises and elections, and then published as a whole when the war was well advanced or complete.

The hostilities all took place in regions lying north of the province of Narbonese Gaul. That is to say, the war was fought outside the Roman empire as hitherto constituted. The whole area between the rivers Garonne and Seine—modern France without its extreme south-western and north-eastern parts—was inhabited by some two hundred separate tribes of Celtic Gauls: the descendants of people who had migrated across the Rhine some seven or eight hundred years previously, subordinating the earlier inhabitants. The total population of the territory may perhaps have amounted to between ten and fifteen million. Extreme administrative weakness not only prevented unity, but made the central executives of each small tribe highly unstable. Government was usually in the hands of pairs of elected officials analogous to the Roman consuls, though there were also surviving examples of an earlier system of hereditary chieftainships. Tribes were more or less compact collections of smaller communities linked with one another by blood-relationship or geographical proximity. The most promising sign of cohesion was a strong factor of loyalty like the client system of Rome, which united rich patrons with their poor dependants, and likewise bound weaker states to their stronger neighbours.

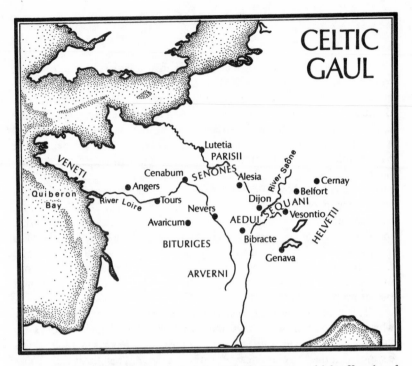

CELTIC GAUL

Apart from this perilous administrative feebleness, which offered such an enticing invitation to invaders, the civilisation of the Gauls was relatively advanced. Agriculture achieved good results, the breeding of imported stocks of horses and pigs was elaborately developed, and metallurgy reached such heights that Gallic swords were equalled in no other country but Spain. In the plains there were scores of hamlets, and on the hills above them stood small but well fortified towns. The superb rivers of Gaul encouraged a trade which is demonstrated by the extensive and varied coinage of many tribes, copying Greek and Roman coins but also displaying fine patterns of distinctively Celtic style. Artefacts included painted pottery, mirrors and openwork horse-trappings, and the Gauls loved ballads and rated clever speaking second only to prowess in war.

But in war they were showy rather than truly dangerous. Ancient invasions of Italy had given them an impressive reputation at Rome, and there was still something frightening about the first charge of their trousered, tartan-shirted infantry, with its long cutting swords and wooden or wattle shields. But after an initial setback these foot-soldiers deteriorated rapidly into unwieldy, useless mobs, 'more than men at the first onslaught, less than women after a severe repulse'; neither as ferocious as barbarians nor as well-organised as Romans. Besides, leading Gauls regarded the infantry as unsmart, and tended to leave it to the earlier races that had become their serfs. The Gaulish leaders themselves, in their rings, bracelets, gold collars, plumed helmets and chain-armour, preferred to serve in the cavalry—which was far more formidable, though rarely good enough to beat well-disciplined enemies.

Much the most powerful tribes, and those in which the Romans were principally interested, were the Sequani of Franche-Comté and the Aedui of Burgundy. These peoples lay, respectively, north-east and north of the Roman province of Narbonese Gaul. The province had owed its existence to the threat which the Arverni (Auvergne), in the second century BC, had presented to Rome's Greek ally, Massilia. At that time the tribe, based on the fortress-capital Gergovia, had spread its dominions as far as the Pyrenees and the Atlantic. But the Romans had prevented them from expanding to the Mediterranean, and thereafter the empire of the Arverni was limited to suzerainty over smaller tribes in their immediate vicinity. In its appeal to Rome, Massilia had been joined by the Aedui; and that people henceforward constituted the chief Gallic ally of Rome, which always liked to keep a *cordon sanitaire* of such dependent states beyond its formal borders, maintaining with them a client relationship akin to the client-patron connection which played so large a part in the social and political life of Rome and Gaul alike. The capital of the Aedui was Bibracte (Mont Beuvray), situated on a hill above Augustodunum (later Autun). Bibracte possessed quite a highly-developed urban and industrial life, and excavations have revealed rectangular houses made of stone compacted with clay and equipped with courtyards and internal staircases, and central heating systems.

The Sequani and Aedui, each surrounded by a ring of dependencies, perpetuated Gallic disunity but created a certain precarious balance in the country. Now, however, that was threatened by a more easterly tribe, the Helvetii. These people were Celts who had gradually been driven from south Germany into Switzerland. But there, too, the land they occupied was under constant pressure from the Germans, and in 61 they had decided to migrate westwards in a body, from end to end of Gaul, in order to establish new homes on the Atlantic coast. Although the Helvetii were old enemies of Rome—the great-grandfather of Caesar's wife had lost his life in a disastrous battle against them—this proposed evacuation of Switzerland was unwelcome since they had served as a useful barrier between Italy and the fierce German tribes beyond. Besides, the most convenient route for their trek would run through the northern part of the Narbonese province, where tribes exasperated by oppressive Roman government might be encouraged by their presence to make trouble. The Romans also felt anxiety about the infantry of the Helvetii, which was unusually strong for a Celtic tribe.

During the years immediately preceding Caesar's governorship there had been several scares about the Helvetian migration; indeed, the prospect of trouble was what made him want to include the Transalpine area in his command. Now, in March 58, he hastened to Genava (Geneva) in eight days (covering ninety miles a day) and at once arranged for its bridge across the Rhône to be demolished, and for other westward routes to be blocked as well. The Helvetii, seeing that they could not pass through Narbonese Gaul, decided instead to proceed to the Atlantic by a more northerly route, which did not touch upon the province. This might have seemed to deprive Caesar of the pretext for a fight. But in order not to lose his opportunity of military distinction he chose to see this route, too, as a threat to the province; and indeed contemporary political doctrine maintained that Rome was obliged to enforce its power in the quasi-dependent regions beyond its borders. Moreover, after a lightning transfer of troops from north Italy, he found himself with a less implausible excuse for military intervention, since the pro-Roman faction in control of the Aedui was induced to appeal to him formally for aid against the Helvetic menace.

With this exemplary justification, Caesar fell upon the migrants on the Saône, and slaughtered a quarter of their number. After an unsuccessful attempt to negotiate, the remainder of the Helvetii, who, unlike their unfortunate compatriots, had succeeded in getting across the river, continued northwards for two weeks with the Romans following five miles behind. But Caesar's cavalry, which had been swelled by Aeduan horsemen to the total of four thousand, suffered a rebuff. Moreover, the corn-supply, which the Gauls had undertaken to provide for him, broke down, apparently because of the treachery of an anti-Roman party among the Aedui. Consequently Caesar was obliged to make a detour to their capital Bibracte, seventeen miles off his road, in order to obtain food from there. Encouraged by this apparent retreat, the Helvetii started to harass the column. However, in the fierce battle that followed they were overwhelmed. Their waggon camp was captured, and those who managed to escape were forced to surrender.

The survivors were compelled to go back to their original homes. Caesar estimates their number at 110,000, and indicates that those who had met their deaths numbered about 258,000. This figure may be accurate, or it may have been exaggerated for purposes of publicity. If the latter is the case, Caesar was calculating that Roman public opinion would like to hear of the slaughter of as many barbarians as possible. What is worse, he explicitly adds, with a distasteful regard for the truth, that a large number of the casualties were women, old people and children. This detail was evidently just another picturesque touch in an account which confronted his enemies at Rome with a rising reputation for martial glory. And the other Gaulish tribes, spared the mass migration through their midst, were likewise pleased.

The second victory of 58 was won not against Gauls but Germans. Rome had not forgotten the frightening invasions of half a century ago, when German hordes had penetrated to southern France and even down into Italy in gigantic numbers, and had overwhelmed several Roman armies before they themselves were finally annihilated by Marius. Caesar, to emphasise that the current menace was equally grave, perhaps overstresses the contrast between the comparative culture of Gauls and the savage ferocity of Germans. The Rhine was not the dramatic frontier that might be imagined from his pages, since there were still Celts or Celticised peoples on either side of the river, and indeed it had only recently been appreciated that the Germans could be described as a 'nation' in the same sort of sense as the Gauls. Here Caesar was following the Graeco-Syrian scholar, Posidonius, of the previous generation; and the Germans, as a power confronting the Gauls from across the Rhine, can be regarded as the two men's invention.

It is true, however, that the German nomads known as Suebi, who early in the first century BC had migrated from east Germany towards the Marne and Rhine, were tough characters who spent their lives fighting and hunting, though they also showed an increasing interest in land. In the later seventies or a little later, Ariovistus, a chieftain of the Suebi or a kindred tribe, had resumed the drive, bringing pressure upon the Celts of eastern France and Switzerland. In particular the Sequani, a large tribe extending between the Aeduan border and Alsace, found Ariovistus encroaching considerably on their territory. Nevertheless, appreciating rather sadly the superior military efficiency of the Germans, they made use of him as an ally, enabling them to win an important victory in 61 against the Aedui, with whom they had a difference of opinion about the customs dues of the Saône valley. But after the victory Ariovistus proved even harder to dislodge than before, demanding more and more Sequanian territory. Although the matter related to regions far outside the borders of the province, this caused disquiet in Rome. The government played for time, apparently on Caesar's initiative, by recognising Ariovistus as king and friend of the Roman people.

That was in 59, but in the following year, after Caesar had dealt with the Helvetii, he saw an opportunity for another spectacular campaign. Again Rome's allies, the Aedui, had conveniently appealed for intervention; and it was always possible to scare Rome with the threat of fresh German invasions of Italy. Negotiations with Ariovistus ended in an ultimatum which he could not be expected to accept, and he moved west towards the Sequanian capital, Vesontio (Besançon), a fortress surrounded on three sides by water. Caesar got there first and occupied the place, but then a momentary setback occurred, because of bad morale among some of the Roman officers. Caesar somewhat ironically singles out the young men from good families whom it was customary for generals to take onto their staffs. He claims they were frightened by the stature and prowess of the Germans, but it is also very likely that the trouble was fomented by political enemies at Rome, making capital out of the unnecessary nature of the campaign. The German war was not, perhaps, exactly illegal, since, in spite of a treason law insisting that governors must not fight outside their provinces, a two-year-old enactment specifically authorised any measure that might be needed to help Rome's allies the Aedui. Yet the whole encounter with Ariovistus could very well, and indeed justly, be represented as being mainly directed towards the greater prestige of Caesar himself. He does not say how he dealt with the temporary officers; they no doubt suffered later from his inconveniently long memory. But he records that the more professional centurions, to whom the disaffection had partially spread, were summoned in order to hear his confident prognostications of victory.

Next came a conference with Ariovistus, at which Caesar, distrusting his Gallic cavalry, transferred their horses to legionaries, whom he employed as an escort. After Ariovistus had sneeringly disclosed that he knew all about Caesar's enemies at Rome, the talk came to nothing, just as Caesar had intended. He was in a hurry, with autumn ahead, and a pretext was quickly found for claiming a breach of truce and launching a major attack on the Germans. This extremely hazardous battle, which perhaps took place near Cernay or Belfort, was mainly won for the Romans by a youthful officer, Publius the younger son of Crassus, who, acting on his own initiative, sent in Caesar's last reserves to save the endangered left wing. The German army, numbering possibly a hundred and twenty thousand men, was almost totally obliterated. Among those hunted down and killed by Caesar's Gallic cavalry were Ariovistus' two wives. He himself escaped in a small boat, and died soon afterwards. Three German tribes were allowed to stay west of the Rhine, and the middle areas of the zone, protected by dense forests, remained at peace for many years.

When the dispatches about these events reached Rome, Caesar's father-in-law, who was consul, did not succeed in arousing a very enthusiastic reaction. But the capital was in the grip of gang warfare directed by Clodius, and fighting in the streets became general when his enemies, ostensibly acting in defence of society, likewise organised powerful rival bands.

Meanwhile Caesar was embarking on a fresh phase of his Gallic enterprise. When he established his winter quarters among the Sequani, they saw they had only replaced one foreign master by another, and the local popularity he had gained from his victories over the Helvetii and the Germans turned to disaffection. During the winter he learnt that this hostile attitude had spread to the Belgic peoples beyond the Marne and Seine. These Belgae, who had settled in north-eastern France and Belgium about a century and a half earlier—the most advanced tribes being those on the near side of the Ardennes—were proud of their German origins and retained German customs such as cremation. But they had intermingled with the Celts, and were

BELGIC GAUL
AND GERMANY

now Celticised in many of their institutions and in their language, which dif-
fered only slightly from that of their neighbours.

Although they were now amassing against Caesar a force estimated at
three hundred thousand men, this news was welcome to him rather than
alarming, because it seemed to offer the chance of overrunning the whole
vast region of Transalpine Gaul north of the existing Narbonese province:
the opportunity, that is to say, of winning victories as great as Pompey's, if
not greater, with a corresponding effect upon Rome. And so Caesar, at the
turn of the year, recruited two new legions in his Cisalpine territory, bringing
his army to double the size authorised by the Roman government.

Meanwhile the Belgae entrusted the supreme command of their federal
force to the king of the Suessiones (Soissons). However, their neighbours the
Remi (Rheims), discontented because they were subordinate to the
Suessiones, formed an alliance with Caesar; and, although their hopes of
keeping out of the fighting proved vain, they remained his most loyal allies
in Gaul, or, to look at it the other way, the most infamous collaborators in
the country. The Aedui were also induced to help the Romans again. But
after Caesar had moved northwards to a point on the Aisne, probably Berry-
au-Bac where a camp had been identified, only minor hostilities were necessary before the huge Belgic host ludicrously broke up owing to the collapse,
or rather non-existence, of its system of food supplies. The tribes were

allowed to survive, on a tributary basis, and Caesar pressed rapidly onwards
in a north-easterly direction against the most formidable Belgic tribes which
had not yet been engaged. These were the Nervii of Hainault and Flanders.
Their country was protected by a criss-cross of high hedges which made
mounted action impracticable, and the Nervii were unique for their first-class
infantry. This was waiting for Caesar behind the shallow river Sambre, near
Neuf Mesnil (Maubeuge) on the Franco-Belgian frontier. The battle which
followed was one of the most perilous Caesar ever fought, because he was
completely surprised by the proximity of the Nervian army in a thick wood,
unrevealed by the cavalry screen of the Romans. Their losses due to this
reconnaissance failure were alarming—one cohort lost all six of its
centurions—but the situation was saved by one of those displays of spectacular personal initiative and heroism with which Caesar had a talent for retriev-
ing desperate emergencies. And so, he reports, 'the name of the Nervii was
almost blotted out from the face of the earth'. The old men of the tribe, who
had been hiding with the women and children in the creeks and marshes,
told him that out of sixty thousand men capable of bearing arms scarcely five
hundred had survived. Later events, in fact, suggested that the carnage was
not quite so severe as that, but Caesar was proud to report the figure to Rome.
     The campaign was rounded off by an onslaught on the eastern neighbours
of the defeated Nervii. These people, the Atuatuci, who laughed at the Romans
for their diminutive size, had made a move to join the Nervii, but on hearing
news of the battle they had returned to their homes in the neighbourhood of
Namur. There, intimidated by the siege machinery of the Romans, they gave in,
but then unwisely broke the truce, giving Caesar a pretext for ferocious retal-
iation. After repelling their sortie, he proceeded to sell all the fifty-three thousand inhabitants of the place by auction as slaves, in a single lot. He tells us this
himself, and would no doubt have maintained that the example was necessary,
and that these were too barbarous a people to be relied upon.
     Meanwhile the young Publius Crassus had marched into north-western
Gaul and received the submission of the coastal tribes of Normandy and
Brittany. The invasion of this area was unprovoked, and apparently indicates
that Caesar's mind was now set on the annexation of the whole country, or
at least on the creation of a network of dependent states such as Pompey had
established around his Asian conquests. During the winter, while he himself
went at last to pay some attention to the Illyrian part of his province, Gaul
was held down by garrisons in the north—beside the Loire near Angers,
Tours and Orléans (the ancient Cenabum) and in the western regions of
Switzerland. He regarded the war as virtually over.

These achievements had by now aroused considerable excitement at Rome.
The new vistas they opened up were sensational, and some of the enormous

booty was already filtering through to the capital. Most senators felt that such resounding successes erased all memory of earlier illegalities. Pompey proposed the longest thanksgiving on record, and Cicero agreed to second the proposal. He took this accommodating line out of gratitude to Pompey—who had recently brought him back from exile, since the orator's enemy, Clodius, had proved highly unreliable, not only attacking the dubious events of Caesar's consulship but offering Pompey himself grave personal intimidation. But now Clodius was to a large extent incapacitated, since his popularity, which largely depended on the free food distributions he had sponsored, was weakened by a serious shortage of grain, the result of a bad harvest and intrigues by unscrupulous speculators. Clodius also claimed, though probably without justification, that the dearth was deliberately worsened by Pompey himself, since one of its effects was the conferment upon him of a special commission to remedy the situation. Although a tribune suggested that this post should carry universal and overriding military authority, it is not likely that he himself sponsored the idea, and no such powers were in fact attached to the appointment. But its duration was to be for five years, of which the final two would outlast the period at present allotted to Caesar's governorship. The mutual trust between the triumvirs was not complete enough for him to envisage those two years in Pompey's power. There was already a suspicion that the poor job Pompey had made of maintaining order, as well as food supplies, might have been prompted by his hope of being called upon as saviour and dictator. Moreover, for all his honorific proposals in Caesar's favour, even a less vain man than he was could not fail to have felt slight pangs of jealousy about the victories in Gaul, which were beginning to rival his own eastern successes. Was that, perhaps, why he seemed in no hurry to read Caesar's dispatches in the senate? It was even being suggested that he should divorce Julia and rejoin the conservative cause. He refused, but became, meanwhile, extremely unfriendly with Crassus, whom he regarded as responsible for Clodius' insults and even accused of attempting to murder him.

Naturally all this was very welcome to the diehards. Moreover, they had secured the appointment for 56 of a consul who hated the triumvirs; and they hoped that in the following year a consulship would go to Ahenobarbus, who coveted Caesar's Narbonese province. In these circumstances Cicero, too, regained confidence. When he returned from exile, there had been an understanding that he would back the triumvirs, but now, instead, he began to exert himself to drive a wedge between Pompey and Caesar. He described the law which had conferred the latter's province as a massacre of the ancestral constitution. Moreover, in the spring of 56 he announced his intention of supporting a tribune who had assailed the notorious Campanian land-law of Caesar's consulship.

Here, however, he overplayed his hand, for this only served to remind all the triumvirs that they still needed one another's help. Though the tribune attacking Caesar's land-law was believed to be a partisan of Pompey, his initiative conflicted with Pompey's interests, which were vitally bound up with the settlement of his veterans by this law. Crassus, too, evidently came to the conclusion that his investment in the triumvirate was far too heavy to be thrown overboard, since he still needed the friendship of both his colleagues to secure his ultimate ambition: a military command which would give him glory equal to theirs, and would double his financial worth.

Accordingly Crassus proceeded in April to Ravenna, just inside Cisalpine Gaul, where he met Caesar and warned him of Cicero's hostile intentions. The next step was a meeting between all three triumvirs, and by the middle of the month they were in conference together at Luca (Lucca), which like Ravenna was on the border of the Cisalpine province. All disagreements were patched up for the time being, and the comprehensive plans made there, though for the time being remaining secret, became gradually all too clear during the following year. The slogan CONCORDIA which appeared on a coin about this time meant, in effect, that the Republic was to remain in abeyance, and that the allegedly one hundred and twenty senators who had flocked to the little town of Luca must just wait and see and obey.

First, it was decided that Caesar's acts should be confirmed, and that the treasury should pay for his four new legions—a somewhat malicious gesture in the face of his critics, since Caesar was now wealthy and the exchequer poor. He was to be given time to finish the exploitation of his province, Pompey would remain in sole charge of Rome, and Crassus was assured the overseas appointment that he wanted. Even Clodius, though he could not be relied upon, felt it desirable to support Pompey's candidates for office. As for Cicero, he was effectively reduced to compliance because his brother, Quintus, was serving in Sardinia under Pompey, who made his hold over the orator painfully apparent. Furthermore, Quintus next passed into the service of Caesar, whose treatment of him again varied in direct relation with his brother's obedience. Though the orator wrote privately that he was ashamed to behave in such a way, he now engaged in grovelling recantations, including a speech in which he listed every possible reason why Caesar was still the right man for a country with the geopolitical significance of Gaul. Caesar may have raised an eyebrow at the description of himself as a former anti-conservative who had now seen the light. Nevertheless, as a reward he allowed Cicero to let off steam by delivering an abusive attack on the father of his wife Calpurnia, a man the orator hated for failing, as consul, to prevent his banishment.

The *carte blanche* conferred on Caesar's Gallic operations at Luca proved welcome and indeed necessary, because, whatever imposing successes he may have planned for 56, they had to be postponed when it became clear that the country was nothing like pacified after all. During the winter, perhaps believing that Caesar's authority was undermined at Rome, the tribes of Brittany had begun to have second thoughts about their submission. The initiative was taken by the warlike Veneti, an Atlantic people of Morbihan, scarcely touched by Celtic culture. They took the perilous step of detaining Roman requisitioning officers, and their eastern and southern neighbours offered support, so that the Roman forces had to be divided between the various regions concerned. The coastal towns of the Veneti were situated on jutting promontories cut off by the tides and unapproachable by land, and Caesar could find no means of capturing them until, from his headquarters at Angers, he had supervised the construction of warships on the Loire, and the mobilisation of others from seafaring tribes between Loire and Garonne.

The Veneti were not only the principal sea-traders of Gaul, possessing a virtual monopoly of the importation of British tin, but they were also the leading Gaulish sea-power. At first the relatively light Roman warships found themselves at a disadvantage in dealing with the heavy oak barges of the Veneti, which had shallower draughts to weather shoals at low water, and leather sails able to withstand Atlantic gales. But they carried no rowers or archers, and the Romans ingeniously invented long poles with pointed hooks to sever their halyards and make it impossible for them to move. In a decisive engagement in Quiberon Bay the luck of a sudden dead calm did the rest, and the hopelessly drifting barges were boarded and captured. The Veneti surrendered, and Caesar himself reports that he had all their councillors executed and the rest of the population sold as slaves. This gruesome act was no doubt prompted by a desire to indicate that tribes which had once submitted did not do well to revolt. But Caesar's attempted justification of the deed on the grounds of a violation of diplomatic rights by the Veneti was threadbare, since his requisitioning officers had been concerned only with obtaining corn and supplies, and possessed no ambassadorial role, nor had they suffered any harm.

Meanwhile repressive military action in Normandy was equally successful, and the young Publius Crassus also triumphantly achieved an unprovoked aggression among the Iberian Aquitani between the Garonne and the Pyrenees; the first words of the *Gallic War*, 'All Gaul is divided into three parts', famous among generations of schoolboys, refers to the Gauls (Celts), Belgae and Aquitani. Further to the north, the season ended with something of an anti-climax in thickly-wooded, waterlogged Pas de Calais and Flanders, where Caesar, like others after him, was checked by rain and mud.

It was probably the campaigns of 56 which finally convinced him that the permanent military occupation of northern as well as central Gaul was inevitable. He had comparatively few political worries about Rome at this time, because opposition was severely impeded by the renewed understanding between the triumvirs. They had agreed that Pompey and Crassus should be consuls for 55, and although a hostile predecessor tried to prevent their candidature on the grounds of inadequate notice, urging the electorate to behave freely while it still had the chance, they arranged for a tribune to prevent the elections for the rest of the year, so that these could take place after the obstructive official's term of office had come to an end. The delay had the further advantage that Crassus' younger son was now free to bring a thousand of Caesar's soldiers down to Rome 'on leave'. They assured the result, though Cato was wounded in the process.

The first thing the new consuls did was to block Cato's candidature for a praetorship of the year by bribery and the declaration of unfavourable omens. Then they moved rapidly into positive action. A bill by the tribune Gaius Trebonius secured that, after the end of their term of office, they should be voted the two Spains and Syria for five years, the lot being manipulated so as to give Spain to Pompey and Syria to Crassus. Both received huge powers to raise troops and make war and peace, and at once mobilised recruits and sent officers to take over their provinces. In spite of Cato's continued resistance the bill went through, amid riots that cost four fatal casualties: Crassus himself drew a senator's blood. Caesar's friends were at first said to have been worried by the law, but if so they were misinformed, since immediately afterwards a bill sponsored by the consuls themselves renewed his command also—likewise for a further five years, until late 50 or early in 49, thus giving him parity with his fellow-triumvirs during the foreseeable future. Cohesion was all the more necessary because the conservatives were still strong enough, in the elections for the following year, to win Ahenobarbus and Cato the consulship and praetorship for which they had respectively waited. Pompey remained near the city 'to maintain order'. This was not exactly unconstitutional, but it was an anomalous and arbitrary situation for a man who had been appointed governor of Spain: the formula was noted later by emperors, as a means of maintaining autocratic powers under a Republican façade. As for Crassus, he departed for the east in November. Before he left, aware that his prestige was not large enough to ensure durable popularity, he distributed to every citizen of Rome enough money to live on for three months, boasting that even after that he still had seven and a half million pounds left.

All the triumvirs were now enormously rich. But they still needed further gigantic sums in order to maintain and expand their positions against the world and each other. Crassus hoped for this windfall from Parthia, and Pompey and Caesar looked towards the wealthiest country of the ancient world, the kingdom of Egypt. Four years earlier they had undertaken to secure the official Roman recognition of its monarch, Ptolemy XII the Oboe Player, in exchange for an absolutely enormous payment. Ptolemy, for all his immense resources, had found it necessary to borrow this *douceur* from the Roman knight Rabirius Postumus, the prince of blatant speculative bankers, who was accustomed to placing loans of such a kind, though scarcely on such a scale, throughout the Mediterranean world. But in 58, immediately after recompensing Pompey and Caesar from this source, Ptolemy had been expelled by his Alexandrian subjects. Now, therefore, the potentially lucrative question of restoring him was in the air all over again. Friends of both Pompey and Crassus had hinted that their patrons might like the job; enemies of Pompey even suggested it was actually he who had arranged for the king's expulsion, so that he could profitably put him back on the throne. However, Crassus was now to be occupied raising funds elsewhere, and at Luca it was decided that his fellow-triumvirs should arrange the matter. This was not, however, to be done personally: the current restoration was to be undertaken by Pompey's henchman, Gabinius, who was now to become governor of Syria, and then he and his master were to share the spoils with Caesar. Rabirius, who had not yet got his vast loan back from Ptolemy, was authorised to accompany Gabinius in order to recoup himself and have a finger in the new pie as well. In the event Ptolemy, unable to pay, made him his minister of finance, so that he could raise the money for himself by various means, including trade in cloth and glass.

But meanwhile Gabinius had committed the dangerous offence of annoying the Roman knights who had Syria in their financial clutches. He had done this by being too fair to the native population of Syria, and as a result the knights complained about the bribe which he in his turn now received from the Egyptian king. Rabirius, when he returned home, declared he himself was a poor man; but this was hard to believe, and both he and Gabinius were prosecuted for illicit gains. Cicero previously described Gabinius, who like his fellow-consul Piso had done all too little to prevent his exile, as a treacherous, thieving, effeminate ballet boy in curlers. But now his obligations to the triumvirs forced him to forget this and speak up for the man—though his defence was not accepted. Rabirius, whom he defended more successfully, apparently had his unsatisfied claim upon Egypt transferred to Caesar. It seemed only proper for Caesar to stand by Rabirius, since the latter was only indebted because Caesar had laid his hands on so much Egyptian money five years earlier. Besides, if (as may have been the case) Rabirius was not as poor as he seemed, Caesar probably received from him not only an unclaimed debt but a large sum of money as well.

Meanwhile Caesar had returned from Cisalpine to Narbonese Gaul earlier than usual in the season. This was because an incursion from the east had

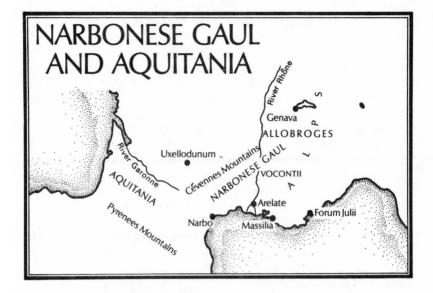

NARBONESE GAUL
AND AQUITANIA

given him an opportunity to get to grips a second time with the Germans. Welcomed by several Gallic tribes, two large German peoples, the Usipetes and Tencteri, had crossed the Rhine in a mass from Westphalia, and as they moved west and south they sent Caesar a request for land on the left bank of the river. Instead he offered them territory on the right bank, with curiously little consideration for the tribe already residing there, which was an ally of Rome. During a period of truce for further negotiations, a cavalry engagement somehow began. Caesar rightly or wrongly blamed the Germans for starting the fight, and to make it worse they defeated his Gallic horse, although outnumbered six to one. When the entire body of German chiefs and elders came to apologise, Caesar arrested them all, fell on their camp in the neighbourhood of Maastricht, and annihilated the whole of the two tribes. 'There was also a great crowd of women and children in the camp,' remarked Caesar, 'since they had brought all their families with them when they left home and crossed the Rhine. These began to flee in all directions, and were hunted down by the cavalry which were sent out for the purpose'. Stopped by the confluence of the Rhine and the Moselle, the exhausted refugees were killed or drowned. In this deed of genocide, the enemy dead were estimated as high as four hundred and thirty thousand: and it was claimed that on the Roman side there was not a single casualty.

Subsequently the praetor-elect, Cato, declared in the senate that, far from being honoured with a thanksgiving for this carnage, Caesar should be handed over to the enemy as an act of atonement. The grounds for this proposal were not so much humanitarian as political: conservative hatred of Caesar, and perhaps old-fashioned anti-annexationism. But the main motive was religious, because Cato asserted that the breach of faith which he believed

Caesar to have committed would bring down a curse, and this ought to be made to fall not on Rome but on the guilty party. If the gods must be thanked, he declared, this should be because they had not allowed the folly and delusion of the general to be visited on his soldiers, and because they had spared the city of Rome from retribution. Handing over governors to wronged foreigners for this religious reason was in the news; only a very short time before, Cicero had made a similar proposal regarding Caesar's father-in-law. Nothing, of course, came of the idea of punishing either, nor, apparently, of another proposal to the effect that a commission should be sent to investigate the continual enlargements of Caesar's military activity. But Cato was one of the few people capable of stinging him, and he wrote furiously to the senate complaining of Cato's speech. No doubt he argued that, unless an example were made of these hordes of German invaders, Gallic appeals could never be met and Roman conquests never stabilised. Cato refuted his arguments, and the relevant passage of Caesar's *Commentaries*, in which the blame for the outrage is elaborately ascribed to the Germans, may only have assumed its final form as a result of these irritating events.

CHAPTER FIVE

Raids on Britain
and Germany

*B*efore the discussion about Caesar's brutalities to the Germans took place, he had strengthened his position by two further exploits which, although impermanent, were highly spectacular. The first of these enterprises was the bridging and crossing of that barrier hitherto untraversed by Roman armies, the Rhine. The pretext was that some cavalry of the Usipetes and Tencteri, which escaped the battle because they were out foraging, had crossed to the east bank and taken refuge with another German tribe. And so, within ten days from beginning to cut the timber, Caesar's engineers completed a trestle-bridge across the river. The bridge, near Coblenz or Andernach or Cologne or Xanten, was fifteen hundred feet long and forty wide; never had so wide or rapid or deep a river been bridged before. Once across, however, Caesar did very little. No hostile Germans put in an appearance, and after eighteen days he marched back across the bridge and had it demolished behind him. But this novel adventure, intended to rival the achievements of Pompey in unexplored lands, excited Rome. It also served notice on the neighbours of the Gauls that Rome expected them to be as docile as the newly subjected peoples themselves, and that Roman strength had no need to accept any demarcation line as a natural border.

In the same year (55) came an even more sensational excitement: the crossing not of a mere river, but of the very ocean itself that surrounded the known earth. Caesar had sailed upon the outer seas when he was governor of Further Spain, and more recently the British expedition upon which he now embarked may already have been in his thoughts when he was building ships on the Loire to use against the Veneti of Brittany. The latter tribe had possessed a monopoly of British trade, but Caesar found them unwilling to disclose any reliable information about the island. Nor did he have greater success with spies and intermediaries. The Gaulish king, Commius of the Atrebates (Arras), one of his collaborators, was arrested when he crossed the Channel, and a Roman officer sent to reconnoitre had a five-day sea-trip but did not manage to land on the inhospitable British shores at all. Some even maintained that the country was a complete fabrication, but those who gave credit to its existence were inclined to believe it was very rich. In particular, Caesar himself like many others hoped for lavish loot of gold and silver and above all pearls. From about 75, south-east England had been gradually over-run from the continent by Belgae, who at this time were just beginning to form their tribes into larger unions. Caesar claimed that they had helped his Gallic enemies, and whether that was true or not they showed a provoking tendency to harbour Gaulish resistance movements.

The time-factor was vital for an operation of this kind, since the Romans must not run the risk of being stranded by winter; and Caesar informs us that his expedition took on board no grain for such a contingency, intending to live off British corn and cattle, and then return before the bad weather set in. However, after the eventful months in the Rhineland, he was not able to start until late August, that is, according to the seasons (which were out of step with the calendar), mid-July. Without waiting for his cavalry, which was delayed, he embarked after midnight from Portus Itius (Boulogne or Wissant) with eighty transports carrying two legions. The fleet arrived off Dover at about nine in the morning, but failed to land in the face of a mob of Britons stationed in a position from which they could rake the beach with their javelins. The British armies also included strong cavalry, whereas Caesar only had thirty horsemen with him; and unlike the Gauls they still made use of war-chariots. The Roman force sailed on to some point near Walmer or Deal, where they effected a most uncomfortable landing in the afternoon. Once they saw the legionaries on shore, the nearest British tribes soon sub-mitted, but they started fighting again when the beached Roman warships and anchored transports were heavily damaged by high tides, which Caesar admits had not been foreseen. A perilous ambush launched against foraging Romans was successfully dealt with, and Caesar was able to make the gesture of doubling his demand for hostages before returning his whole force to Gaul, only eighteen days after he had landed.

Very few hostages were in fact sent by the British, and apart from the briefest reconnaissance in force nothing practical had been achieved. All the same, Roman arms had penetrated for the first time to a legendary land quite separated from the continental mass. Pompey was later recorded as saying that the Channel was not really ocean but tidal mud-flats, but the fantastic nature of the expedition stirred the imagination of most people at Rome. It was at this stage that Cato reminded his fellow-senators of Caesar's cruelty towards the Germans. But he struck an untimely note, and as a token of con-gratulations for the year's campaigns the senate voted Caesar a thanksgiving to last for the singular duration of twenty days.

* * *

He and his lieutenants had now completed four seasons beyond the province. The pattern of the *Commentaries*, although it makes room for tributes to individual acts of gallantry in the lower ranks, does not admit the inclusion of very much detail about his senior officers whose professional competence was so indispensable. Caesar's principal deputy commander was Labienus, whom he left in charge every winter while he himself moved to the Cisalpine part of his province. Labienus came from Picenum like Pompey, with whom, like other members of Caesar's staff, he had previously served. Labienus seems to have come into contact with Caesar for the first time during the latter's brief term of service in Cilicia in 78, and he worked in collaboration with him in 63. He was a man who inspired fear more than devotion, and later events suggest that, although Caesar greatly enriched him, his ostentatiously expressed subordination may have concealed a repressed jealousy or dislike for his commander. But he possessed ability of a very high order. In spite of miscalculations, his information service was excellent, he adapted himself rapidly to sudden changes of plan, and above all he was in advance of almost all his contemporaries in the handling of cavalry, an arm generally neglected hitherto, for which the Roman army was now beginning to recruit Gauls and Germans.

Caesar's chief of staff was Mamurra of Formiae, who had again probably fought under Pompey in the east; then he served with Caesar in Spain. Like Labienus, he was a first-class officer, and like him he made a great deal of money out of the war. Cicero tells us that his town house set unprecedented standards for luxury. Both he and his general earned the acute distaste of the smart young poet Catullus. Both, he said, are tarred with the same brush, joint competitors in the women's market. Another poem, probably written in the autumn of 55, referred to the invader of Britain as a pansy Romulus, and spoke of Mamurra, who, the poet said, had made millions out of his commander, in terms of the most savage coarseness. Almost worse, in a way, was Catullus' further epigram:

> Utter indifference to your welfare, Caesar,
> Is matched only by ignorance of who you are.[1]

Caesar was, not unnaturally, displeased, but Catullus' father was his friend and host at Verona, a city which played a considerable part in Cisalpine arrangements and plans. So Catullus was somehow induced to apologise, and Caesar invited him to dinner on the same day. Another youthful poet, Calvus, who specialised in attacking not only the triumvirs but the scrofulous Vatinius, had friends who approached Caesar in the hope of reconciling him to the young man, and the general himself made the first move to bring this about. The homosexual allegations on which these poets dwelt were the stock-in-trade of such abuse, but Caesar's own soldiers later sang a song referring to another aspect of his sex life in Gaul:

Home we bring our bald whoremonger;
Romans lock your wives away!
All the bags of gold you lent him
Went his Gallic tarts to pay.[2]

And in the following century a man from near Dijon (Dibio) claimed that his great-grandmother had been Caesar's mistress, and that he himself possessed Julian blood.

Scurrilous attacks ignored the fact that staff officers like Mamurra got through a great deal of highly efficient work. And so, no doubt, did the office for political correspondence at Caesar's headquarters. This was at first directed by Pompeius Trogus, a Gaul from the Vocontii (Vaison) who was an expert on Celtic affairs. In about 54 he was succeeded by Aulus Hirtius, a scholarly man without great military knowledge, who later incurred Cicero's disapproval as idle and effeminate but was entrusted by Caesar with the writing of the last book of his *Commentaries on the Gallic War*. Hirtius was also a gourmet, famous for the sauces produced by his chef; people were frightened of asking him to dinner. He cannot, in this respect, have greatly enjoyed life at the headquarters of Caesar, who drank very moderately and was singularly indifferent to food. At a dinner-party he once attended in Milan the asparagus arrived covered with scent instead of olive oil. Caesar ate this quite calmly, and rebuked the bad manners of his staff who could not manage to get it down. A feature of Caesar's own dinners was that they were served in two rooms, so that he would not have to endure the company of the more boring among his guests.

The eyes of Hirtius and his office, like those of his commander, were naturally directed all the time towards Rome, since Gallic wars were fought not so much to conquer Gaul as to advance Caesar's ambitions in the capital. To Rome, incessantly, went a mass of letters fixing elections, exhorting friends, cajoling or threatening enemies and neutrals and waverers. Even from Britain came a continual flow of communications, taking only three or four weeks on their way; and in winter, from the greater proximity of Cisalpine Gaul, the effort was always intensified. Caesar continued to dictate letters even on horseback, keeping two or even more secretaries fully employed. It is not surprising that a young Roman lawyer, enrolled on the legal staff in Gaul, complained to Cicero, who had recommended him for the post, that is was scarcely ever possible to secure an interview with the great man himself.

Not only was the outward mail enormous, but vast quantities of communications were also coming in to headquarters from Italy. Cicero warned Atticus to be careful what he wrote even in his private letters, since it would be sure to get to the ears of Caesar. His office in Rome was kept very busy maintaining this flow of intelligence, and getting his candidates into jobs. The bureau was in charge of Balbus and his inseparable and equally tireless colleague Oppius, who belonged to a substantial banking family of knights and spent his spare time writing biographies.

Cicero was meanwhile receiving flattering attentions from Caesar and his staff, and within a mere five weeks of the busy year 54 he heard from him on no less than three occasions. All this helped to keep the orator up to the mark. He was still bound to his recantation in favour of the triumvirs, which he justified to a correspondent at enormous length, and he hoped, in vain as it turned out, that his brother, who was now on Caesar's staff, might become consul. Accordingly Cicero went to court to defend Vatinius whom, like his other new client, Gabinius, he had attacked with gusto only two years earlier. And Caesar made it worth his while. He lent Cicero a substantial sum, and appointed him to a lucrative co-directorship of the huge contracts for a new Forum Julium that Oppius was planning for him beside the old Roman Forum. The land earmarked for the new building complex cost a very great deal, and with so much money going about there was sure to be something for the directors.

And yet, however graciously Cicero was treated—and Pompey was nothing like so nice to him—he always felt profoundly uncomfortable about Caesar's politics. Caesar could insinuate that his exile had been the conservatives' fault, and yet Cicero remained evasive and impervious, and made frantic attempts to safeguard the last remnants of his independence by keeping their association on a personal level. There was never any difficulty about a cultural exchange, since Caesar was not only an orator who with practice could almost have rivalled Cicero himself, but had many other literary tastes in common with him too. What other man leading Caesar's public life could have written a weighty treatise on grammar in the middle of the Gallic War, apparently while crossing the Alps in a carriage?

This work, of which fragments have survived, was dedicated to Cicero. They could agree about Caesar's insistence on avoiding rare and obsolete words, and they would be able to feel a civilised difference of opinion about historical schools, and about the contrast between Caesar's stylistic ideals of bare clarity and Cicero's own more rounded and resonant diction. Possibly a surviving piece of Caesar's poetry, comprising a literary critique of another purist, the dramatic poet Terence, was also an offering to Cicero. He in his turn sent Caesar a poem praising his own consulship. Subsequently, he wrote nervously asking his brother what the great man had meant when he tempered superlative praise of the first part by the suggestion that the second, at certain points, could have profited from rather more elaboration. Did he refer to subject or style? Their literary relationship must indeed have been easy if Caesar could criticise Cicero's verses without offence, as he clearly could: for Cicero rather endearingly told his brother that he would not think any the less of his poem whatever the answer might be.

Meanwhile Caesar cannot have found the situation at Rome as reassuring as it had previously been. No doubt he and Pompey maintained contact through their usual liaison officer, the latter's adjutant Lucius Vibullius Rufus, but nevertheless, Pompey's position in Italy had become too powerful to inspire confidence among his rivals. He duly declined the suggestion of a loyal cousin, Hirrus, that he might become dictator. All the same, although he was officially governor of Spain, he remained in the neighbourhood of the capital. His pretext was that he needed this central position to organise his second job, the superintendence of the corn-supply of Rome. Apart from a bid for popularity at the opening of his new theatre, at which the entertainments included an elephant fight and the massacre of five hundred lions, he kept out of metropolitan affairs. But this in itself was held against him, since it was alleged, as before, that he was deliberately allowing the Republic to lurch into anarchy so that he would have to be invited to set matters right.

The summer of 54 was so hot that Cato appeared in court wearing only his toga and loin-cloth and no tunic, characteristically claiming this to have been the costume of the Romans of remote antiquity. Even that comic touch, however, did not lighten the ominous atmosphere, in which Cicero wrote despairing that the constitution, the senate and the law courts had now become nothing but deadlocked and disorderly shams. In August occurred the tragic death of Julia, Caesar's daughter and Pompey's wife. A year or two earlier she had suffered a miscarriage after catching sight of her husband's cloak covered with blood after a violent public meeting. A further childbirth proved too much for her, and her baby died a few days after herself. Pompey had intended to bury her on his property near Alba Longa, but enormous crowds at her funeral, defying the consul Ahenobarbus, carried off her body and gave it an imposing cremation in the Field of Mars. The people of Rome were intending by this gesture to celebrate her distant father's victories. Yet they may also have dimly realised that her death was a national disaster, for she had been an invaluable and unique intermediary between the two potentates.

Caesar had spent the earlier months of the year not only in Cisalpine Gaul but in the Illyrian part of his province, where tribes raiding from the southeast had to be brought to submission. Meanwhile ships were being constructed for a second and more convincing expedition to Britain. But Caesar did not return north across the Alps until late spring, and even then he found it imperative to lead four legions against the powerful Belgic tribe of the

Treviri (Trier). They had kept aloof from all Caesar's conferences, and this could not be ignored since their cavalry was the most powerful in Gaul. Their hostile chief, Indutiomarus, hampered by a rival, offered apparent submission, gave three hundred hostages, and was punished by demotion from the principal chieftainship. But further delay occurred when the leader of the nationalist movement among the Aedui, Dumnorix, refused to cooperate with Caesar's plan that the heads of the Gaulish tribes should accompany him across the Channel. He tried to get away but was cut down by Roman cavalry, and died with the defiant cry 'I am the free citizen of a free country!' This was the first occasion on which Caesar's authority was openly flouted by a member of a supposedly allied community.

Because of such incidents, coming on top of adverse winds which had already held up departure for three weeks, the start for Britain was again rather late, though about a month earlier than in the previous year. On this occasion, however, the force was far larger, comprising five legions and two thousand cavalry, escorted by twenty-eight warships and carried in nearly six hundred transports, in addition to perhaps nearly two hundred further vessels contributed by private Roman financiers in exchange for a share of the eventual plunder. The ships to carry the horses were made unusually broad, and the rest had lower decks than those of the previous enterprise in order to expedite unloading and beaching. Oars as well as sails were taken on board, and tackle specially devised and adapted for British conditions.

Starting from the same port as before, the invaders landed near Sandwich in easternmost Kent. Disembarkation took all day, and after midnight the march inland began, illuminated by a full moon and guided by Mandubracius of the Trinobantes (Essex), a collaborator who was earmarked for the leadership of a pro-Roman federation. By dawn the force had moved as far westwards as Sturry on the Great Stour. The Britons, who had accepted Cassivellaunus of the Catuvellauni (north-west of London) as their commander-in-chief, did not succeed in holding Caesar up. However, he was delayed by the news that the British weather had repeated its temperamental behaviour of the previous year by severely damaging his fleet and destroying forty ships. In spite of his earlier experiences, he had still found no suitable harbour, and had again failed to beach his vessels effectively.

This impatient reliance upon luck now had to be remedied. What remained of the fleet was pulled up on to the beach and protected by a fortification. Carpenters were extracted from the legionary ranks, and Labienus, in Gaul, was ordered to send over fresh ships and materials. Then Caesar, beating off guerrillas as he went, forced his way across the Thames and stormed the capital of Cassivellaunus, which was probably at Wheathampstead, north of St. Albans. The Kentish princes failed to establish a diversion in the rear, and Cassivellaunus formally submitted and provided hostages. Then, in the latter part of September, Caesar returned to Gaul.

Before doing so, he made arrangements to maintain British tribes in varying degrees of quasi-subordination. But they came to nothing, and the island remained independent for another hundred years. At Rome, Caesar was able to make much of the fact that the princes of such remote and exotic regions had ostensibly submitted to himself and the Republic. Yet any idea he may have cherished of conquering any part of Britain, as a counterblast to Crassus' expected eastern conquests, was now abandoned. When he landed for the second time in 54 he evidently had some such hopes, since otherwise the expedition would scarcely have been repeated. But at some point during the inland march he must have decided that permanent occupation was after all impracticable—and he was too realistic to believe seriously that the submission of the tribes would have any meaning once he had gone. Still, propaganda for Rome was the main thing, and in this, as usual, he did his best. But there was also some disappointment in the capital. During the first optimistic days Cicero had written to his brother requesting material for a glorious epic description of the conquered island. But soon he was admitting to Atticus that the hoped-for supplies of looted silver were non-existent. He had also been looking forward to British slaves, he told Atticus: 'though I don't fancy you'll find any with literary or musical talents among them'. But this hope, too, was presumably unfulfilled. Neither Caesar nor anyone else made anything out of Britain, which did not become a Roman province until southern England was conquered a hundred years later.

CHAPTER SIX

Crises in Gaul and Rome

*I*n the Gaul to which Caesar returned from Britain in the autumn of 54 it soon became clear that the supposed pacification was unreal. The trouble started among the Carnutes who lived round Cenabum (Orléans). Their country, containing dark and impenetrable forests, was the principal headquarters and annual meeting-place of the Druids. This privileged religious hierarchy, extending throughout Celtic Gaul, exercised judicial, educational and administrative functions, possessed a monopoly of writing—using the Greek script—and was excused from taxation and military service. The Druids were also rumoured, though with doubtful justification, to play a leading part in the custom of human sacrifice which still occasionally took place.

Three years earlier Caesar had appointed a king of this important tribe of the Carnutes; and now they proceeded to assassinate his nominee. Caesar detached troops straightaway in order to deal with the situation, but did not deviate from the plan, which he had formed previously, to divide up the winter quarters of his armies among a number of different centres. This division was convenient because of a bad harvest and the consequent difficulty of securing food, but it was also dictated by precautionary considerations, since most of the places selected for troop concentrations were located in the north-eastern regions of Gaul, the home of the formidable tribes of the Belgae. Disaster struck promptly when the easternmost of these garrisons at Aduatuca (Tongeren, near the Meuse, north of Liège) was overwhelmed, and the one and a half legions that formed its garrison, consisting mostly of raw recruits, were annihilated. This calamity, an unprecedented experience for Caesar, was the work of Ambiorix, the determined king of a relatively small Belgic tribe, the Eburones, who inhabited the hills and woods of the Ardennes. 'How', he remarked, as he tore the arms and clothing from the local Roman commander before striking him down with his javelin, 'can creatures like you hope to rule over great men like us?' Word spread to those of the Nervii who had survived the Roman massacre three years earlier, and Cicero's brother, Quintus, in command of the garrison surrounded at Namur, enjoyed his finest hour when he got a loyal slave through to Caesar's head-quarters at Samarobriva (Amiens), and held out until his general brought relief. But first Caesar experienced a moment of alarm, when he saw before Quintus Cicero's camp the impressive siege machines that Ambiorix had imitated from the Romans.

For the Gauls were proving good learners, and the disaffection spread. In particular Labienus, stationed near Sedan, found himself faced by open revolt from Indutiomarus of the Treviri, who had never genuinely submitted and had instigated Ambiorix. Labienus' Gallic cavalry put Indutiomarus to death, but it was clear that the whole structure of 'pacified' Gaul had collapsed and that only the Aedui and Remi could still be relied upon to collaborate. In the winter of 54–3 Caesar abandoned his usual departure across the Alps, and stayed in the neighbourhood of Amiens instead. But he recruited two new legions in his Cisalpine province, and Pompey gave him another which he himself had enrolled but not called up.

After the catastrophe Caesar allowed his hair and beard to grow, declaring he would never cut them until vengeance had been taken. This conveyed a clear message to the Gauls who attended the general conference he summoned at Amiens early in 53. Nevertheless, many northern and central tribes stayed away. In order to be nearer the danger-zone, Caesar moved his headquarters and the whole meeting of chiefs to Lutetia (Paris), which he now visited for the first time. Thereupon the Carnutes and the Senones (Sens), who had likewise risen, rapidly submitted. The Treviri, deprived of their leader, were crushed by Labienus. Caesar, after crossing the Rhine once again—a gesture which he records with a 'background' description intended to rival Pompey's eastern penetrations—first isolated the Eburones and then started to blot them out, easily inducing their neighbours to join in the carnage. He had invited them to do so, he explained, in order to spare Roman legionaries the danger of warfare in thickly-wooded country.

But a principal purpose of all this punitive activity failed, because Ambiorix himself escaped. The numerous horsemen who were scouring the countryside failed to catch him, and he and four faithful attendants got away. However, Caesar regarded it as essential to frighten his compatriots by some act of revenge, and since the principal proposed victim was not available, this horrifying fate fell instead upon Acco, the chief of the Senones who had joined the dissident movement. When, in autumn 53, the Gaulish princes were summoned to join Caesar at Rheims (Durocortorum), capital of the collaborationist Remi, they found themselves obliged to watch the execution of Acco in the ancient Roman manner. Before being decapitated, he was stripped, tied by the head in a wooden fork, and beaten to death with rods. The Roman army, whose assembled ranks witnessed this repulsive scene, no doubt felt it was fitting retribution, even if the leading delinquent had regrettably got away. But his own compatriots and fellow-princes, whose presence was required at the ceremony, were not so much cowed as driven to desperation.

Meanwhile, Caesar set out as usual across the Alps to hold the winter assizes and intensify his watch on Rome. The enormous Gaulish wealth he was now coming to possess enabled him to convey heavy bribes to Roman officials and candidates, on the pretext of helping them with their expenses, and he also, we are told, often sent presents to their wives. Strangely enough, one such candidate enjoying his financial support for the consulship in 53 was Memmius, who five years earlier had joined Ahenobarbus in a savage attack on Caesar's own recently concluded term of office as consul. Now, as Caesar and the conservatives outbid one another, bribery for the elections of 53 was so intense that the rate of interest suddenly rose from four to eight per cent. Pompey professed to be shocked, and compelled Memmius to confess to the senate about an outrageous electoral bargain which had been formed between himself, another candidate, and the two existing consuls—including Ahenobarbus who thus, directly or indirectly, had been destined to become the recipient of huge sums from his worst enemy, Caesar. But prosecutions were announced against all concerned, and the consulships went elsewhere.

The same year, 53, also produced a decisive shift in the balance of power. Crassus, old for his age of sixty and rather deaf, had left for his province of Syria with the intention of at last rivalling the military glory of Pompey and Caesar. His intended victim was the only considerable independent power on any of Rome's borders, the Iranian kingdom of Parthia, which feudally governed Persia and Iraq, but had been deprived by Pompey's conquests of its hopes of expanding to the shores of the Mediterranean. Crassus, interested not only in glory but in Babylonian gold and silk, had invaded Mesopotamia without pretext or declaration of war, only to suffer, in June, the worst disaster to Roman arms for a hundred and fifty years. Novel tactics used by the Parthians, who carried on their camels unprecedented quantities of arrows and fired them continuously at double trajectory so that Roman shields were useless, were too much for Crassus, and he, his younger son Publius (sent to him from Gaul by Caesar) and three-quarters of his forty-four thousand men were killed. The death of Julia had meant that the principal bond between Pompey and Caesar disappeared. Since then their direct confrontation had been postponed by Crassus, who was compared to the isthmus of Corinth preventing two great seas from clashing with one another. But now he was gone, and there was nothing to keep them apart.

Continued disorders at Rome had caused more and more people to think in terms of a dictatorship for Pompey; and among them were enemies of

Caesar who were afraid of what he might do when the Gallic Wars came to their approaching end. Even Cicero, in the treatise *On the Republic* which he was composing at this time, saw the need of some sort of personal government, if only to give an occasional masterful turn to the helm and enable the old constitution to forge ahead again. Meanwhile the year 52 again opened without any consuls. When increasing disorders culminated in the murder of Clodius by Milo, the rival gangster who fought for the right wing cause, the senate gave Pompey emergency powers, including authority to mobilise troops. Soon afterwards he was elected consul for the third time—without a colleague. This sole consulship was the most extraordinary office of his career. Finite in duration and not a dictatorship, but not too far from one, it seemed irreconcilable with his absentee governorship of Spain, and it brought Pompey even closer to the emperors of future years. Yet the appointment was conferred on the proposal of the diehard Bibulus, and even Cato felt obliged to lend it reluctant support.

When Pompey had started raising troops, Caesar also began to recruit in Cisalpine Gaul, claiming that it was the least he could do in order to carry out the mobilisation plan the senate had decreed. The situation was now tense. Pompey, who possessed his own confidential circle of literary and other figures without political affiliations, would have preferred to remain uncommitted between Caesar and his implacable conservative enemies; and this would have suited his increasing incapacity to make up his mind. But he now saw ahead of him the uncomfortable possibility of having to make a choice. Meanwhile, he characteristically took one step in one direction and one in the other.

Caesar, expressing approval of Pompey's efforts to restore order, had launched an endeavour to renew their compact by suggesting a new matrimonial alliance. He offered to divorce his childless wife, Calpurnia, whose father had served his turn as consul, in order to wed Pompey's daughter, while Pompey was to marry Caesar's grandniece, Octavia. Both the proposed brides were married already (or one was married and the other engaged), but in politics that was immaterial. However, Pompey refused the bargain, and instead married Cornelia, the daughter of the greatest aristocrat in Rome, Metellus Scipio. Through him, a Cornelius by birth and a Caecilius Metellus by adoption, Pompey repaired his family alliance with the Metelli, broken by his divorce of one of their number eight years earlier. Moreover, in contrast to the colourless though virtuous Octavia, Cornelia, the widow of young Publius Crassus, was a most talented person, musical and knowledgeable in geometry and philosophy and yet, we are told, 'not at all tiresome or pretentious like most intellectual girls'. Her father, on the other hand, whether it is true or not that he was the chief guest at a dinner party staged as a brothel—with noble ladies performing—was arrogant, obstinate and deeply corrupt.

Memmius, himself a briber on a monumental scale, had tried to save himself by accusing Mettelus Scipio of the same offence, but Pompey had invited the three hundred and sixty members of the jury to his house and requested acquittal. Metellus Scipio also detested Caesar, so that many found it highly significant when, Pompey, not content with marrying his daughter, chose him during the summer as his associate in the consulship which he had hitherto occupied without a colleague.

And yet at the same time Pompey, a master of mystification, was encouraging measures to relieve Caesar's worst anxiety. Constitutionally, Caesar could not hold another consulship until ten years after he had finished his last one, that is to say in 48. If his governorship ceased before then, there would still be that painful interval of private status during which he would be liable to prosecution and ruin. Now Pompey sponsored legislation to allow him to stand for the consulship in absence so that the two tenures would overlap. The date of transition still remained uncertain: if the Gallic war was finished soon, he *might* need another dispensation, in order to become consul before 48. But Pompey at once confused the issue by adding other bills which lawyers could twist into attempts to remove from Caesar what he had just been given. Furthermore, he himself had his own absentee Spanish command renewed for five more years. True, this was not a direct attack on Caesar, who did not want a parallel enactment for himself. Yet was all this quite in the spirit of Luca? At the very least Pompey was being a little careless—and was responding perceptibly to conservative pressure. Moreover, his attitude, like that of others at Rome, was sensitive to what was happening in Gaul. This was a year of important Gallic battles which first nearly brought ruin to Caesar, and then led him to almost complete triumph: and the political pendulum at home swung in harmony with each vicissitude. The Gauls, too, had their eye on metropolitan affairs. They also drew lessons from what had happened to Romans in other parts of the world, for the downfall of Crassus in the east made them realise that they might be able to get rid of their own aggressor as well; and they had watched the British avoiding annexation with impunity. But according to the *Commentaries* it was the murder of Clodius in January 52, and the subsequent disturbances in the capital, which gave them particular hope, for they believed that Caesar would be too preoccupied by Italian events to rejoin his army in Transalpine Gaul, especially during winter weather.

It was the Carnutes who again triggered off the rebellion, for at their capital, Cenabum, they turned on Caesar's requisitioning officer and murdered him, together with a group of resident Roman business men. But the principal initiative, this time, came from a more southerly tribe which had long been one of the leading peoples of Gaul, the Arverni. The fact that they had never suffered directly from Caesar's interference shows how deep the general discontent had gone. Exasperation at food shortages was widespread, the atrocities which Caesar hoped would intimidate the tribes had produced the opposite effect, and it was only too clear that he was now thinking in terms of permanent annexation and occupation. The leading spirit of the Arverni, who became chief of the whole revolt, was Vercingetorix. This hero of French patriots from Thierry to de Gaulle had joined Caesar's service as a cavalry officer and 'friend' of Rome; and now that he fought for the nationalist cause he displayed strategic, administrative and diplomatic gifts far superior to those of any other Gaul encountered by Caesar throughout the war.

The Arverni were joined by other tribes, and for the first time these armies included a large proletarian element, predictably identified by Caesar as vagabonds and robbers. While he was racing back to the scene of the emergency, bands of partisans sprang up to intercept Roman columns, and even the Roman city of Narbo (Narbonne), capital of the province, was threatened. Caesar had to cross the Cévennes in mid-winter, but a rapid success for the revolt became impossible when he had the pass cleared of its six-foot-deep layer of snow in twenty-four hours, appearing unexpectedly, with a small force, on the northern side of this barrier near the territory of the Arverni themselves. As was expected, his arrival diverted Vercingetorix to his homeland, whereupon Caesar moved into the centre of Gaul with lightning speed, his troops living from hand to mouth on an unrelieved diet of meat. In the land of the Bituriges (Cher), who had risen in support of the rebellion, a body of four hundred German horsemen—in Caesar's service for the first time— routed the nationalist cavalry, and Vercingetorix came to the conclusion that a scorched-earth policy must be adopted and all towns destroyed that could provide the Romans with supplies. It is a tribute to his persuasive leadership that the Gauls accepted this self-sacrifice. The Bituriges alone burnt twenty of their settlements, but pleaded that their capital, Avaricum (Bourges), was capable of defence; and since the town was only approachable by a very narrow passage between streams and marshes Vercingetorix finally, and reluctantly, agreed. However, on the twenty-fifth day of the siege the Romans completed a huge terrace, three hundred and thirty feet wide and eighty feet high, which despite all attempts at undermining gave them entry to the town. The legionaries, who had suffered from inadequate food and heavy rain and were angry about the massacre of their compatriots at Cenabum, 'did not think of making money by taking prisoners', Caesar tells us, and indulged in an indiscriminate slaughter, including old men and women and children alike. Out of the town's total population of about forty thousand, a bare eight hundred who rushed outside the walls at the first alarm got safely through to Vercingetorix. He took them in quietly by night, arranging for their interception and distribution before they reached his lines, so as not to depress morale.

In fact, however, the disaster, since it was just what he had predicted, made the Gauls feel increased confidence in his judgment. Even the Aedui, who had derived little benefit from their traditional collaboration with Rome, were so sharply divided among the adherents of two rival princes that Caesar found them wholly unreliable. He summoned their council, decided which of the contestants should be chieftain, and then considered it safe to move his supply base to their town of Noviodunum (Nevers) on the Loire. However, the extensive range of the revolt made it necessary to take the risk of dividing his troops, so that Labienus marched northwards towards Paris while he himself, with a larger force, moved up the Allier valley to the powerful Arvernian capital of Gergovia, four miles from the present Clermont-Ferrand. This very strong position, on a plateau twelve hundred feet above sea-level, was the central fortress of Vercingetorix, which he could not sacrifice. After dealing leniently with an Aeduan revolt, Caesar proceeded with the formal invest-ment of Gergovia. But his troops were repulsed from the walls with a loss of forty-six centurions and seven hundred other ranks. This defeat, one of the gravest reverses of his career, was blamed by the commander upon an officer and his men who, on receiving orders to capture the Gallic camp out-side the town, had been induced by their desire for glory and loot to exceed their instructions and press on to the town itself; but this may be an attempt, for the benefit of Rome, to minimise his own responsibility for what had hap-pened. At all events, he was now obliged to break off the siege of Gergovia altogether.

The Aedui, in spite of their tactful handling by Caesar, now finally joined the nationalist cause, massacring the Romans at Nevers, seizing their stores, destroying all the corn they could not eat, and setting fire to the town itself so that Caesar could not use it. With the exception of the Treviri and Rome's faithful Remi, almost every tribe now recognised Vercingetorix as commander-in-chief, and resistance movements scoured the country. Caesar now felt it imperative to rejoin Labienus, who had meanwhile moved against Paris—which was burned by the Parisii to prevent him from occu-pying it—and after marching by day and night caught up with him near Auxerre. To replace Aeduan defectors, additional cavalry were summoned from Germany and transferred from their native ponies to Gallic mounts. These reinforcements were all the more necessary since none could be obtained from Italy, from which even Caesar's letters arrived only infre-quently and by devious routes. The Narbonese province was cut off and threatened, and in order to protect its frontiers Caesar's united force started to march towards the south. At this juncture Vercingetorix decided to launch his excited troops against the column. Somewhere near Laignes (Côte d'Or), taking advantage of rather perfunctory reconnaissance arrangements, his cavalry charged the Romans simultaneously from three sides. But the

German horse were too good for them, and the Gauls were defeated with heavy losses.

Vercingetorix was now obliged to fall back to a base he had fortified a few miles away on the isolated, elevated plateau of Alesia (Alise-Sainte-Reine on Mt. Auxois), a minor town belonging to a dependency of the Aedui. Before Caesar could close a ring round the place, Vercingetorix, who had felt it necessary to withdraw his whole force into the fortress, sent away every horseman he possessed. This served the dual purpose of lessening his food problem and enabling the cavalry to scatter far and wide to summon a relief force from the tribes. It might have seemed more sensible to keep a small squadron for sorties and unhorse the rest, using their mounts as food, since five thousand horses could have fed the eighty thousand inhabitants for more than a month. But presumably the Gauls of that time felt an aversion to horsemeat which their commander believed it beyond his power to change, even in a crisis of this magnitude.

Roman legions were tremendous entrenchers, accustomed to building large camps for themselves every day, and no great general had ever used the spade more than Caesar. Since Alesia was hard to take by storm but lent itself to methodical siege tactics, he surrounded the town by a continuous circle of fortifications ten miles long. Furthermore, this circle was itself ringed by three outer lines, fourteen miles in circumference, so that on the arrival of the expected relief force of the Gauls, his troops could face inwards and outwards simultaneously. Meanwhile he also performed the vast task of laying in a supply of corn and forage sufficient to feed his ten legions for thirty days.

The besieged, on the other hand, were so short of food that they expelled everyone whose age and infirmity made them unfit for fighting; and since the Roman camp closed its gates to them, they must have come to an unpleasant end. Meanwhile the relieving host was approaching. Its numbers were very large, though probably not so large as Caesar's estimate of a quarter of a million infantry and eight thousand cavalry, provided by no less than forty-three Gaulish tribes. The Roman army now came under full-scale attack from both directions over a period of four days, but a movement by Labienus to stem a breach in the outer line prevented disaster, and then a rear attack by Caesar's German cavalry, wheeling round outside the fortifications under his own leadership, proved decisive. The relief army, owing to its cumbrous size, for the most part had not been engaged, and was becoming very difficult to feed; and now, under two of its Aeduan leaders, it melted away.

Vercingetorix surrendered, to be saved up for execution after Caesar's Triumph six years later. Most of the other prisoners were distributed among the Roman soldiers as slaves, one to each man. But although the Aedui and Arverni had harmed him more than any other tribes, Caesar decided against their extermination since they were still needed as the keys to the political system of central Gaul. So the captives belonging to those peoples were reprieved, and it was hoped that they would serve as a bait and bribe to their compatriots. If not exactly clemency, this at least seemed a sign of appreciation that the previous policy of bloodthirsty terror had produced the opposite results to those desired.

The Gallic War was not yet over, but the Great Revolt had been crushed. It had failed to achieve the degree of national co-ordination for which its leader hoped, since even his gifts could not overcome Gallic incapacity for discipline and the organisation of supplies. He had been compelled to exploit the favour of the Gauls at the moment when it was on the boil; but this meant that the timing was unfortunate, since, if the rebellion had taken place two years later, it would have caught Caesar on the verge of a Roman civil war.

Moreover, many Belgic tribes, who had borne the brunt in earlier years, had stayed aloof owing to self-sufficient arrogance, or decided to help too late in the day. For example, the Bellovaci (Beauvais), whom Caesar described as the best fighters in Gaul, should have sent more than the two thousand men they contributed to the relief force at Alesia. Now, in the first months of 51, came their own tardy and isolated independent effort. Ahenobarbus, at Rome, was full of hopes that this new revolt might put an end to Caesar altogether, but it collapsed when its heroic leader, Correus, found an unexpectedly large Roman force too much for him and was killed. Next Caesar moved north-east to vent his hatred against the Eburones, but their leader, Ambiorix, continued imprudently to elude him.

Caesar now found it necessary, with what exertions can be imagined, to march his army right to the other end of Gaul, for a terrible and culminating struggle. Even at this late date, determined chieftains of various tribes, joined by two thousand fanatical irreconcilables, had revived a plan to attack Rome's Narbonese province. But they were forced to take refuse in the hill-fortress of Uxellodunum (Puy d'Issolu, Dordogne). The place was almost impregnable, but Caesar diverted its water-supply, and the Gauls, blaming supernatural powers, surrendered. Describing this final drama, Hirtius notes Caesar's feeling that pacification would be impossible if this sort of thing were allowed to continue. He therefore cut off the hands of everyone in the place who had carried arms, and then, after this culminating atrocity had shown that clemency was not yet, after all, the order of the day, he let them go so that people could see it did not pay to challenge Rome.

And yet even now, at the other extremity of Gaul from which Caesar had so recently departed, one chieftain fought on in his Belgic homeland until the end of the year. This was Commius of the Atrebates (Arras). At first one of Caesar's most loyal supporters, he had been rewarded in 57 by exemption from tribute and a grant of suzerainty over a neighbouring coastal state. It was he who had gone ahead to Britain on Caesar's behalf and had endured arrest there, and he became a useful cavalry leader. But then recognition of what Caesar's far-reaching intentions must be, reinforced, perhaps, by the dreadful treatment of a fellow-chief, had caused Commius to reverse his attitude. In the Great Revolt he whipped up certain recruits for the nationalist relief force at Alesia and served among its generals, and in the subsequent rising of the Bellovaci he was again one of the commanders. On the collapse of the rebellion he still did not give up hope, but retreated to Germany to raise more men. At this juncture, Labienus sent a centurion to stage an interview and strike him down. 'But either', suggests Hirtius, with a hint of criticism at such sordid proceedings, 'the centurion's nerve failed him because he was unaccustomed to such work, or Commius' friends were too quick for him. In any case the Gaul, though severely wounded in the head, escaped.'

Even after the collapse of all other Gaulish resistance, the Atrebates continued to hold out and attack Roman convoys, and now the same centurion made a further attempt to catch Commius, but failed again and was badly wounded in the thigh. Commius, deciding honour was satisfied, now came to terms, stipulating only that he should never again be required to come into the presence of any Roman. In the following year, he managed to escape to Britain, where he established a kingdom in Berkshire: the most successful among the few survivors of Caesar's wrath.

But meanwhile the Gallic War was at last at an end. It was maintained, no doubt with some exaggeration, that Caesar had fought thirty pitched battles, captured over eight hundred towns, and fought against three or four million men, of whom he had captured a million and killed a million more: the victorious general himself assessed enemy deaths at 1,192,000. Commenting on his appalling treatment of the final resisters, Caesar declared, according to Hirtius, that it would not be misunderstood, because everyone knew what a humane man he was. Macaulay and John Buchan applauded and agreed, the latter, admittedly, with certain reservations. Boileau and Rousseau were nearer the mark in detecting repeated acts of nauseous and treacherous brutality. This, as has been seen, often exceeded and defeated its intimidatory purpose; though Caesar no doubt pointed out that it paid in the end, since Gaul was duly conquered, and did not rise again in force for many years.

Its conquest, like that of British India, was largely brought about by internal dissensions. The tribes could not abandon their quarrels, so in a world where there was nothing to stop aggression by stronger powers they were too weak to retain corporate independence on their own account; and if it was a choice of being controlled by other Gaulish tribes or by Rome, many of them would have felt more humiliated to obey Celts than an alien ruler. Besides, if the Romans had not stepped in, the Germans would have

continued their encroachments. Rome had been able to clothe its initial interventions in the all-too-familiar guise of response to an appeal from an ally.
But the whole war, in each of its successive expansions, was in fact wanton
aggression to win renown for Caesar at Rome.

Yet the repercussions of what had been done went very far beyond any
considerations limited to his personal career. The area now annexed was twice
the size of contemporary Italy and far more populous than Spain. Even more
decisively than Pompey in the previous decade, Caesar had changed the whole
idea and nature of the Roman dominion. It had ceased to be merely a
Mediterranean maritime strip, and had become a vast land empire of which
Gaul was to be the hinge. The conqueror had opened up the continent to
his peculiar brand of civilisation. He had laid the foundations of modern
France. He had ended the prehistory of western Europe, and started its history, of which we are the heirs.

At Nemetacum (Arras), during the winter of 51–50, he gave the newly
conquered country, Long-Haired Gaul (Gallia Comata), its new organisation.
The annual tribute that the country must pay was assessed at two million
pounds. At first sight, in comparison with the sums extorted from eastern
regions, this seems a fairly modest figure. A more extortionate claim was
avoided because Caesar would need the support, or at least the quiescence,
of Gaul during the trials which were now to await him elsewhere. However,
the sum is not really so very small. The territory had been bled white and
was for the time being exhausted, and the assessment amounted to as much
as one-eighth of the total revenue Rome had derived from all its ten provinces
two decades previously.

Provided this new Gaul paid its taxes, Caesar did not intend to interfere
too much. He proposed, it is true, to utilise its manpower, and had already
set a precedent for raising infantry as well as cavalry by his recruitment of
the Legion of Larks in Narbonese Gaul. However, in pursuance of the example of Pompey, who had mulcted the east without imposing regimentation,
the stupid and stultifying direct oppressions which had caused such distress
in the Narbonese province were to be avoided in the freshly conquered territory. Under the loose supervision of a Roman governor, aided by local collaborationist régimes, the tribes were allowed to retain their own
organisations, and the horrifyingly bloodthirsty acts of recent years, having
served or failed to serve their purpose, were shelved, now that the war was
over, in favour of more judicious handling.

The entire operation had lasted for eight seasons. The duration could
have been even shorter if Caesar had not felt obliged to stage spectacular
adventures in order to play to the gallery at home. Even so, it was not a long
time for the annexation of two hundred thousand square miles occupied by
a dense population which, though for the most part pathetically inadequate

against Roman arms, was nevertheless determined, at least fitfully, to maintain its independence.

Of course, the main reason why Caesar conquered Gaul was because he was one of the greatest generals of ancient times and, indeed, in the whole history of the world. Byron, Constant and Stendhal compared Caesar with Napoleon, and Napoleon himself, in the *Précis des Guerres de César* that he wrote at St. Helena, detected in the Roman an affinity almost amounting to identification. But the problems of the two commanders were different. The Roman army consisted to an enormous extent of heavy infantry. (Light infantry were peripheral—archers, slingers and javelin men, undisciplined and often poorly armed.) A legion only included three hundred horses, and in spite of the expertise of Labienus another three centuries passed before this arm was taken seriously. The dead weight of military tradition must have played a part here, because the Romans needed cavalry, especially against the Gauls, and when the Aedui proved unreliable they obtained Germans, who made several decisive interventions.

With armies consisting overwhelmingly of fully-armed infantry, battles could be adequately conducted against any commander who was not of exceptional calibre by satisfying the few basic conditions—courage, supplies and training. Any good drill-master, therefore, was a fairly good general: Caesar was an excellent drill-master, with continual awareness of the importance of knowing and mastering details and subordinating means to ends. But the man who went one better than the drill-master was not so much the producer of competent plans as the general who had the ability to change them at short notice. This ability Caesar possessed to an extraordinary degree, and he combined it with exceptionally skilful timing of his lethal blows, that natural capacity to read the battlefield which German strategists call the 'finger-tip feeling'.

This was just a part of his most noteworthy characteristic—speed. The Roman army's custom of constructing an elaborate camp each night normally reduced its mobility by three or four hours a day, so that its enemies did not expect very rapid movement. But time after time Caesar won an engagement before it started, because he and his force had already arrived where they had no business to be. He himself rode fast and well, and possessed abnormal endurance. He got most of his sleep in litters or carriages, and even in those light four-wheelers of the day, bumpily jolting along rough roads, he was capable of travelling at the killing rate of a hundred miles a day, twice the pace that might be averaged by an ordinary man. This uncanny quickness of movement went with an equal quickness of mind, ruefully recognised by Cicero: 'the wariness and energy of that bogeyman are terrifying!' Rapidity was the secret of his success, though it occasionally became rashness—several times when reconnaissance was dispensed with, in Britain when the ships were twice not beached, and at Gergovia when his stroke was delivered too soon. But no stroke was ever delivered too late.

Caesar repeatedly staked everything on a single throw. This was his famous luck. Luck was much in the minds of Romans, and was indeed one of the principal deities of this disillusioned age. Sulla had elevated the quality into a sort of mystical personal characteristic, closely associated with merit. Now, as the years went on, and Caesar still survived these hair's-breadth victories, there was much talk of his Fortune as the most necessary qualification of a successful general. And the point was taken by Shakespeare:

> Danger knows full well
> That Caesar is more dangerous than he.[3]

He himself was no philosopher and no mystic, but he was instinctively a gambler who never paused to tremble at the odds but relied on his capacity to force them to his will. Luck is never far below the surface of his *Commentaries*; it is the movement of small weights which produces great vicissitudes. Indeed he often sees the historic process itself as a drama of sudden reversals of fortune. And yet this is not fatalism, since he leaves little doubt that they are reversals which his own abnormal talents, confronted with the efforts of lesser men, could help to mould.

The vast role played by his generals does not really emerge from his narrative. Still less do we learn about the commanders of individual legions, though Caesar did much to lend a new and professional character to their functions. Their acts are noted, with only occasional praise or blame. Caesar records few conferences with senior staff. Except in unanticipated crises they were allowed little individual scope for departing from their instructions, and there is small evidence of requests for their advice.

On the other hand the reader becomes aware that much depended on the courage, loyalty and initiative of those formidable blends of company officers and sergeant majors, the centurions, who, six to each cohort and one its commander, formed the backbone of his army.

Although grouped with officers in rank, they are united with other ranks in the intimate and ungrudging affection which Caesar felt for them, and which indeed was probably the strongest personal emotion of his life—a feeling, apparently, which had only dawned on him after years among the less rewarding emotions of Roman metropolitan politics. It could be said of Caesar as of Rommel, 'between him and his troops was that mutual understanding which cannot be explained and analysed, but which is the gift of the gods'. Caesar, it has been remarked, saw the long line of the legions as an extension of his own personality. In the *Commentaries* this peculiar bond is conveyed through the conventional medium of speeches to the troops. Such communications, which must in fact have been addressed to officers rather than to other ranks, were spiced by well-judged personal appearances of the general himself, bald and bare-headed in sun or rain, leading the army on foot or making intrepid interventions to turn the scale of hazardous engagements. And there was always a chance, especially for centurions or standard-bearers, of receiving one of those honourable mentions in the *Commentaries* which ring like medal citations. One might even get some witty remark recorded, and thus perpetuated for thousands of years, if it served Caesar's purpose sufficiently.

An officer serving in one of his subsequent wars tries to explain this magnetic sentimental relationship between Caesar and his men when speaking of a brief period in which he was separated from his army. 'They missed the sight of their commander, his vigour and wonderful good spirits. He held his head high and radiated confidence.' In modern terms he behaved less like a general with his troops than like a certain type of industrialist with his workers. Discipline did not bother him at all except when there was work to be done. Severity and indulgence were combined in a heady blend which an army would nowadays find disconcerting. A blind eye was turned to offences, except disloyalty in the form of desertion or mutiny, which was penalised relentlessly or, if punishments seemed untimely, remained unforgotten. After battles Caesar found it advisable to allow a great deal of licence. 'My troops are crack fighters,' he said, 'even when they stink of scent.' In a later campaign the oceans of wine they drank while sacking a town was said to have greatly improved their standard of health when they resumed the march.

But more solid rewards than that were needed. The history of recent years had shown only too clearly that in these days of semi-private armies the soldiers simply had to be recompensed very heavily indeed. Most of them were volunteers. Something like a voluntary system had begun to supplement conscription during the wars of the second century BC, and at the same time there had been a gradual lowering of the earlier requirement that only men with a property qualification of two thousand pounds could be enlisted. Marius had instituted reforms which in the crisis of the eighties gradually pushed the door open and officially admitted landless proletarians. From then onwards the supply of volunteers was so large that, except in times of civil war, there was rarely any need to fall back on compulsion. This meant that the army had become a career and that soldiers, therefore, had to be correspondingly remunerated both during and after their service. But who was going to make sure they got these rewards? Not the Roman senate, which might indeed be strongly opposed to their generals. It was rather from those generals themselves, their immediate employers, that the largesse had to be expected—from the commanders who increasingly behaved like independent warlords, and exerted whatever pressures they could upon the government of Rome. It was in response to this situation that the old oath of allegiance to the standards was increasingly supplemented and superseded by a more highly charged and personal oath of obedience to the general himself. His soldiers became his personal dependants or clients: and the cliental relationship was a two-way link in which the patron not only expected service but had to give as good as he received.

Lucullus, who fought against Mithridates before Pompey was given the command, had been a sad example of an otherwise excellent general who had failed because he was too devoted to the ideals of an earlier age to appreciate or accept this point; and he had lost his army and his job. Caesar did not make the same mistake. It is true that the plunder, which was gigantic, included a very large amount that went to himself. Indeed, he obtained so much gold that in Italy he was selling it at £150 to the pound weight—only about two thirds of the usual price. But this superabundance of loot meant that a great deal of wealth also found its way to the men who were serving under him. In the first place, this reflected itself in their wages. By all previous standards he paid them well. At some stage, perhaps at the end of the Gallic War, he doubled their tiny annual pay of just over twenty-two pounds. But even this gave them only what the cheapest labourer got, and much more had to be done. So, while the officers became rich men and the generals became millionaires, an enormous quantity of slaves and other booty, including the plunder of wealthy Gaulish shrines, went to the legionaries as well: and on retirement they would have to receive grants of land. The Duke of Wellington remarked that the 'want of power to reward' was a fatal handicap for a general, and Caesar was always aware that his soldiers, like those of other commanders, might at some stage or other become uncontrollably impatient for remuneration; and this applied most of all to the legions he had raised specially and temporarily for the purpose of the war. 'If you lack soldiers, you will have no money', he said; 'but if you lack money there will be no soldiers'. Caesar spent a very large part of his life raising funds, but now there was no lack. The vast sums of money available, combined with the skilful stage-management with which he projected his personality, were enough to retain the devotion of his legionaries.

These little men constituted one of the greatest military machines of history, and inspired terror. Within the legion of six thousand men, the principal unit since the time of Marius was the six-hundred-strong cohort, which provided a fighting line of unprecedented solidity. When battle was pending, legions were usually formed up into three lines with four cohorts in the first rank and three each in the second and third—a triple formation of fighters, support and reserves in which, at any one time, two-thirds of the legion remained outside the zone of peril and exhaustion. For these battles were close-order individual duels, in which the whole burden of the fighting fell on the front rank. Losses from death and wounds in this first line were heavy, and in any case even Roman soldiers did not possess unlimited physical endurance, so that a great deal depended on the calm efficiency with which replacements could be moved in.

The legionaries wore sleeveless woollen shirts, and sometimes strips of cloth round their thighs and legs. Their bodies were further protected by metal-ribbed leather cuirasses and by helmets and rectangular or oval shields. Until the second century BC a thrusting spear had been their main weapon, but thereafter it was largely replaced or supplemented, probably under Gaulish influence, by a six-foot throwing javelin. This had a barbed and hardened point fastened to a soft iron blade, which bent on impact so that the missile could not easily be extracted from a shield.

When it is borne in mind that soldiers might have to carry two of these javelins, and a cut-and-thrust Spanish sword or dagger as well, and that when it was cold or wet they also wore cloaks, it is alarming to learn from Dr. Rice Holmes that over his left shoulder the legionary on the march also 'bore a pole to which were fastened in a bundle his ration of grain, his cooking vessel, cup, saw, basket, hatchet, sickle, pick and spade.' But it has now been suggested, with plausibility, that while the column was on the move most of these impedimenta were carried by pack animals, which no doubt also came in useful to transport the heavy loads of loot which he had collected.

Presumably, however, the soldier did carry his cooking-vessel on his own person, or at any rate his portable hand-mill, because when the march ended he very soon needed it. His staple food was wheat, issued in the grain, and this he himself had to grind over hot stones or embers, making a rough bread like the Indian chupatty. The provision of sufficient supplies of this corn was a gigantic and often dominant problem, and although Caesar's *Commentaries* record frequent preoccupation with this anxiety, we hear hardly anything about the details of its organisation. We must make do with casual references to supply and grain depots, though there are more frequent allusions to requisitioning which suggest that the occupying forces expected to live off the tribes in whose country they found themselves.

Nor is it compatible with the scheme and dignity of the *Commentaries* to tell us about the supply of prosaic details like uniforms and boots. Yet two new legions needed twelve thousand pairs of boots, and evidently they were at once available. That can only have been made possible by the existence of elaborate administrative arrangements, and these, perhaps, were the responsibility of men like Publius Ventidius. A former prisoner of war of Pompey's father, sneered at as an upstart and muleteer, he played a vital role as contractor and manager of Caesar's army supplies. Nameless and faceless,

on the other hand, are the engineers who, their smiths and artificers waste-
fully fighting as ordinary legionaries when not required, organised Caesar's
elaborate camps such as Nointel near Clermont de l'Oise: the men who built
the bridge over the Rhine and who provided the rams, catapults and stone-
throwers corresponding to the siege guns, field guns and howitzers of modern
times. Unidentifiable, again, are the shipwrights who constructed the novel
vessels required to fight the Veneti and land in Britain. It may be suspected
that all these activities were conducted under the watchful eye of the chief-
of-staff, Mamurra, whose office was described by the traditional title of pre-
fect of smiths or engineers. But of such organisational matters the
Commentaries have nothing to say.

That remarkable work, probably known already to a limited circle from successive instalments, seems to have been published in the capital as a complete
work during the last months of 51. Its account of the war, seen as a whole,
stressed the immensity of what had been done, and hinted that no one should
try to tamper with the autonomous power and prestige which Caesar had won
for himself by means of his devoted army. Yet when, early in the year, perhaps
deliberately at the very time when the *Commentaries* were published, he suggested that his governorship should be renewed in order to tide him over until
the consulate of 48 at which he aimed, the dispensation was refused. A clique,
declared Caesar and Hirtius, was preventing the senate from expressing its
true opinion, which would otherwise have been favourable. The leader of
the right-wing opposition, to whom Cato now subordinated himself, was the
consul Marcus Marcellus, whose unstable family the Claudii Marcelli, during
this rising crisis which needed all the diplomacy that could be mustered,
disastrously emerged from the shadows to provide three successive warmon-
gering consuls, the leading 'hawks' of their day.

During the months and years that lay ahead most people wished to
heaven that one or the other of the two over-powerful marshals would leave
for the east to avenge Crassus and get out of the way. But they did not do
so, and the Marcelli constantly forced the political pace against Caesar, while
Pompey weakly protested or conceded a point in his disfavour here and there.
Marcus Marcellus declared that the war had ended, and that Gaul no longer
needed a general. He also deliberately challenged Caesar's measures in
Cisalpine Gaul by having a man of Novum Comum flogged, a punishment
not legitimate for the Roman citizens into whom Caesar claimed to have converted its population. Pompey, who like Caesar regarded himself as a patron
of Cisalpine Gaul, was angry. Nevertheless he agreed that the question of the
provinces to be allotted to ex-consuls—that is to say, the question of a successor to Caesar—might be discussed before very long: to be exact, on 1
March of the coming year, 50. When asked what he would do if an attempt

were made to veto a decision, he suggested that this would be the equivalent of rebellion. Then someone enquired what would happen if Caesar wanted to be consul and yet to keep his army at the same time. From this question Pompey shied away with the mild reply, 'what if my own son tried to hit me with a stick?'. He must still have been hoping that Caesar would not insist on remaining governor until he became consul; though, if so, he had been induced to lose his grip of realities, since acceptance of such a condition would have meant exile or even death.

Meanwhile Caesar was intensifying the uphill struggle to obtain influential support at Rome. One of the consuls for 50 was his bitter enemy Gaius Marcellus, who had never forgiven him for trying to take away his wife, Octavia, and give her to Pompey. But the other consul for the year, Lucius Aemilius Paullus, was won over to Caesar's cause by a very large bribe, enough to pay for the reconstruction of the Basilica Aemilia still traceable in the Forum today. Even more significant, however, was Caesar's acquisition of a tribune, Curio. One of the most brilliant and unscrupulous young men of the day, an eloquent master of propaganda already possessing invaluable popular support, Curio had previously been a savage opponent of Caesar, who, as consul, had retaliated by letting the informer Vettius try to frame him as an alleged conspirator against Pompey's life. Now, however, Curio was extremely heavily in debt, because of his wild life and over-extravagant funeral games in honour of his eccentric or mentally deranged father. At the second attempt, Caesar bought the young man's services for a huge sum of money. Curio was no doubt all the more willing to transfer his allegiance because he was married to a fire-eating woman named Fulvia who liked Caesar for his support of her previous husband, Clodius. Curio also had friendships in Caesar's camp, and bitter feuds with certain conservatives. Nor was he fond of Pompey, whom he accused of vindictive legislation. Cicero, who had reluctantly gone to govern Cilicia, wrote that *he* was the only person who had foreseen that Curio would change sides. At the time it seemed to him a good joke, but the poet Lucan, looking back from an oppressively autocratic régime a hundred years later, saw this vital reinforcement of Caesar as a profoundly ominous turning-point in history.

Curio lost no time in making his effect. Between March and May of 50 the senate's expected debates about Caesar's province raged heatedly, and the young tribune, with sidelong attacks on Pompey, successfully maintained his veto throughout. No new provincial governor was sent out from Rome, and the empire was held up to ransom and paralysed. But at the same time Curio also developed an interesting new argument, namely that Caesar should, as had been requested, give up his province and army, but that Pompey should resign from his absentee governorship of Spain at the same time. Here at last was a suggestion which, though in fact unfair to Pompey whose command was not due to expire, looked both reasonable and simple; even those who were not thoroughly versed in Roman legal quibbles could see the point. It may have been Curio who thought of the idea, but it soon received Caesar's endorsement. The motion met with great success; many senators liked the look of this double withdrawal. But the proposal was firmly blocked by a small group of ultra-conservatives who detected a trap. Finally the senate, under the influence of Pompey, played for both sides at once. When Marcellus, in effect, suggested that a tribune who behaved like Curio should be violently handled, they would not agree. But when, on the other hand, danger on the eastern frontier made it necessary to send two legions to Syria, they concurred with Pompey's view that the first of these units should come from Caesar, and the second should be the one that Caesar had been lent by himself three years earlier. Caesar complied, choosing as his own contribution a raw and untried unit. But he gave each of the departing legionaries a personal present, which, even at his new double rates, amounted to more than a whole year's pay.

In May Pompey fell seriously ill at Neapolis (Naples). While he lay on his sick-bed he wrote offering to lay down his powers without awaiting an expiry date; and then he suggested that Caesar should do the same. But vagueness about dates made this look like a trick. As Pompey got better, he received many friendly popular demonstrations, which, combined with misleading information about low morale in Caesar's army, gave him an exaggerated idea of the support he himself would receive in the event of a showdown. He allowed two diehards to be elected to the consulships for 49. However, Caesar at least managed to secure the appointment of a tribune to pursue his interests, namely Marcus Antonius, for whose youthful looks his predecessor in the tribunate, Curio, had a passionate admiration. 'Mark Antony', for so Shakespeare has handed his name down to history, was a debauched, impetuous, brave and intelligent young nobleman whose mother was a distant relative of Caesar.

Shortly before the date at which he was due to retire in favour of his friend (10 December 50), Curio produced his most successful coup. The consul Gaius Marcellus failed to persuade the senate to put him in his place, but obtained approval for proposals that Caesar should give up his command, but that Pompey should not do so. And yet immediately afterwards, the senate were persuaded by Curio to decree, with complete inconsistency and incoherence, that both Caesar and Pompey should retire from their commands simultaneously. The decision was made by three hundred and seventy votes to twenty-two. This enormous majority confirmed Cicero's opinion that almost everyone he knew would rather give way to Caesar than fight him—the man ought to have been attacked when he was weak, the orator added, for now he was too strong.

It is a sad commentary on the rundown of the Republican government that so nearly unanimous an opinion remained ineffective. For on the following day, amid hysterical rumours that Caesar was already marching on Rome, Gaius Marcellus, accompanied by both consuls-elect, stormed out of the senate and the city, and upon his own responsibility, without any official sanction, charged Pompey to take all necessary measures to defend the state. He accepted the commission, with a final equivocal proviso, 'unless a better way can be found', and also accepted the responsibility of recruiting additional troops. The two legions which Caesar had sent for transmission to Syria had been held back in Italy, and now they were placed under Pompey's command.

At this juncture the senate's attitude began to stiffen, perhaps, as Caesar suggested, because it was intimidated by these measures of mobilisation. After spending two hours with him on 9 or 10 December, Cicero said that Pompey was convinced that a breach was inevitable, since Hirtius, on a visit from Gaul, had left again without visiting himself. Hirtius had, in fact, failed to call on Pompey because he learnt, on arrival, of the new emergency command, which seemed to make discussions useless. However, while in Rome, Hirtius conveyed through Metellus Scipio a suggestion that Caesar, whilst waiting for his consulship, might be content with only Cisalpine Gaul and Illyricum and two legions, or even Illyricum and a single legion. But Pompey, when informed of this, declined to agree to any such private bargain. No doubt he was under strong pressure from the war party, but his own attitude was hardening as well. For on 25 or 26 December, at a further long talk with Cicero at Formiae, he had evidently been deeply affronted by a violent speech Antony had made, and he gave the impression that he no longer had any real desire for peace, which he felt could now be nothing but a manoeuvre directed against the Republic and himself.

Meanwhile Curio hastened to Caesar's new headquarters at Ravenna in Cisalpine Gaul, and then speeded back to Rome—completing the hundred-and-forty-mile return journey in three days. He brought with him to the capital a letter in which Caesar, after reviewing his own patriotic services, reiterated that, if he had to retire, Pompey must do the same. But Pompey now let it be known that he expected the senators to take a tough line. Consequently, at the meeting on 1 January 49, the tribune Antony and a colleague, Quintus Cassius Longinus, could barely even secure a hearing for Caesar's message, and a very large majority supported a motion by Metellus Scipio that Caesar should lay down his command by a fixed date, or be declared a public enemy. The two tribunes vetoed the proposal and during four days of subsequent excited discussion in the senate (largely concerned with questions of legality) Cicero engaged in peace talks behind the scenes, keeping alive Caesar's compromise proposal that he might retain Illyricum and nothing else. These private talks, however, came to nothing, and on 7 January the senate passed an emergency decree which confirmed and legalised Pompey's commission by requesting all major officials to protect the state. Before this decree was passed, Antony and Quintus Cassius were warned to leave the senate-house and Rome itself, since after the declaration of martial law they would be subject to severe penalties.

Declaring that their rights as tribunes were infringed and their inviolability threatened, the two young men departed for Caesar's camp, accompanied by Curio and Cicero's young correspondent, Caelius. The senate next proceeded to appoint governors to provinces. Metellus Scipio was sent to Syria to win over the east, and formal arrangements were made to supersede Caesar, an ex-praetor being allotted Cisalpine Gaul and Ahenobarbus receiving the Narbonese province which he had coveted for so long.

CHAPTER SEVEN

War against Pompey

When the news of the fateful senatorial decision reached Caesar, he concluded that he could now derive no benefits from any further diplomatic approaches without first making a show of force. And so, unobtrusively leaving a dinner-party on the night of 10 January 49 (the calendar was seven weeks ahead of the seasons), he slipped across the Rubicon (Fiumicino), the little Adriatic stream forming the boundary between Cisalpine Gaul and Italy. Horses were set free as a religious offering, to dispel fears of sacrilege which the evidently unconstitutional and therefore blasphemous act of invading the homeland might have lodged in the soldiers' minds. Caesar was accompanied by a single legion, the only unit he had with him in the Cisalpine province since he had been unwilling to encourage hostile mobilisation measures by forming troop concentrations south of the Alps. Nevertheless, he had finally taken the precaution of instructing two legions in the newly conquered Gallic territories to join him, as well as twenty-two recently recruited cohorts; and he had stationed three legions in Narbonese Gaul to deal with possible threats from Pompey's Spanish army.

Caesar split up his small force into two equal columns, of which one marched towards Ariminum (Rimini) and the other moved in the direction of Arretium (Arezzo). At Ariminum the tribunes Antony and Quintus Cassius, who had arrived from Rome, were dramatically presented to the troops in the slaves' disguise which they had allegedly been obliged to adopt in order to get away in safety. But the battle-cry of violated tribunes' rights was principally directed towards civilian opinion in Rome.

There consternation reigned. Calculating that no reinforcements from Gaul could reach Caesar for a fortnight, the senate had expected him to wait for these before taking any action. But he did not do so, and the appalling ordeal of a major civil war was no longer a threat but a reality. In the eyes of the conservatives, it constituted a rebellion of Caesar against the senate, but in practice it was a clash between the personal armies of Caesar and Pompey. In spite of enormous superiority at sea and whole hosts of

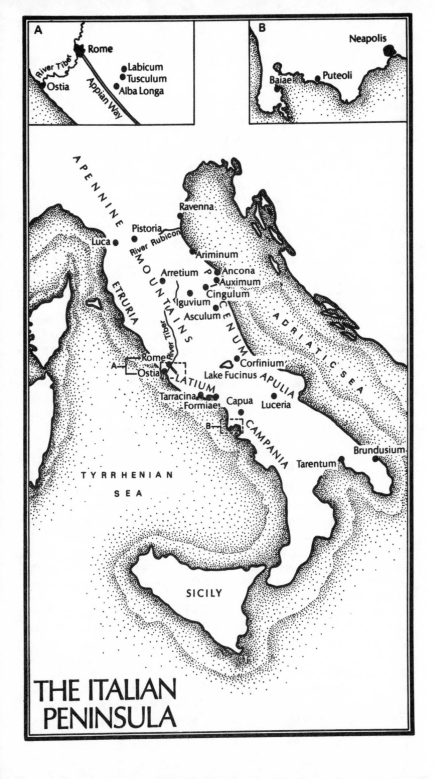

A

River Tiber
Rome
Labicum
Tusculum
Ostia
Alba Longa
Appian Way

B

Neapolis
Baiae
Puteoli

Ravenna

Pistoria
Luca
River Rubicon
Ariminum
Ancona
Arretium
Auximum
Iguvium
Cingulum
Asculum

APENNINE

MOUNTAINS

ETRURIA

River Tiber

Rome
Ostia
LATIUM
Corfinium
Lake Fucinus
APULIA
Tarracina
Formiae
Capua
Luceria
CAMPANIA
Brundusium
Tarentum

ADRIATIC SEA

TYRRHENIAN
SEA

SICILY

THE ITALIAN
PENINSULA

dependants whom he could call up in the east, excessive optimism had caused Pompey to make a bad start. It was he who had encouraged the senators to believe that Caesar would not invade with a single legion. Moreover, there seemed little basis for this claim that he himself had ten legions ready, unless one counted the Spanish army, which was by no means on the spot. Furthermore, as Caesar moved south it immediately became clear that Pompey had gravely overestimated his own support in the municipalities of Italy. Nor was he master of his own associates, for the Republicans, although they needed him against the common enemy, remembered how he had undermined them in the past, and continued to feel insuperable doubts about his constitutional soundness. And so Pompey, his growing tendency to indecision accentuated by ill-health, was induced to place his great authority at the service of an incompetent senate which had no intention of automatically accepting his advice.

They did not, therefore, make him commander-in-chief; though even as determined a Republican as Cato saw that this was the only sensible thing to do. For Cato distrusted Caesar even more than he distrusted Pompey. His hatred for Caesar was longstanding and unwavering, and fuel had been added to the flames by a defeat for the consulship in which Caesar had recently played a leading part. Yet, even so, Cato's support for Pompey was limited to the immediate aim of a military victory, for in respect of the man himself he shared the general misgiving about his ultimate motives:

> Scarce had it been worth while to stimulate
> A civil war, if neither were to rule.[4]

Cato remarked that he foresaw death if the winner was Caesar and voluntary exile if it was Pompey. He intended, if possible, to see that the winner should be neither of them, but the Republic. Meanwhile, he sharply criticised every aspect of the war, though it was he who had opposed every proposal that would lead to peace, had scorned every dove and encouraged every hawk. Nevertheless, while almost everyone else was fighting for loot, Cato was one of the very few men who could identify relevant points of principle and formulate them in imposing terms.

Most of the other conservative leaders were almost too bad to be true. Lentulus Crus, the consul for 49, who had guided the January debate towards war, was a crafty parliamentarian but abusive, idle, and steeped in all the pretentiousness for which his family was a byword. His extravagance had plunged him so deep in debt that his friends, seeing his open and covetous venality, were afraid that he might be bought for Caesar by Balbus, who was connected with the house of Lentulus (and, bearing like him the name Cornelius, may even have owed him his status as citizen of Rome). This suspicion, however, did Lentulus an injustice, because the last thing he wanted was to avert civil war, which would give him a splendid chance to plunder a province and sell kingships to Asian princes. Similar hopes stirred in Pompey's uniquely blue-blooded father-in-law, Metellus Scipio, whose many failings included an indebtedness so grave that it was rumoured his creditors were about to sell him up. The same was also said about two other relations of Pompey by marriage, the father-in-law of his younger son, and the husband of his daughter. Debts, then, were an important reason why many ex-consuls and nobles wanted war, in the hope that it would bring them plunder. But the more senior officials and former officials could not face war on Caesar's side, after the fearful hatreds of the last two decades or more, and so opted instead for the man they hoped they might later be able to discard.

Yet how disappointing it was for Caesar, and how infuriating, that in spite of his own immense prestige and unremitting, well-financed endeavours to win friends, the vital inner circle of consulars should now after all, almost without exception, choose the other camp. Caesar explained this by saying he had inherited all Pompey's enemies at the time of their marriage alliance. But it still looked bad, and produced an impression that there was something sinister and repulsive about Caesar's cause.

A worse blow still, though not wholly unanticipated, was the defection of Caesar's own second-in-command, Labienus. Or, rather, it was not a defection but a return, for Labienus had come from Pompey's own country, Picenum, and had risen from humble origins to make his name under the protection of the powerful Pompeian house. Nevertheless he had been Caesar's most trusted deputy for eight long Gallic years. Somehow or other his leader's magic in the end failed to work. Although a commander of exceptional ability, Labienus was a harsh and rather difficult man, ill-at-ease when not fighting and unappreciative of subtle or ostensibly conciliatory policies. Perhaps the personalities of the two men were incompatible; and social class could have had something to do with it. Labienus might well have become impatient with Caesar's effortless superiority and aristocratic culture. Moreover, the rise of his general's smart young noble protégés, like Curio and Antony, may have made him feel that his own immense activities, to which due credit is scarcely given in the *Commentaries*, were inadequately appreciated, and that the enormous wealth that came into his hands was not sufficient recompense. Or perhaps he merely chose the side he thought would win. For, curiously enough, his unique inside knowledge of what was happening in Caesar's army left him with an unfavourable impression of its morale, which was to prove highly misleading information in the hands of his new allies. Meanwhile, however, Cicero, though commenting on his lack of 'rank', hailed his defection as splendid news. And indeed, except for

Pompey himself, Labienus was the only first-class general the Republicans had. The news that he was about to come over had proved a great encouragement to the warmongers; although after his arrival, owing to differences of background and temperament, the conservatives paid less attention to his military expertise than it deserved. Except for Cicero's own brother—who was smarting under a rebuke—no other senior officer of Caesar abandoned him throughout the civil war.

Nor did he lack noble supporters of his own. But they were younger, and their careers would have cut much less of a dash in *Who's Who*. They included members of decayed patrician families, who had lately found public office hard to obtain and tenaciously sided against the great, grandiose, plebeian noble houses, especially as Caesar was known to favour their cause, which was, after all, his own. Moreover, the propertied classes and financiers, who were unimpressed by a debt-ridden Metellus Scipio or Lentulus, supported Caesar, as did their satellites. 'The tax-collectors,' said Cicero, 'have never been loyal, and are now very friendly with Caesar.'

Indeed, his adherents, although so regrettably weak in ex-consuls, were drawn from an exceptionally wide circle. Among them—as Cicero and his correspondents continually emphasised with alarm—were all sorts of bankrupts and adventurers, people with shady pasts and compromised futures, 'men of fear and little hope', whom Atticus described as the kingdom of the dead emerging from the shades to drain their fellow-Romans' blood. Caesar was known to be perfectly prepared to enlist even the dregs of the population if need be, with money no object. This was what the clever young Caelius reported; he himself joined Caesar's cause because, unlike Labienus, he believed it was the side that was going to win.

But the more obscure supporters of Caesar were very far from all being young opportunists, or seedy and useless rascals. The impoverished, war-like areas of Italy, which had suffered from Sulla and liked Caesar's Marian sympathies, gave him the centurions and middle-class professionals who were the nucleus of his army. He had also worked harder than anyone ever before, and with a very great measure of success, to engage on his side the people who ran the Italian country towns. These included, throughout the peninsula, many bankers and other solid men who were now beginning to count in Roman affairs for the first time. Like the soldiers, they remembered with unappeased hatred the oppressions, disasters and devastations they had endured from Sulla and his henchmen. They welcomed Caesar all the more because, like his uncle, Marius, he had crushed the traditional northern enemies on their borders.

This situation became distressingly clear to the Pompeians when Caesar's advance into Italy proceeded with wholly unforeseen speed. By 14 January, only three days after the operation began, Arretium and Ancona had already fallen. Town after town opened its gates and expelled Pompey's troops; and when at Iguvium (Gubbio) and Auximum (Osimo) the civilian population began to show this attitude, the garrisons melted away and went over to Caesar.

Although he was still far away, Pompey (who as proconsul could not enter the capital) decided to retreat southwards toward Capua in Campania. At Rome the consuls, like many others, were horrified at this withdrawal. But they followed—so precipitately that Lentulus failed to carry out his orders to take with him the massive reserve treasury in the Temple of Saturn. Cicero recalled that even before hostilities began Pompey, despite his apparent confidence, had mentioned that the capital might become impossible to hold. He was also nervous of the effect on Roman opinion of the insidious peace moves that Caesar continued to launch. Nor did he feel that the two legions sent him only recently by Caesar, with large gratuities, could be relied upon to maintain a resolute defence of the city. But his decision was mainly strategic, and from that point of view, despite its ill-effects on morale, the evacuation was soon shown to be justified and indeed unavoidable.

An exceptionally alarming sign was the crumbling, almost without a blow, of Pompey's own home country, Picenum. Evidently the pattern of feudal patronage was a mixed one here; the rise of Pompey's father and himself must have been accompanied by friction and faction. Cingulum (Cingoli) had been refounded and built by Labienus at his own expense, and yet even this town quickly sent word that it proposed to give Caesar its support. One of the legions he had summoned from beyond the Alps caught up with him as he approached Asculum (Ascoli Piceno), and here too, though it was the strongpoint of the region, resistance melted away. Early in February the whole of Picenum was in Caesar's hands.

His second legion from Gaul, together with the twenty-two recently raised cohorts, joined him in front of the fortress of Corfinium, near Pentima in the Abruzzi, almost due east of Rome. At this town, forty years earlier the capital of the Italian rebels against Rome, the man who detested Caesar as much as anyone, Ahenobarbus, decided to make a stand. Although appointed to succeed his foe in Gaul, he had not yet attempted to leave Italy, and now commanded nearly twenty thousand men, including legionaries and dependent workers from his own vast estates in the area, where he encouraged mobilisation by promises of land. Pompey, who had now gone on to Luceria (Lucera), a hundred and thirty miles away in the south-eastern corner of Italy, urgently requested Ahenobarbus not to attempt resistance on his own account but to move back and effect a junction with himself. But Ahenobarbus, as governor-elect of a province, was technically independent of him, and refused to obey. He was afraid that Pompey now intended to leave Italy altogether, and he was supported by five senators who agreed that this would be a disastrous decision (and did not fancy the sea-journey in winter weather). Pompey, whose intentions were precisely as he thought, had evidently not taken Ahenobarbus into his full confidence, no doubt dreading his indiscretion and obstinacy. However, the attempted stand at Corfinium collapsed within a week, after scarcely a blow had been struck. At the last moment Ahenobarbus was arrested by his own officers and troops, who had found out that he was planning to get away without them; and a general surrender followed.

After the capitulation of Corfinium there was tense curiosity throughout Caesar's army about the treatment he would mete out to the Roman enemies who fell into his hands. When these senators, knights and officers, and the officials of the municipalities, were brought to him outside the town, he protected them from his soldiers, who were unkindly suggesting that the nobles who had taken up arms against their general should be sent into the slave market. Then, after commenting mildly that they had shown him inadequate gratitude, Caesar let them go free—even Ahenobarbus, on whom he heaped further coals of fire by letting him have back three hundred thousand pounds he had deposited in the local treasury.

This novel policy of leniency came as a sensation to all those who remembered Caesar's atrocious brutalities towards the Gauls. He himself too, was very conscious of the innovation, and wrote of it to Balbus and Oppius at Rome as the initial move in a carefully thought out programme. 'Let us see if by moderation we can win all hearts and secure a lasting victory, since by cruelty others have been unable to escape from hatred and have failed to maintain their victory for any length of time—except Sulla, whose example I do not intend to follow. This is a new way of conquering, to strengthen one's position by kindness and generosity.'

It was indeed a new way. Caesar was later said to have observed that the remembrance of cruelty is poor equipment for old age. He had also no doubt noticed that his savagery towards the Gauls may have retarded rather than accelerated the final settlement. Besides, they had been barbarians: whereas these were Roman nobles and citizens, men of the classes whom he was always trying to win over. Curio, although his supporter, somewhat disloyally said that Caesar was not by nature averse to cruelty, and would be cruel again if he began to lose support, but that his present belief was that mild measures would win him popularity. Mercy had its calculated part in the personal traditions of Roman politics. A general conferred a favour on the men he allowed to go free, and if thereafter they behaved unappreciatively—and Ahenobarbus, for example, immediately went off to renew the war elsewhere—he could arouse sympathy by demonstrating their ingratitude. Cato was infuriated by this policy, protesting that he had no right whatever to 'pardon' people who were not his subordinates. Yet the clemency of Caesar became legendary among his supporters, and one of the first things sympathisers did after his death was to build a temple in its honour and commemorate it on a coin.

Meanwhile Caesar was beginning to produce a new literary masterpiece exploiting his incomparable talent for depicting his own actions and motives in a favourable light. This sequel to his account of the Gallic campaigns, the second part of his *Commentaries*, was entitled the *Civil War*, but only covers the first two years of its operations. Although the date of final release is disputed, it is likely enough, once again, that each annual instalment became known among people of significance soon after the events which they described. As in the *Gallic War*, this view seems to be confirmed by the unusually emphatic note of self-justification in the account of the initial campaigns. The argument, throughout, is that Caesar's enemies, because of their insistence on pursuing a personal vendetta, had forced upon his shoulders a war he never wanted. The other side, of course, could just as convincingly have demonstrated Caesar's dubious past and suspect aims, if they had possessed the artist to do it. But Caesar was at least right in describing his really determined enemies as a small minority of reactionary senators who had forced their wishes upon the rest.

   Although anger and scorn are not far beneath the surface, his lucid, concise calmness is calculated to contrast impressively with the hate-ridden gossip which was raging against him. The emphasis on peacefulness is almost feverish. He insists that he is fighting not to destroy his enemies but to reconcile existing differences with as little bloodshed as possible. That was why, some three weeks before the Rubicon, he refused Curio's suggestion of a surprise attack, because it was important that everyone should know that he had done everything possible to avoid hostilities. He was obliged to carry his soldiers with him, since in these days of personal armies he must be assured of their consent, their trust in adequate rewards to come, and their conviction that he, their general to whom they were bound by oath, had suffered an injustice. But, as ever, the main target of propaganda, of insidiously blended legal and emotional appeals, was Rome. In February 49, Caesar defined his war-aims as the freedom of the Roman people from oppression by a small clique, the restoration of the tribunes who had been illegally driven from the city, and the protection of his own person from undeserved humiliation by his enemies. He thought it absurd to say that the revolutionary was himself and the constitutionalist was Pompey, whose career showed the opposite and whose youthful murders must be avenged. This may not have cut too much ice with those who noted the dignified, correct Pompey of the present day, but the cause of the wronged tribunes enabled Caesar also to declare that the free workings of the Roman constitution possessed no more stalwart supporter than himself.

All this double-talk was more effective than the corresponding Pompeian efforts, since Caesar already had successes to reinforce what he was saying, in addition to agents more experienced in its persuasive presentation. Throughout these months he kept up a deadly barrage of special envoys and informal peace missions, about which the cunning *Civil War* cannot be depended upon to tell the whole unadulterated truth. However, it is possible that his desire for peace, at this juncture, was genuine. For he was even speaking of a possible recognition of Pompey's nominal supremacy, under which, after his recent victories, he himself could easily have assumed the leading role.

One of Caesar's peace feelers was conducted by Balbus' nephew, as colourful and active a figure as his uncle: his object was to win over his family's bankrupt noble patron, the consul Lentulus. But the young man was too late because Lentulus had already left Italy. For the loss of Ahenobarbus' troops had tilted the numerical balance against Pompey and hastened his withdrawal to Brundusium (Brindisi); and then, on 4 March, the two consuls had set out across the Adriatic with part of the army.

This was highly irritating for Caesar, since the absence of the consuls made his legal façade look even flimsier than before, and raised complications about the election to next year's consulship, which remained an integral part of his programme. Nevertheless, Pompey was still at Brundusium. Caesar, too, arrived before the city a few days later with six legions and, after more peace soundings had failed, tried to blockade him in the harbour. But his engineers lacked the necessary naval support, and Pompey, with great skill, forced his way out to sea on 17 March, and made for the Balkan coast.

Although Cicero, and indeed Napoleon, regarded his decision to leave Italy as a mistake, it is hard to see what else he could have done. His armies and dependants in Italy had proved unreliable. On the other hand, the vast resources of Spain and the east still remained to be drawn upon: the east being the better destination of the two because it was richer and because Spain could be cut off by Caesar's troops in Gaul. Pompey held command of the sea, and his intention was to return victorious from the east as he had returned thirteen years earlier.

Meanwhile, he had gone, and Caesar must for the time being give up any plans of detaching him, as on several occasions, from his precarious conservative alliance. The future, then, remained anxious. But meanwhile there was much to be thankful for. He had conquered all Italy in sixty-five days almost without striking a single blow. And now at once he showed recognition that Italy, to him, meant not only the peninsula itself but also the north which had not hitherto been regarded as part of the home country. Caesar knew how much of his success he owed to his base in Cisalpine Gaul and to the magnificent troops he had recruited there. An end must be put to the humiliating situation by which the towns across the Po were only thought of as possessing a halfway status towards the full citizenship of Rome. Now, only a week after Pompey had left the Italian shores, Caesar arranged for a praetor to confer on these townships the full Roman franchise which their services so fully justified.

Meanwhile he had immediately set out from Brundusium in the direction of the capital. On the way, he insisted on seeing Cicero, and they met for the first time in ten years. It was imperative that this golden-tongued senior ex-consul should be converted to political friendship or at least passivity. Balbus and other intermediaries had already been working on Cicero, and Caesar himself had corresponded with him at length, courteously emphasising the common bond of their friendship with Cicero's patrician son-in-law, Dolabella (who was, however, treating Cicero's daughter, Tullia, abominably), and congratulating him on a thanksgiving which had somewhat ludicrously been awarded to the orator after minor skirmishes with brigands during his governorship of Cilicia. Caesar could not, however, forbear to point out that Cicero's ally, Cato, had objected to the thanksgiving. Cicero, for his part, replied in many phrases of exquisite Latin which displayed an equal or even larger amount of insincerity. For while he fulsomely congratulated Caesar on his clemency at Corfinium, he was simultaneously writing to Atticus that this leniency was entirely bogus and that the man was a loathsome bandit who would stick at no abomination and indeed would leave very few members of the upper classes alive.

But there were also several reasons, in addition to plain fear of Caesar, which prompted Cicero to avoid showing this hostility openly. In the first place he felt pretty sure that a victory of the diehards would be scarcely less bloodthirsty than a victory of Caesar; they frequently said as much themselves, with gloating satisfaction. Secondly, like Cato and others, he was very nearly as gloomy about Pompey's autocratic intentions as about Caesar's, especially as people kept on reminding him that Pompey had let him down badly over his exile. Furthermore, Caesar had lent him a great deal of money. The orator had repeatedly urged the long-suffering Atticus to repay it on his behalf, pointing out that it looked ugly to be in debt to a man whose politics one wanted to attack. On the other hand another financial factor pulled embarrassingly in the opposite direction. During his governorship Cicero had made personal gains amounting to a hundred and ten thousand pounds, apparently without incurring any violent criticism. On returning to Italy he had left this sum for the time being in Anatolia and was afraid, justifiably as it turned out, that the Pompeians—or rather the destitute and grasping conservative leaders—would seize the sum.

The conversation between the two men took place at Formiae, on about 28 March. It was not a success. Caesar urged Cicero to be present at the senate meeting he was going to convene at Rome, since his eloquence and example would be invaluable. Cicero quotes himself as saying that if he attended he would feel obliged to express sorrow at what had happened to Pompey, and would deplore any plan by Caesar to invade Spain or Greece. 'That', replied Caesar, who had been suggesting no more than neutrality, 'is not what I want'. For it was, indeed, his intention to invade both those countries, one after the other. It was left that Cicero would think the matter over, but Caesar's final words showed that his politeness was wearing a little thin. If he could not get counsel from Cicero, he said, he would take it from wherever he could, 'and would be obliged to descend to any sort of measure'. But Cicero adhered to his decision, and stayed away on 1 April.

In every town the tribunes Antony and Quintus Cassius, who were back in office, had arranged for notices to be posted requesting senators to be present on that day. But when Caesar arrived at the meeting, which was held outside the city because he was a governor, the attendance was depressingly poor, especially in the higher ranks. Only two ex-consuls were present, and one of them, the eminent non-political jurist, Servius Sulpicius Rufus, struck the same unfortunate note as Cicero by replying to the victorious general's long propaganda oration by a plea that he should not carry the war to Spain. In response, Caesar offered to send yet another deputation to Pompey. This, however, was a somewhat empty gesture; volunteers were unlikely, now that Pompey had declared all senators who remained in Italy to be his enemies. Then Caesar uttered, according to his own account, the following combination of an offer and a threat: 'I earnestly invite you to join with me in carrying on the government of Rome. If, however, timidity makes you shrink from the task, I shall trouble you no more. For in that case I shall govern by myself.' 'The man no longer refuses to be called a tyrant,' wrote Cicero to Atticus: 'in fact he practically demands it, and that is just what he is.' And he was reported to loathe the infuriatingly lukewarm senators like poison.

Next, Caesar spoke to the Roman assembly, promising food and money bonuses. Then he turned to methods of raising funds in order to meet this expenditure and pay his troops. In this major crisis all the wealth he had won in Gaul was no longer enough. He was very short of coin, which he even borrowed from his officers—thus killing two birds with one stone, since this had the additional advantage of guaranteeing their loyalty. The senate obediently tried to pass a measure authorising him to draw money from the reserve treasury in the Temple of Saturn, which the Pompeians had failed to ransack as they hurriedly left. The events that now followed are not mentioned in the *Commentaries*, which are, at this point, less than frank. Caesar refers vaguely to an obstruction and plot by a tribune, Lucius Caecilius Metellus, who was suborned by hostile elements and wasted several days. Apparently Metellus vetoed the senate's proposal, and when this was ignored he even barred the locked door of the temple with his own person. This impertinent and courageous action, taken by a man belonging to the most eminent family in Rome, had the effect of bringing Caesar himself into the city. He had not been there for nine years, and as a governor he possessed no legal right to be there now; this was a strangely unceremonious occasion for the great conqueror's re-entry. Metellus indicated that, according to ancient tradition, the reserve treasury should only be used for fighting against the Gauls. Caesar attempted to meet this antiquarian point by recalling that this is just what he had been doing. But then his patience snapped, and he continued, 'I've a good mind to kill you, young man. You may not realise it, but I should find the act even easier than the threat!' Metellus was brushed aside, after being persuaded to abandon his resistance, so it is said, by a fellow-tribune who pointed out that it is up to a tyrant to relieve his subjects of all financial worries. And so Caesar was able to cart away 4,135 lb. of gold, 900,000 lb. of silver, and one and a half million pounds in cash. But there had nearly been bloodshed, and the incident was particularly unfortunate because one of Caesar's principal constitutional claims was his sponsorship of the freedom and sacrosanctity of the tribunes. This sort of high-handed action was so unpopular with the Roman public that, on the conclusion of his brief visit, Caesar was obliged to abandon his farewell speech. He left in a state of extreme irritation.

It had been clear to him for some time that the only way to keep this unpopularity within bounds was to guarantee metropolitan food supplies, which were gravely threatened by the supremacy of Pompey on the seas. The corn-producing islands of Sardinia and Sicily had to be occupied, and this was promptly done. In Sardinia there was a rising in his favour even before his troops landed, and Sicily, which provided a stepping stone towards the even larger granary of Pompeian north Africa, was swiftly seized by Curio from Cato, who evacuated the island in early May with disagreeable remarks about Pompey's lack of military preparations.

But although Sardinia and Sicily had gone one way, Cicero now finally made up his mind to go the other. The complex brew of principles, personal sentiments and financial considerations which was seething within his breast had finally coalesced to produce a decision. Caesar's bad reception at Rome seemed to show he could not last. The man was his own worst enemy, Cicero wrote to Atticus on 2 May: 'and fall he must, either through the agency of his enemies or of himself.' When, therefore, Pompey summoned all senators to join him at Thessalonica (Salonica), Cicero, on 7 June, wound up many reams of closely argued hesitancy by obeying. Yet even now, as he set sail from Caieta and rounded the foot of Italy to cross the Adriatic, he intended to keep out of whatever fighting there might be.

Cicero was partly influenced in this decision by a rumour that Pompey had arrived in Africa, which was false, and a report that the Caesarian cause had suffered a setback at Massilia (Marseille), which was true. After his short and unsatisfactory visit to Rome, Caesar set out by land in the direction of Spain. His spirits had risen, and he joked that he was going to fight an army without a general, after which he would go and deal with a general who had no army. But when shortly after mid-April he arrived before Massilia, he found that the people of this historic and wealthy Greek city-state were not disposed to offer any cooperation. Ahenobarbus, pardoned after the fiasco at Corfinium, was on his way to renew his hereditary friendship with the Massilians, and they had recently sent envoys to Pompey. But Caesar, too, had been generous to them after the Gallic War, and so the city council diplomatically informed him that their equal obligation to both parties constrained them to neutrality. But this was scarcely sincere, since as soon as Ahenobarbus arrived by sea he was admitted and given control of the city's defences.

The place was a serious obstruction to Caesar, since it lay right across his lines of communication. If it were allowed to remain hostile, the communities in Spain, even in the Further province where two tenures of office had left him many dependants, were unlikely to come out openly in his favour. By land, however, the conquest of Massilia proved impossible, and ships had to be constructed at Arelate (Arles) in order to invest the city by sea as well. In June they were ready, and Caesar felt sufficiently confident of the outcome to proceed with his westward journey.

On 22 June he reached his six legions which had been transferred to Spain from Gallic camps. They confronted five Pompeian legions based on Ilerda (Lerida) on a northern tributary of the Ebro. This force, which as Caesar commented must have been raised, such was its size, not to garrison Spain but specifically to make war upon himself, was under the orders of Lucius Afranius and Marcus Petreius. Afranius was an unpolitical character whose only civilian accomplishment was dancing. He had been a ludicrously bad consul eleven years earlier, after achieving election through enormous bribes by Pompey, whose homeland, Picenum, he shared. But he was a very experienced officer who had seen much military service under Pompey in Spain as well as elsewhere. Petreius seems to have been the son of a centurion from south of Rome. It was he who had defeated and killed Catiline in the field, and later, when Caesar as consul ordered Cato off to prison, Petreius had ostentatiously gone with him, observing that he preferred Cato's company in prison to Caesar's in the senate.

Both sides possessed strong auxiliary forces, including cavalry, an élite contingent of which came with Caesar from Gaul. He needed to act quickly, because Italy was severed from him by Massilia, and had been left inadequately garrisoned; he was also afraid that Pompey himself might appear in Spain. But rapid action was difficult, because Ilerda possessed strong natural protection and the Pompeians had learnt from local guerrilla wars how to adopt fluid tactics of charging in open order or scattered units, regrouping speedily thereafter. Moreover, Caesar was suffering seriously from the weather. According to the calendar it was late in June, but since the calendar was out of joint with the seasons, spring was not yet over, and the snow was still melting on the mountains and flooding the rivers. Caesar's two pontoon bridges were broken, and he was cut off on a peninsula between two swollen tributaries. Public opinion at Rome was highly sensitive to each successive development, and when this news reached the capital many senators who had hitherto hesitated felt it was time to follow Cicero and join Pompey in Greece.

But they had, once again, underestimated Caesar, who managed to cross one of the streams by constructing light coracles of wood, wattle and hides such as he had seen in Britain. His escape from the trap, combined with the news of a naval victory off Massilia, brought over to his side several important Spanish towns north of the Ebro, including Osca which remembered proudly that it had been the headquarters of the inspiring anti-conservative Sertorius when he was fighting against the heirs of Sulla, including Pompey. Impeded by this local hostility and by Caesar's cavalry, Afranius and Petreius decided to retire to the highlands south of the Ebro, where Pompey, during the same campaigns, had won a powerful following. On their march towards the river, however, they were encircled and brought to a halt. Yet Caesar did not attack. His troops wanted to get to grips and lay their hands on plunder; but he foresaw that food shortages would do his work for him. Then the armies began to fraternise. At this point, however, Petreius, showing greater determination than his colleague, put a stop to the rot, executing the soldiers of Caesar whom he caught in his lines; though that proved a mistake, since it gave the enemy a useful propaganda weapon.

The Pompeians were obliged to turn back towards Ilerda. But Caesar maintained continuous pressure and when they next encamped it was to have their supply of water cut off. This proved the end, and on 27 August they capitulated. Forty days had been enough for another almost bloodless victory. In accordance with his policy of clemency to fellow-Romans, Caesar set Afranius and Petreius free and sent them away from Spain. Their soldiers were discharged in Spain and Gaul. Varro, the leading scholar of the day, whose unavailing attempts to hold Further Spain for Pompey earned mild amusement in the *Commentaries*, surrendered and was replaced by Quintus Cassius who had served Caesar so well as tribune earlier in the year.

After raising large sums, Caesar returned to Massilia. The city had been forced to capitulate, Ahenobarbus escaping to fight unsuccessfully on yet another front. Although the city's defenders broke the armistice, they were spared the atrocities of retribution which the barbarian regions of Gaul had so often experienced. But their venerable city-state, in spite of its centuries of loyalty to Rome, was deprived of most of its territory, and ceased to exist as a political force.

On his way back to Rome, Caesar, though we do not learn of this from the *Commentaries*, had to turn aside to deal with a serious mutiny at Placentia (Piacenza). Apart from a minor flurry among officers at the beginning of the Gallic War, this was the first time in his military career that such a thing had happened. The leaders of the subversive movement belonged to a legion which had suffered severe losses in Spain. The soldiers fighting there had been poorly fed and had resented the prolongation of the campaign by Caesar's avoidance of battle. In spite of all the money he had seized, the amount of loot that had reached themselves was scanty, and the new policy of clemency had made it scantier; while even payments of wages had been delayed. The troops knew very well that Caesar, who was after all a rebel against his government, could not do without them. But they needed him just as much, since otherwise there would be no booty for them, and no land grants on retirement. After reminding them that they were, in fact, the best and most regularly paid army in the whole of Roman history, Caesar decided that a certain show of severity was both desirable and practicable. The offending legion was sentenced to the archaic, historic punishment of the execution of every tenth man. But then their general, who had never seriously intended to inflict such a wasteful, unpopular penalty, relented to the extent of demanding the names of a hundred and twenty ringleaders. These had their details filed for future reference, with the exception of twelve, who were put to death. Ostensibly they were chosen by lot, but Caesar's political life had taught him how to ensure that lots did not fall by chance alone. Moreover, a popular gesture could be salvaged even from this unwelcome incident, because when one of the condemned men complained he was innocent and had been falsely accused by his centurion, the centurion was executed in his place.

Meanwhile the Spanish success had been further offset by disasters of Caesar's lieutenants elsewhere. In the Adriatic, where Pompeian fleets were predominant, Dolabella was driven back on to the coast and defeated, and Antony's brother was forced to capitulate upon an island. Even worse, Curio, after taking Sicily from Cato, had been destroyed with the whole of his two legions in north Africa. The victor was Juba, king of the large state of Numidia (Algeria). He had inherited a bond of friendship with Pompey, and, besides, during a legal hearing in the senate thirteen years earlier, a sneer by Juba at the affected clothes worn by Caesar had caused the latter, in a moment of anger, to grasp and pull the prince's beard.

Juba also had a grudge against Curio, who had recently proposed that Rome should take over his kingdom. On his arrival in Africa, Curio had not believed he would be attacked by Juba, who was assumed to be too much discouraged by the news of Caesar's victory in Spain. But the invader was lured into a trap in the Medjerda (Bagradas) valley, where he moved too far and too fast, and like Crassus in Parthia found himself surrounded by cavalry on unfavourable ground. Many fell, and among them was Curio himself; most of the rest were captured and executed by Juba. For the time being, then, the enormous corn-supplies of Africa remained in Pompeian hands. But Caesar's publicity was able to dwell upon the fact that the enemy cause depended so much on this unsavoury, sadistic foreigner, whom he proceeded to declare an enemy of the state.

> Romans, what madness, what huge lust of war
> Hath made barbarians drunk with Latin blood?[5]

Making more of Spain than of these disasters, Caesar now paid his second visit of the year to Rome. He was still determined to become consul for 48 in constitutional fashion, and since the absence of the current consuls had made a normal election impossible he was obliged to secure this aim by having brief recourse to the emergency institution of dictator. He was nominated to the dictatorship by a law proposed by Marcus Aemilius Lepidus, who was married to the daughter of his lifelong friend, Servilia. Although Lepidus was a shifty and pompous light-weight, he was chosen by Caesar as his principal deputy in Italy because of his extremely blue blood—a rare commodity among Caesar's senior officials—and because his father had opposed Sulla and in 78 BC led the first movement against his heritage.

Caesar used this first dictatorship specifically in order to hold the necessary consular elections, and not for the more general and sweeping purposes discredited by the harsh régime of Sulla. He also proceeded to tackle a nagging problem which had been intensified by the civil war and presented a grave menace to the entire structure of society. This was the problem of debt. It affected, to varying extents, the vast majority of Romans and Italians, and Caesar himself had acquired considerable knowledge of the problem both from his personal experiences as one of the heaviest debtors of the day and from the reforms he had undertaken during his administration of Spain before the Gallic War. As far back as the eighties, politicians had tried to do something to rescue the numberless debtors, whom harsh laws allowed to be bled white by money-lenders. But these efforts were limited by the need to ensure that the operation did not deteriorate into a general attack on credit and private possessions, which was widely dreaded by property-owners throughout the country.

Debt again played a leading part in the discontents which brought Catiline to the surface, and now civil war had created a credit crisis of dangerous proportions. One of the chief problems seems to have been a shortage of cash. An enormous quantity of coin was taken to pay the rival armies, and because of general insecurity huge amounts had also disappeared from circulation into hoards. Consequently, money had become so scarce that there was none available to be repaid. Creditors were frantically trying to recover their loans, but the borrowers, quite unable to satisfy them, were obliged to forfeit their mortgaged estates and allotments instead. But this only caused additional hardship, because creditors were not interested in these properties, which therefore fetched miserable prices. And meanwhile, all the time, the savage, antique laws against debtors were oppressively at work.

What Caesar now produced was a measure which forbade the hoarding of cash but at the same time obliged creditors to accept land and movable goods in repayment. To avoid disputes about prices, this property was to be assessed at pre-war values, determinable by special official valuers who were to be appointed by the city praetor. It was also laid down that interest already paid out in money or securities should be deducted from the debts. At Rome the interest rate had normally been about 4 per cent. Bribery at elections had raised it to 8 per cent, and lately it had been nearer 12 per cent. The decision that interest might be deducted was therefore a substantial concession. It may not have taken place, however, at exactly this time, since Caesar continued for the rest of his life to pass further measures endeavouring to deal with this acute crisis, and it is not easy to distinguish their chronology. But it was already possible in 49 to see what his general attitude was going to be.

His suspected intentions had caused great alarm among the wealthier classes. Even one of the ex-consuls who had remained in Italy, Servius Sulpicius Rufus, had written to Cicero that, whichever side won, money difficulties would inevitably necessitate disastrous attacks on private property. Abolition of debts was the most truly popular item in the anti-conservative programme with which Caesar had long professed to associate himself—and he was believed to have assured debtors that a civil war, fought on his side, would set them on their feet. But, since so many financiers were numbered among his supporters, the story may not have been true. Or, if it was, his behaviour now belied his words, since the widespread fear that he would take revolutionary action in favour of the penniless proved quite wrong. It was true that his debt law meant that creditors suffered, on an average, a loss of perhaps a quarter of their legal entitlement. This seems a lot, and indeed they complained greatly, but it was less than they had expected. Consoled by Caesar's insistence that none of their slaves would be rewarded for denouncing breaches of the law, they soon decided that it was still profitable to lend, and continued to do so briskly.

Caesar had shown that he was committed to no particular class. While anxious that dangerous abuses should be checked, he felt no desire for the abolition of debts. After all, it was far more convenient that most of the money should get back to the creditors. They were men of substance: the sort of people from whom he would find it easiest to extract funds when the time came. They were, in fact, his partisans, and at the same time he swelled their numbers by arranging that sentences of exile the Republicans had passed against his friends should be rescinded.

Then, after an exceedingly active eleven days at Rome, he proceeded southwards in the direction of Brundusium.

People were afraid that Pompey might at any moment start back from Greece and land in Italy. In fact however, this, like the earlier rumours that he would be going to Spain or Africa, did not represent his current intentions at all. Pompey's favourite strategy, like that of General Grant and Lord Montgomery, was to attack from a built-up position of superior strength. Rather, therefore, than launch attacks of a more spectacular kind, he preferred the slower but surer method of mobilising the vast forces of the east before making any further move at all. He was spending the winter at Thessalonica, and although on hearing of Caesar's arrival at Brundusium he had begun to move westwards, he did not expect him to succeed in crossing the Ionian Sea during the season when navigation was normally suspended.

There, however, he was wrong. Admittedly Caesar, too, experienced a grave disappointment—indeed, one which in his view prevented the early conclusion of the war. For at Brundusium he found that the number of available ships was quite insufficient to carry his whole force across the Adriatic. Nevertheless, on 4 January 48 (early November by the season), profiting by a brief spell of calm sea and favourable wind, he crammed twenty thousand men and six hundred cavalry on board and hurried across the sea, landing at Palaeste (Palissa) on the open coast of Epirus, south of Vloné (Valona) in what is now Albania. Pompey's admiral in the Adriatic, Bibulus, who was in command of a hundred and ten ships based on Corcyra (Corfu), did not, to his own frenzied annoyance, intercept the convoy of his hated enemy. He had to be content with destroying thirty of their ships on their way back to Italy, and brutally killing their crews. Then he returned to the Adriatic coast to conduct a naval blockade of Caesar's newly arrived force, which in turn deprived him of fresh water. Bibulus, whose ships, like all ancient men-of-war, were ill-suited for patrol work since they could not stay at sea for very long,

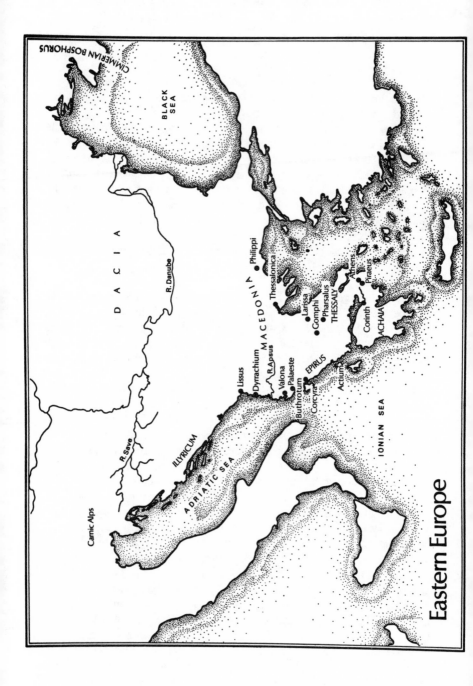

Eastern Europe

soon afterwards died of cold and over-exertion, receiving a brief but gentlemanly obituary note in Caesar's *Civil War*.

Napoleon maintained that Caesar ought to have invaded the Balkans by land and not by sea, on which he was so greatly inferior. But it is doubtful if even Caesar could have managed so long a trek, since he had found his troops at Brundusium exhausted, sick, and inclined to desert; and indeed, had he started on the long landward detour, Pompey would surely have re-invaded Italy across the Adriatic after all. Moreover, Caesar's arrival by sea came as a most unpleasant surprise, and indeed caused something like panic in the enemy army, which now did everything possible to speed up its westward march. Noting this disarray, Caesar reverted to his familiar barrage of peace moves, even releasing and dispatching to Pompey a captured senior officer (Vibullius Rufus, formerly liaison officer between the two leaders), whose inevitable disclosure of information about Caesar's movements, though it seems a big risk to have taken, was presumably compensated by the weakening of purpose and morale which his mission caused in Pompey's ranks.

The two armies came face to face across the river Semani (Apsus), Caesar to the south of the stream and Pompey to its north. Caesar was so anxious about the failure of his reinforcements to reach him from Italy that he himself attempted to re-cross in a small ship in order to urge action, but he was turned back by bad weather. On 10 April (late February according to the season), this agonising period of delay came to an end when Antony succeeded in bringing four legions and eight hundred cavalry across the strait. An extremely lucky change of wind enabled him to evade the enemy fleet and land near Lissus (Lesh). This place was seventy-five miles north of where Caesar was waiting, but Antony managed to join him.

Both armies now converged upon Dyrrhachium (Durrës, Durazzo), which contained Pompey's stores and munitions and was the key to his naval blockade. Further delay was not in Caesar's interests, since his enemy could draw upon the whole of Asia, while his own hopes of further reinforcements were now slender. Some of his transports had been destroyed at sea; and Gabinius (who had deserted Pompey for Caesar) failed to reach him by the land-route, and died of illness while besieged in Illyricum on the way. Consequently Caesar hoped to force Pompey to fight by threatening the vital point of Dyrrhachium. However, this attempt failed by the narrowest of margins, since Pompey, still very seriously to be reckoned with as a general, won the race by a few hours and just had time to seize the high ground six miles south of the town. Caesar pushed his way between Pompey and Dyrrhachium, so that both sides were now cut off from their bases—Caesar from Italy by Pompey's navy, and Pompey from Dyrrhachium by Caesar's army.

The enemy force was too close at hand for Caesar to launch a siege.

Instead he surrounded the fourteen-mile line of the enemy entrenchments with his own seventeen-mile circuit of land fortifications. This immense piece of spadework, scarcely equalled except in the American Civil War, was a remarkable expedient for an army outnumbered by four to three. Caesar explains that his motives were to secure his own foragers, to restrict the grazing of the enemy's cavalry, and to make Pompey look ridiculous, so as to give himself an advantage in the propagandist peace moves which continued meanwhile. Napoleon criticised the operation, and although he was writing at a time when large-scale trench warfare was out of fashion, it is true that the blockade could never have been a total success, because Pompey retained access to the sea; for this reason Dyrrhachium could scarcely become another Alesia. Moreover, Caesar's food situation was very poor, as the harvest had not yet ripened (since early July was still May according to the season), and he could not wait for it to do so.

On about 8 July, therefore, he attacked the enemy lines at six different points on a single day, but failed to break in. Some nine days later, Pompey struck back. Advised by Gaulish deserters, he sent six legions and light auxiliaries across by sea to puncture Caesar's line at its southern extremity on the coast, and these troops succeeded in fortifying a camp which completely frustrated the investment. Caesar's counter-attack was a disastrous failure, in which at least a thousand men and thirty-two standards were lost. Labienus, in order to convince his new conservative allies he was loyal, insulted and then murdered the prisoners. But for some reason Pompey failed to follow up his success. This was probably because, amid this difficult network of fortifications, he did not realise just how great his victory had been. He can scarcely have believed those who maintained that the war was already practically over; though Caesar declared that it would have been, if the other side had possessed on that day a man who understood how to win it.

However, the blockade had been broken, and Caesar recoiled rapidly inland. He had already stationed detachments in Thessaly, as in other regions of northern Greece, in order to spread the pressure on food-supplies and to encourage local anti-Pompeian parties, formed to some extent of people to whose families he himself had performed services during his career. And so now it was Thessaly that he made for. There he was successfully joined by two legions under the former consul, Calvinus, while Pompey's forces were likewise increased when Metellus Scipio, coming from his province of Syria, met him at the Thessalian capital, Larissa. If Pompey had decided, after Dyrrhachium, that the time had come to sail back to Italy, Caesar would have been obliged, whatever the dangers, to go after him by the overland route. But he had surmised that his enemy would feel unable to abandon Metellus Scipio, and he was right. Pompey, too, was in Thessaly—far from his maritime bases—and there were hopes of a decisive battle. After Caesar had allowed his hard-worked and ill-fed soldiers an orgy of looting, drinking and killing at the recalcitrant small town of Gomphi, the two armies confronted one another in the plain of Pharsalus. Pompey's forces were now more than twice the size of Caesar's, and they were stationed in an elevated position. Nevertheless, for day after sweltering summer day, the smaller force offered battle, even on unfavourable ground, without eliciting any response. Indeed, Caesar was actually on the point of breaking away—in the hope that his superior mobility might give him some advantage—when he saw to his delight that the opposing army was preparing for battle. He cancelled the movement order, and formed his line.

Caesar suggests that Pompey had finally decided to fight under pressure from the conservative politicians in his camp. They were contentious and ill-tempered, interested only in vengeance, spoils and jobs, and quarrelling violently about who would get Caesar's post of chief priest. And, above all, they were reluctant to treat or tolerate Pompey as their commander. He had found it advisable to give Metellus Scipio the honours due to an independent general. Yet Ahenobarbus, like others of similar opinion, was full of sneers about their 'king of kings', who might be rapidly dispensed with if only a decisive battle could be fought. And meanwhile Pompey himself was also induced by an over-sanguine belief in his enemies' low morale to agree that a battle would be successful.

This misleading intelligence came from his best general, Labienus. It was he, again, who secured the adoption of a scheme by which his seven-thousand-strong cavalry were to win the victory (sparing legionary losses) by a flank attack on Caesar's right wing after the legions on both sides had engaged. Caesar, however, anticipated this danger by forming a reserve corps of three or four thousand infantrymen—one cohort from the third line of each legion—and posting them obliquely in support of the threatened wing, which he himself commanded. Caesar's Gaulish experiences had given him an inclination to incorporate rear attacks in battle plans. Although the reserve was out of sight, it seems curious that Pompey did not foresee this apparently rather obvious strategy: perhaps some of the pieces in the precarious jigsaw of our information are missing. At all events, when the battle took place on 9 August, Caesar's stratagem was completely successful. Confronted suddenly with prickly hedge spikes presented by the reserve line, which had been ordered to use its javelins for stabbing instead of throwing, Pompey's cavalry, instead of circling round the unexpected formation, panicked and fled. After that, it was easy to outflank and roll back his legions. Then Caesar's soldiers, though exhausted in the great heat, pushed on and captured the enemy camp, from which Pompey himself got away (just as they were entering) and made his escape from the battlefield and from Greece. Fifteen thousand of his men had been killed, including six thousand Roman citizens, whereas Caesar's losses were negligible. On the next morning over twenty thousand Pompeian survivors, after painfully retreating some six miles during the night, offered their surrender. The army had ceased to exist.

Pompey was obsessed by the failure of his cavalry, on whom he had confidently counted. He suspected treachery, but in fact he had merely judged wrong, although the initiative had been in his hands; while Caesar had judged right. Only cavalry in overwhelming numbers can make an impression on the finest infantry, and Pompey's horse were not quite numerous enough. Furthermore, his army was too mixed, and although Gauls and Spaniards on his side fought well the oriental levies had proved a disappointment.

The battle of Pharsalus was hastily improvised, rapid and overwhelmingly complete. It is true that, except for Ahenobarbus who was killed, most of the leading Pompeians escaped to fight another day. Nevertheless, the total ruin which had fallen upon Pompey himself demolished the balance of power in the empire, and made this one of the decisive engagements of history.

> Nor Fortune lingered, but decreed the doom
> which swept the ruins of a world away.[6]

The engagement possessed the gloomy distinction of being the largest ever fought between Romans, and Caesar found it advisable not to mention this victory in any official statement, and never to celebrate it in a Triumph. But he managed, all the same, to derive from the occasion political advantages in addition to those which came naturally from an overwhelming military success. First, even before the battle was over, he had created an impression by ordering his soldiers to spare their own countrymen, and this had removed any chance that Pompey's legionaries might rally. Next, on reaching the enemy camp (where he ate the dinner that had been prepared for his rival) he was able to note and point out the unseemly luxury of the tents of Lentulus and others, surrounded by artificial arbours and fresh turf, festooned with ivy, and crammed with silver plate. On capturing the correspondence of Pompey and Metellus Scipio, he burnt it unread. Finally, an inspection of the battlefield elicited a widely reported utterance which repeated one of the most persistent themes of his propaganda. If he had refrained from appealing to his army for help, he declared, all his achievements would not have saved him from condemnation in the courts.

Caesar gazed at all the dead bodies and pronounced the words: *They asked for it.*

CHAPTER EIGHT

The Wealth and Charm of Cleopatra

*A*fter Pompey's disappearance from Greece, Caesar seized ten enemy warships in the Hellespont (Dardanelles), and landed in Anatolia. It was imperative for him to raise huge sums in order to pay for the upkeep of his armies. Fortunately the country was rich enough to stand a further bout of contributions. Caesar took the view that all money raised for Pompey must be handed over to himself, and the communities were also encouraged to make voluntary gifts of heavy golden crowns. But all was not extortion, since he was eager not to seem to be repeating the oppressive behaviour for which Metellus Scipio had become notorious during his westward journey through these territories. So Caesar accompanied his impositions by a measure calculated to lighten the lot of the provincials. Although funds were so greatly needed, he relieved the province of Asia of the attentions of the Roman tax-farmers, instead allowing the local authorities themselves to raise their own tribute in the form of a fixed land-tax; and the total burden was thereby reduced by as much as one-third. The reform was bound to upset financiers at Rome, but Caesar considered he had treated them well by his debt law and that he could therefore stand a little indignation from them now.

The *Commentaries* also record how the treasury of the Temple of Artemis at Ephesus, reprieved when Metellus Scipio had no time to seize it before leaving to join Pompey in Greece, was now saved by Caesar for the second time. An inscription from that city describes him as 'god manifest and common saviour of mankind'. Nothing is said about this sort of thing in the *Commentaries*, since it is far removed from the niceties of Roman constitutionalism. But the Asian cities found no difficulty in equating Caesar, like Pompey and even at a pinch Metellus Scipio, with the Hellenistic monarchs to whom they were accustomed. Moreover, Caesar invited comparison with Alexander by visiting Troy in his footsteps. But the pilgrimage of Caesar struck a more intimate and Roman note, because of the Julian family's alleged descent from the goddess Venus through the Trojan prince, Aeneas.

Meanwhile Pompey, after riding away from the disastrous battlefield of

Pharsalus, had embarked for Macedonia. He did not touch the Anatolian mainland, but sailed straight on to the island of Lesbos, where he collected his wife and younger son. He might then have made for the principal province remaining loyal to him, Africa (Tunisia) with its great supplies of corn. Napoleon thought that this is what he should have done, since many of his leading supporters were gathering there. But he may not have been certain they would continue to resist, and he cannot have cared for the idea of having to depend on a foreigner as unlikeable as Juba of Numidia. It seemed best, therefore, to continue to rely on such eastern resources as could still be mobilised—and at least it would be possible to organise them without interference from headstrong diehards.

However, some foreign aid would certainly have to be enlisted, since not much help was going to come from the Roman provinces of the region; Syria, for example, promptly requested him to go elsewhere. It was said that he first thought of proceeding to Parthia in order to make common cause with the national enemy, but gave up the idea because his wife Cornelia had been the daughter-in-law of Parthia's hated invader, Crassus. But the story that he considered joining the Parthians ought to be rejected as Caesarian propaganda, since Pompey knew they still did not forget that he had once double-crossed them. Indeed, they had sharply reminded Crassus of the fact after his defeat; and they had detained Pompey's envoy. At all events, he accepted the advice of his Greek counsellor, Theophanes, and decided that the best destination was the semi-independent kingdom of Egypt. He had played a leading part in the reinstatement of its king, thereby keeping the dynasty on the throne and preventing its annexation by Rome. When visited by Pompey's elder son the year before, the Egyptian government had contributed fifty ships and five hundred men. And many of Pompey's old soldiers were living there. They had come when Gabinius intervened eight years ago, and they had stayed on; now they could be re-enrolled as the nucleus of a new army to carry on the fight against Caesar.

But what undoubtedly tempted him most was the great wealth of the country. Although this had declined in recent years, largely owing to the gigantic sums which Pompey himself and other Romans had forced the rulers to disgorge, the potential riches of Egypt still dwarfed all the rest of the Mediterranean. Its world-monopoly of papyrus was an unparalleled asset, and there was a great trade in glass, linen and precious metals. Egyptian emeralds, topazes, amethysts and onyx fetched very high prices, and scented essences, ointments and perfumes were exported far and wide. Moreover, Egypt could almost compete with Tunisia in corn production; it was capable of supplying enough grain to feed Rome for four months of every year. Such were the reasons why predatory Roman eyes had so often in recent years looked towards Egypt, and they explain why Pompey, after his defeat, turned in the same direction. He had diverted huge sums of Egyptian money into his own hands eleven years before, and his future now depended upon a repetition of this achievement.

The unfortunate monarch Ptolemy XII the Oboe Player had died three years earlier, and the governing group of the Egypt to which Pompey now made his way was divided into two hostile camps, supporting his two successors against one another. These were his fifteen-year-old son Ptolemy XIII and his sister-bride Cleopatra VII aged twenty-one. Their armies were encamped opposite each other beside the coastal town of Pelusium, south-east of Port Said.

Alexandria was in the hands of Ptolemy, or rather of his chief minister, the eunuch Pothinus, and a general named Achillas. On 28 September 48, as Pompey's ship approached this alien coast—near Jupiter's temple at Casium, on Egypt's eastern border—Achillas and two Roman officers were rowed out to meet him, and presented a friendly message from the king. Leaving his wife on board, Pompey stepped into the boat, accompanied by a freedman and three slaves. As the oarsmen made for the shore, one of the Romans, a certain Septimius who had served under him against the pirates, stabbed him in the back, and he fell forward into the hull and died. The government of Ptolemy had noted who was the victor in the civil war, and had decided to demonstrate in this conclusive fashion that, even if it had sent ships to his enemy, it was now whole-heartedly on the winning side.

Only four days later Caesar arrived from Rhodes, and sailed into Alexandria harbour with his small force of three thousand two hundred infantry and eight hundred cavalry. The king's tutor, Theodotus, a professor of rhetoric from Chios, came out to meet his flagship, and offered him welcoming gifts: the signet-ring of Pompey and also his head, which, he explained, had been embalmed on the young king's order.

All Caesar says about this is that 'he learned of Pompey's death'. But the grisly incident gave other writers free rein to depict his noble emotions of abhorrence. His feelings were in fact likely to be somewhat mixed. It was not a good precedent for Roman leaders to be murdered by non-Romans, and, besides, his death might perpetuate the hostilities of the civil war and lead to a vendetta.

> Not till his country's swords transfix the heart
> Of Caesar, shall great Pompey be avenged.[7]

Moreover, Caesar had hastened to the spot in the hope of catching his enemy alive. For to spare him—though nothing more humiliating could be imagined—would have been an apt culmination of his deliberate programme of clemency. On the other hand, the death of his principal enemy, as well as Lentulus whom he likewise failed to save, surely brought the end of the civil war nearer, if indeed it had not terminated it altogether.

However, pursuit of Pompey was by no means Caesar's only reason for coming to Egypt. He also needed money. His politic moderation to the eastern provinces after Pharsalus made it all the more necessary to lay hands on Egyptian funds, which, since they were foreign, could be seized with less delicacy. The vast wealth of the kingdom was the magnet which had brought Pompey to Egypt, and so it was with Caesar. In particular, he maintained that the country owed him an extremely large sum. The debt was a strange one. Caesar and Pompey had claimed vast compensation from the previous Ptolemy for his reinstatement, and he had borrowed from the financial wizard Rabirius Postumus to pay them. But even after installation as Egyptian finance minister, Rabirius claimed he had never been repaid by the king. Though there was some doubt about the accuracy of that statement, Caesar seems to have accepted the responsibility of extracting the sum. On the death of Ptolemy, he had with a somewhat ironical generosity to that monarch's heirs reduced his claims to a little over half the original claim—still an enormous amount—and this he had now arrived to collect. He needed the sum, he said, for the upkeep of his army, and he did not fail to point out that Egypt, before assassinating Pompey, had given him material help.

Moreover, Caesar maintained that there existed a highly altruistic justification for his intervention in the internal affairs of this ostensibly autonomous state. For the late king was reported to have called upon the Roman government to see that his will proclaiming the joint heirs was carried out; and the story is not improbable, for he may have felt this was the best way to avoid Roman annexation, which his own predecessor was said to have actually requested. Caesar, therefore, to use his own rather disingenuous phrase, 'was most anxious, as a friend of both sides and as arbitrator, to settle the disputes in the royal family'. Once that had been done, the extraction of the funds would be much more decorous and easy. Surprise has been expressed that he stayed in Egypt at all; but he certainly intended to stay long enough to get the money. Besides, it is only with hindsight that we can see that the civil war was not over. And in any case it was physically impossible for him to leave Egypt just yet, since the beginning of October, when he arrived, was still July according to the seasons, so that two months lay ahead during which sailings from this coast were frustrated by unfavourable north winds.

So Caesar came ostensibly as arbitrator, in response to the dead king's alleged plea; and in order to demonstrate that this civil business was his purpose, and that he had no military aims, he landed in the insignia of a Roman consul attended by twelve official attendants.

But Caesar's performance was a failure with the Alexandrians, who deeply resented such a display by a Roman in their independent state. Indeed, by landing with such a tiny force and nonchalantly interfering, with the obvious intention to raise cash, Caesar had this time chanced his luck once too often. Nevertheless, in response to his request, the young king called on him, attended by his chief minister, Pothinus. When confronted with Caesar's request the minister contrived to insinuate that Caesar surely had more pressing business to undertake in other lands. After this had been badly received, Pothinus arranged that his monarch's table should henceforward carry only the shabbiest of crockery, so that it might be apparent to all that Caesar, stopping at nothing, had even got his hands upon the royal plate.

Within a few weeks, however, Caesar, now lodged in the palace of Alexandria, received another caller. This was Cleopatra, who smuggled herself through the city to him in disguise (concealed in a carpet according to a story dear to films), since if Caesar was arbitrating it was only fair that he should see her too. She had already sent him a report when he was in Anatolia, and now, as the historian Dio Cassius observed, 'she thought it was very important to meet Caesar face to face, since she considered her looks her greatest asset'. Cleopatra was not unacquainted with Roman leaders, since she had already intrigued Pompey's elder son when he had come in the previous year to call on Egypt for assistance. But Caesar, though older, was very much more interesting, and possessed the further inestimable advantage of being a great deal more powerful. He was, of course, also profoundly susceptible. Although Cleopatra was the product of many brother-and-sister marriages, her successes bear sufficient witness to her charms. In the words of Shakespeare,

> Other women cloy
> The appetites they feed, but she makes hungry
> Where most she satisfies.[8]

Her intellect, too, was imposing, and so was her determination. All this beauty, brain and drive were devoted to the revival, under her control, of the glory of Egypt, whose language she alone of all her line could speak—in addition to a wide variety of other African and Asian tongues. Although any Macedonian, as she was by birth, had much to avenge on Rome, alliance with Caesar was far the best available way to fulfil her ambitions.

The impression she made on him was immediate, and she moved into the palace as his mistress. Lucan's story that his first dinner-party in her company was spent in deep antiquarian conversation with his colleague the high priest of Isis seems improbable. More to the point,

> In the midst of rage and madness,
> Within the palace trod by Pompey's ghost,
> Soiled with the blood of Pharsalus, he loved
> Amid his cares.[9]

The poet also comments that it was a real achievement to fire a heart as flinty as Caesar's. Of course, she fascinated him, yet there was also an element of politics in the attraction. It was arguable that the most effective way to conduct his arbitration was by taking sides, since he would place at least one of the parties under an obligation. And it was by no means a disadvantage that he was able to achieve this with the party hostile to Pothinus, who had aided Pompey before murdering him, and had then shown insolence to Caesar himself. It is impossible to detect any occasion on which Caesar acted against his own interests because of infatuation with Cleopatra. As Shakespeare makes Brutus observe,

> To speak truth of Caesar,
> I have not known when his affections swayed
> More than his reason.[10]

It was a delight to have her with him; but in any case he could not get away from Alexandria, first owing to the unfavourable winds and the need to raise funds, and then because he became enveloped in a savage little war.

Ptolemy could not be expected to like this liaison with his hated sister-wife, and he angrily left the palace and whipped up the crowds of Alexandria, which were notoriously prone to violence. Caesar affected a relaxed air, visiting the sights of the city and mixing with the crowd to hear university lectures. But so difficult was his position that, when the time came to arbitrate, he thought it advisable to offer the Egyptian establishment a remarkable and lucrative privilege. While confirming the joint sovereignty of the two young monarchs Ptolemy XIII and Cleopatra, he at the same time presented their younger brother and their sister Arsinoe with the island of Cyprus. It was only ten years since Cyprus had been converted into a Roman province by Cato, and to reverse the annexation was a deliberate insult to him. Whether Caesar intended the gift to be permanent or even intended it to be implemented at all, we cannot be sure. But in any case such a restoration of Roman territory to foreign rule was bound to incur much criticism from his own compatriots; certainly he himself later made a great deal out of it when his enemies were believed to be planning something similar elsewhere. But now, evidently, he judged the situation to require this extraordinary concession.

For Ptolemy's general Achillas, who after Caesar's arrival left Alexandria to rejoin his army at Pelusium, had now been summoned back by Pothinus. With him came a hostile force of twenty thousand men—veteran legionaries, outlaws, retired pirates, bandits, runaway slaves and two thousand cavalry. Caesar, outnumbered five to one, dispatched an urgent appeal to his officers and supporters in the Levant and Anatolia for reinforcements. Meanwhile Achillas penned Caesar inside the palace quarter, and savage fighting broke out, in the course of which four (or perhaps seven) hundred thousand books, stacked on the quays, were destroyed, though probably not, as was asserted, the famous Alexandrian library itself. Caesar took charge of the king, in the hope of making it seem that the enemy were mere rebels unconnected with the régime. He also found it advisable to put an end to Pothinus. But the young Arsinoe, who rivalled Ptolemy in her detestation of their sister Cleopatra, managed to escape with her eunuch chamberlain, Ganymedes, who did away with Achillas but proved very effective as his successor, pumping sea-water into the Roman-wells, bringing a fleet into action, and blocking off Caesar's headquarters by armed posts and road-blocks. All this and much else is told us by the anonymous and not incompetent author of the *Alexandrian War*.

Caesar felt able to take more positive action after a legion of surrendered Pompeians from Asia arrived to reinforce his diminutive army. At first all went well when his able Rhodian admiral, Euphranor, captured the Pharos Island which stood with its famous lighthouse in front of the harbour. But then, in February 47, an effort to complete his control over the causeway which linked the island to the city proved a disastrous failure. Caesar himself experienced the strangest of all his predicaments, since he had to jump into the sea from an overloaded boat and swim two hundred yards for his life, from one craft to another, amid a hail of missiles. According to one account, he pulled his purple cloak after him with this teeth, so that his enemies should not get hold of such a trophy. A more probable story is that, as he swam, he held some documents above water so that they should not get wet: in which case work would have been wasted.

Caesar now attempted a characteristic propaganda stroke. The Alexandrians complained they had had enough of Ganymedes and his young firebrand princess, Arsinoe. They therefore urged that the king should be released—and Caesar agreed. His own officers and troops, we are told, regarded this as a starry-eyed and guileless move, which seems hardly likely since they must have known their commander too well. In fact, this display of generosity was intended to disrupt the enemy command by fostering the inevitable dissension between the advisers of Ptolemy and Arsinoe. In this it failed, since the Egyptians continued their resistance with unabated vigour. But the gesture was designed to serve another purpose as well, for after eventual victory it would now be much easier to depose Ptolemy in favour of Caesar's ally, Cleopatra.

Early in March, the relieving army which Caesar had begun to summon soon after his arrival appeared on the eastern desert borders of Egypt. His critical situation had imposed the necessity of calling upon the subject peoples of Rome; and the force of Asian, Syrian and Arabian troops which now arrived was under the control of Mithridates of Pergamum, the son of a Galatian princess and reputedly (though this was doubtful) of King

Mithridates of Pontus, Rome's and Pompey's famous enemy. At Ascalon, we learn from Hebrew sources, this Pergamene was joined by three thousand men under Antipater, the clever and enterprising prime minister of Hyrcanus, the Jewish high priest (who had changed sides after Pharsalus). The news that they were coming helped to bring their compatriots in the Egyptian towns over to Caesar. With the Jewish contingent playing a leading part, Mithridates captured Pelusium, and skirted round the delta to a point near Cairo. Ptolemy had conveyed his army upstream from Alexandria to stop him, but meanwhile Caesar had also moved his own troops out of the city. Transporting them by sea to a point west of Alexandria, he too hastened southwards, and succeeded in joining Mithridates. On 27 March 47, there followed a sharply contested battle in which a pincer movement proved too much for the Egyptians. Caesar rode back to Alexandria on the same evening. An imposing procession of divine images was brought out of the city to meet him; and he was able to convey to Cleopatra the scarcely distressing news that her youthful brother, who was also her official husband, had been drowned. His body, wearing golden armour, had been quickly rescued from the Nile so as to scotch ideas of divinisation which were associated with deaths in that river.

Sentimental or prurient ancient historians at this point bestow upon Caesar and Cleopatra a holiday cruise of two or even three months up the Nile, with every conceivable trapping of exotic luxury. However, if such a trip took place, it was not as long as that, and it was not just a joy ride—for one thing, Cleopatra may well have been in an advanced state of pregnancy, since her son Caesarion (so-called because she claimed Caesar was his father) may, as we shall see, have been born in June of the same year. Nevertheless, a political and military demonstration up the Nile was by no means out of place. But Caesar was also urgently needed elsewhere, and within a fortnight after the battle he seems to have departed from Egypt altogether.

Before then, he had provided the country with its immediate future. His alliance with Cleopatra staved off, for the time being, the ever-present threat of Roman annexation, which in any case Caesar did not want since he could trust no governor with such a plum. Since, however, the Egyptians were not accustomed to sole rule by a woman, he officially associated her with a new brother-husband, the twelve-year-old Ptolemy XIV. This was the boy to whom, in conjunction with Arsinoe, the island of Cyprus had recently been given. But now the gift was withdrawn, since there was no longer any crisis to require such a largesse. And Arsinoe, being extremely unacceptable to the queen, was removed from the scene; she was destined to be paraded later in a Roman Triumph.

We may assume that Caesar collected his debt from Cleopatra's advisers. Next, out of gratitude for the collaboration of Antipater, he seems to have taken some action in favour of the Jews of Alexandria. These were not likely to be popular measures; and in order to enforce them and keep the peace generally, three Roman legions were left behind in Egypt. The country was still to remain ostensibly independent, but its people could scarcely be expected to welcome new and collaborationist régimes. The garrison would also have the effect of removing from the minds of Cleopatra's ministers, or even from the mind of the queen herself, any possible temptation to think later on about taking independent or disloyal action. On the other hand, if no governor of Egypt could be trusted, the same was true, in so tempting a country, of any commander of a substantial force. When, seventeen years later, annexation finally took place, the military command and governorship were never conferred on Roman senators; and Caesar set a precedent for this cautious attitude by leaving his three legions, not under a recognised general, but under a certain Rufio, who was one of his favourite freedmen and thus belonged to a non-political class which had never hitherto been entrusted with armies.

And so ended this extraordinary, irrelevant interlude between the war against Pompey and the war against his sons and supporters which was to follow. Napoleon, who also had reason to know Egypt, was amazed by Caesar's dallying; though as things had turned out it is hard to see how he could have disengaged himself earlier. But the fund-raising excursion, disguised as a pious mission of arbitration, had squandered eight months—longer than any campaign throughout the civil war. This heaven-sent delay gave his enemies the best opportunity in the world to repair their losses and become a formidable force again. Moreover, as a letter of Cicero reveals, Caesar had been totally cut off since December from contact with Italy itself.

Nor did he, even now, go back and deal with his problems in the homeland. A difficult choice had to be made between two necessities, and he decided on balance that, since he was already in the east, it would be a mistake to return home before extracting as much money as possible from Syria and eastern Anatolia, and generally disentangling the affairs of those formerly Pompeian territories. With barely a thousand soldiers he sailed from Alexandria to the port of Ptolemais Ace (Acre, north of Haifa). There large sums were raised on every possible pretext, with special demands upon those who had supported Pompey. At the same time he confirmed the régime of Hyrcanus and Antipater. The Jews were allowed to rebuild Jerusalem, and its natural sea-port Joppa (Jaffa) was given back to them. They were exempted from providing winter quarters for Roman troops and, at least for a time, were excused all tribute. Caesar planned that this Hebrew state should counterbalance Egypt, and dominate a considerable part of the Levant. The arrangement was to prove distinctly irksome to Cleopatra, since Egypt had

ASIA MINOR
(Anatolia)

long had designs upon Palestine. But Caesar gained the goodwill of the Jewish Dispersion, including the influential community at Rome.

Moving on to Antioch, he left the vital border-province of Syria in charge of a young relation, Sextus Caesar. Next, he sailed to Tarsus where representatives of the local communities were summoned. A pardon was extended to a prominent young Pompeian, Gaius Cassius Longinus, reconciled with him through Servilia's son, Brutus, who had himself changed sides after Pharsalus. And now remained Caesar's last major task in the east, the reduction of Pharnaces II, the son of Rome's enemy Mithridates of Pontus, whom he murdered. Pompey had left Pharnaces as ruler of the rich kingdom of the Cimmerian Bosphorus (Crimea), but on seeing the Romans preoccupied by civil war he crossed the Black Sea and emulated his father by seizing an enormous area of northern Anatolia. In the previous year, he had won a victory at Nicopolis (Pürk) over Caesar's general, Cnaeus Domitius Calvinus. (Calvinus was weakened by the transfer of many of his troops to Caesar in Egypt. He had hoped to send him the rest of his force after the battle, but was defeated and had nothing to send.) After this success the king enslaved and castrated Romans and Greeks, and butchered Roman tax-collectors, but a rebellion in the Crimea brought him temporarily to a halt.

As Caesar now approached, Pharnaces remained full of hope that the unwelcome visitor could not stay long, because of troubles at Rome. He

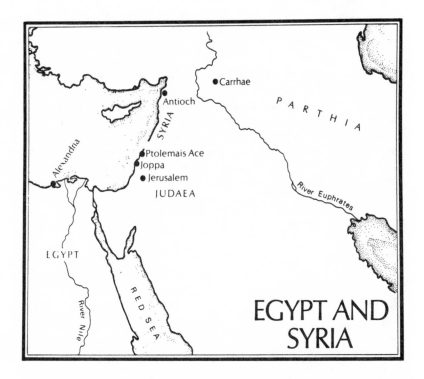

EGYPT AND
SYRIA

therefore played for time. However, his suggestion that Caesar might like to
have his daughter in marriage did not win favour, and the gift of a massive
gold crown, with the assurance that he would do better later on, likewise
proved inadequate. Declaring that nothing could suffice to wipe out the
crimes Pharnaces had committed on Roman territory, Caesar moved forward
to confront him at Zela (Zile) in southern Pontus. It was a place where the
king's father had once defeated the Romans, and Pharnaces was so confident
history would repeat itself that he adopted the remarkable strategy of ordering
his scythed chariots and infantry to charge the Roman legionaries *uphill*. This
proved quite as surprising as Pharnaces had hoped—Caesar could hardly
believe his eyes. Nevertheless, four hours of sharp fighting was enough to
bring the Romans total victory. This battle, fought on 1 August 47, was the
occasion when Caesar, writing to a correspondent in Rome, borrowed from
a Greek writer, said to have been the philosopher Democritus, the immortal,
arrogant epigram 'I came, I saw, I conquered'—intended to outbid a claim
which Pompey had couched in similar terms after his own more protracted
eastern campaigning. (The Emperor Charles v later adapted the saying to
the not wholly modest form 'I came, I saw, God conquered'.)

Pharnaces fled, and succumbed in the Crimea. Then followed a general
redrawing by Caesar of the boundary lines of client kingdoms. An old
Galatian ruler in central Anatolia, Deiotarus, commended by Brutus who

had lent him money, was given a share, together with pardon for his support of Pompey. In contrast to the protracted little Egyptian campaign, Caesar's whole Asian parade had lasted hardly more than two months. Yet, even so, he had spent a whole year since Pharsalus on two campaigns scarcely related to the major civil war which still remained to be fought. On his way home, he indicated to the people of Athens that their glorious dead had saved them from the consequences of siding with his enemies. Meanwhile Vatinius had cleared the Adriactic of Pompeian fleets; and so Caesar returned to Italy.

CHAPTER NINE

The Last Campaigns:
North Africa and Spain

On 24 September 47, Caesar landed at Tarentum (Taranto). One of his first duties in the south of Italy was to meet Cicero. At their last encounter more than two years previously the orator had defied Caesar, and then, in response to an appeal to senators, had joined Pompey in the Balkans. But Cicero had taken no part in the hostilities; when the news of Pharsalus reached him, he was at Corcyra (Corfu). Thereupon he had promptly given in, sending Caesar a letter of capitulation. He had gone back to Italy, but Antony, who had also returned there after the battle and was acting as Caesar's deputy, would not let him move from Brundusium, where he spent eleven miserable months. At last, however, Caesar had written reassuringly, and now, after another of the courteous, insincere conversations in which the two men specialised, he lifted the ban, but only, it seems, at a price. For Cicero now lent a large amount of money to Caesar's shady secretary, Faberius, and it appears from subsequent agonised letters that these sums proved exceedingly hard to recover.

In Italy, while Caesar had been away and out of touch for so long, things did not go at all well. The trouble was due to the debt laws he had passed just before he left. These had only gone part of the way towards meeting an almost desperate situation of hardship. The measures were also too moderate for ambitious young borrowers such as Cicero's correspondent, Caelius, who, behaving as though Caesar no longer existed, gave notice during his prae-torship of a revolutionary total abolition of debts. When this attempt to win popularity and relieve his own financial position was blocked, he made common cause with the gangster Milo, who had returned without permission from exile in Massilia, and the two men stirred up violence in which they both, separately, came to violent ends. However, the youthful tribune, Publius Dolabella, who was even more heavily in debt than Caelius, announced sim-ilar proposals, and Antony blocked them by heavy-handed measures in which eight hundred people were killed. His wife, Fulvia, must have had divided feelings, if, as was said, she was Dolabella's mistress. She had previously been married to Clodius and then Curio.

Caesar, who came back to find that the senate had felt obliged to pass no less than three emergency decrees in his absence, gave both men a chilly reception. Antony was virtually dropped for two years, during which Caesar reverted to Lepidus as his deputy. In the intervals between militancy and debauchery, Antony had been buying up the auctioned property of political exiles and casualties, including the palace and slaves of Pompey himself. He had bought them cheap, and indeed was not expecting to have to pay at all, but Caesar insisted he should at least give the full prices he had bid. Dolabella was made to do the same, and the only purchaser recorded to have obtained exemption was Servilia, whose daughter Junia Tertia, Cicero hinted, had been made available for her mother's old friend the dictator.

Nevertheless the continuing misery of the debtors, however much it may have been exploited by ambitious agitators, was producing a real and mounting pressure which could not be ignored. Caesar noted the warning signal and decided to cancel all interest accrued during the civil war (or from 48 inclusive), and to remit rents for one year, up to a total of one hundred pounds at Rome and thirty pounds in the rest of Italy. This went some distance towards allaying discontent; and Caesar still felt strong enough to avoid plunging into revolutionary abolition of debts.

An even more serious problem was raised by a recurrence of the mutiny of two years before; and this time the outbreak was much worse. The disaffected legionaries were men who had fought under Caesar in the east and were now in Campania. Under the leadership of Gaius Avienus, a senior officer who had served with Labienus and was probably his fellow-countryman, these soldiers refused further service overseas until they had received their promised rewards, and in default of these they demanded to be discharged. Driving a praetor-elect, the historian Sallust, out of their camp, they marched on Rome. Caesar promptly agreed to their discharge—which was not really what they wanted at all. Then, woundingly addressing them as civilians, he indicated that, although they would get their present entitlements, they had obviously disqualified themselves from the distribution of loot which would accompany his eventual Triumph. The mutiny came abruptly to an end. But the names of the instigators were noted for the future; and from now on they were likely to find themselves in the front line when some particularly unpleasant and dangerous engagement was being planned.

This success was very fortunate, indeed indispensable, since a new campaign was urgently imminent. Cicero, whose enthusiasm for the Pompeian cause had died with the death of its leader, was quite depressed about the difficulties in which Caesar was now involved. His long preoccupation with eastern affairs had allowed Pompey's two sons, Cnaeus and Sextus, together with Metellus Scipio, Labienus, Afranius and Petreius, to amass considerable forces in the province of Africa (Tunisia). They had made common cause with the disagreeable Numidian king, Juba, and were also joined by Cato after an epic march from Cyrenaica.

Labienus, although he sometimes miscalculated, was far the most competent of these commanders, and his special knowledge of cavalry was bound to play a vital part in this area. But his humble social origins and the mistrust inspired by his tough personality ruled him out for the post of commander-in-chief, and when squabbles about the appointment developed, Cato felt it best to insist that Metellus Scipio, imposing in rank if not in intellect or character, should take the supreme command. In contrast to Cicero, Cato had become more and more enthusiastic about the struggle: after the death of the suspect Pompey he could pursue the defence of the Republic with a clearer conscience. Yet in order to avoid exacerbating the issue of the supreme command, he himself stayed content to take charge of the headquarters garrison in Utica (Henchir bou Chateur), north of Cape Bon.

The Pompeian army in Africa comprised ten legions (fourteen, if four of Juba's units were included) and fifteen thousand cavalry. This was a large force, not far short of the numbers that had fought at Pharsalus. But against Caesar's leadership it was not overwhelming. Cato, therefore, had good reason to advise Metellus Scipio to adopt a strategy of evasion which would cause the invader difficulties of supply and would 'wither away all the vigour that is the strength of tyranny'.

The *African War* that now followed is narrated to us by an enthusiastic Caesarian, perhaps of low rank since he remains in the dark about the motives for policy decisions. When Caesar had dealt with the Italian mutiny, the season was already mid-September—early December according to the calendar—so that he would have to begin operations just as winter was approaching. In order to avoid further delay he did not even wait for enough ships, food or water, or indeed for his four veteran legions that were on the way, but on 25 December embarked from Lilybaeum (Marsala) in western Sicily, where he had been auctioning Pompeian estates. He took six legions, five of them consisting of new recruits, and a mere two thousand horse. Most of the fleet was carried northwards by a storm, but after a three-day passage he disembarked on the north African coast with scarcely more than three thousand men. He had chosen to land at Hadrumetum (Sousse), south of Cape Bon, because the main body of enemy were beyond the cape in the north of the province.

However, Hadrumetum did not open its gates to him, and so he moved some twenty-five miles south-east to the more welcoming Leptis Minor (Lemta). There some of his missing transports joined him, and he fortified

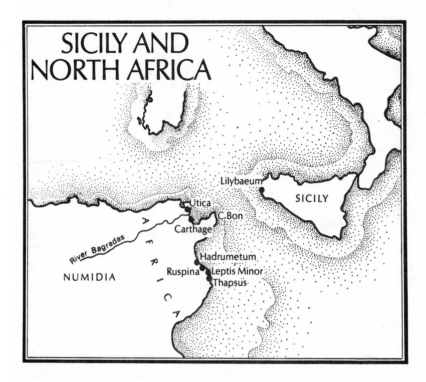

SICILY AND
NORTH AFRICA

Lilybaeum

SICILY

Utica

C.Bon

Carthage

River Bagradas

A F R I C A

Hadrumetum

NUMIDIA

Ruspina

Leptis Minor

Thapsus

a position on the coastal plateau of Ruspina north of the town. The main
problem was to get enough to eat; the whole campaign has been called little
more than a food hunt, and for a time the horses were eating desalinated sea-
weed. On the very day when the last part of his convoy had joined him, a
major foraging expedition had to be launched. It was very nearly overwhelmed by the enemy's Numidian, Gaulish and German cavalry, skilfully
manoeuvred by Labienus and backed up by a rear attack from Petreius. The
situation was only saved by an exemplary drill-book operation by Caesar, in
which alternate cohorts turned about so that the lines faced both ways simultaneously. In the end, under cover of darkness, he managed to get back to
his camp.

Caesar never let much time pass without propaganda, and he had a lot
to say about Metellus Scipio, who, he declared, even lacked the nerve to wear
his Roman purple cloak when the alien Juba was present. Metellus Scipio
retaliated by saying that Caesar had gone to bed with Eunoe, the wife of
Bogudes, one of the two Mauretanian princes who were his allies. Another
of Caesar's friends was an ex-Catilinarian knight from Campania called
Sittius, who had fled his Italian creditors and ended up in Mauretania. There
he had collected together armed bands of adventurers, whom, to his great
profit, he hired out as mercenaries to native princes. Now he put this contingent at Caesar's disposal and joined the Mauretanians in harassing the

territories of Juba, whom he particularly disliked. This disturbance in the rear forced the king to leave Metellus Scipio for a short period, but he soon returned, enticed back, his enemies improbably alleged, by Metellus Scipio's offer of the whole of Roman Africa. With him he brought a force of thirty elephants.

But still Caesar could not bring his enemies to battle. Now that reinforcements had brought his army to a total of nearly thirty thousand, the need for food supplies kept him constantly on the march, and so, beating off Labienus' cavalry, he proceeded seven miles inland. Both sides were now having disciplinary troubles. Caesar's ex-mutineers from Campania had arrived after a terrible, almost foodless crossing, bitterly complaining that their commander Avienus had travelled in luxury, and Caesar seized the opportunity to send this former ringleader of the troubles straight back home. Metellus Scipio, too, was suffering from desertions, which were not remedied by a foolish speech to his troops in which he talked a lot about 'liberating' the Roman people and senate, without saying a word about material rewards.

Meanwhile, Caesar, after continuing to move rapidly from place to place, finally found a way of forcing him to fight. This he achieved by making for the important city of Thapsus (Ras Dimas). He had already instituted its blockade by sea, and, as he anticipated, Metellus Scipio felt he could not afford to lose the considerable garrison and stores which the place contained. Thapsus stood on an isthmus, from one and a half to three miles wide, between the sea and a marshy lake. When Caesar had moved onto this strip, the Pompeians, forgetting Cato's advice to pursue Fabian tactics, believed that they could save Thapsus and corner their enemy at one and the same time. And so they hastened to block the isthmus at either end, Juba and Afranius to the south and Scipio to the north. Caesar, who had chosen a battlefield in which the enemy would be divided and their cavalry tactics severely circumscribed, found Metellus Scipio's army drawn up for battle; presumably he had gained the necessary confidence from the presence of his colleagues at the enemy's rear.

The engagement that followed on 6 April 46 did not at first proceed as Caesar had planned. He himself was later said to have been unwell, and his hungry, ragged soldiers, furious at all the stories of the enemy's opulence, were excited by signs of panic in the opposing ranks, and attacked before Caesar had given the order. However, he made a virtue of necessity, and rode forward with them. The enemy's elephants lent by Juba, harassed by archers and slingers, turned tail and trampled down the infantry behind them, and the African cavalry took fright and retreated. In a few minutes the whole army was routed, and when Juba and Afranius, at the other end of the isthmus, heard the news, they fled as well.

Another campaign of the civil war was over. It ended more unpleasantly than any that had gone before. For Caesar's half-starved veterans had got out of hand. They butchered over ten thousand Pompeians who had wanted to surrender, and then turned savagely against Roman senators and knights, and even against their own officers, whom they accused of softness towards the enemy. Labienus and both the sons of Pompey succeeded once again in getting away. But Cato now decided that, since his only prospect of life was to be spared by Caesar, the time had come to put an end to himself. And so, at Utica, he committed an impressively calm and philosophical suicide, thus creating a legend which was going to prove very inconvenient to Caesar. Metellus Scipio, too, when cornered by Sittius at sea, mortally stabbed himself, dying in the grand style that had eluded him while he had lived. Juba had planned a gigantic self-immolation in which his capital city was expected to serve as the pyre, but the inhabitants proved reluctant to play their part and refused him admission. Accordingly, he and Petreius arranged to dine together and then slay each other in a duel; Juba killed his Roman ally, and then had himself finished off by a slave.

The death-roll was increased by Caesar's own decision to execute one of the enemy's commanders, Afranius, also perhaps Sulla's son. They had been spared once before, and repeated clemency did not extend even to a former consul such as Afranius. In any case clemency was wearing thin. This was found to be the case by a relative of Caesar himself, who was accused of atrocities towards slaves and freedmen and of the scarcely less grave offence of slaughtering animals intended for the funeral games planned in memory of Caesar's daughter, Julia. While awaiting trial, the prisoner died in mysterious circumstances, perhaps on the instructions of his kinsman, towards whom he had shown persistent hostility.

Meanwhile, a brisk reorganisation of northern Africa was under way. Sittius and the Mauretanians were given parts of Juba's kingdom, and the rest, including his Numidian cavalry, was taken over by Rome, which formed a new province of Africa Nova under the historian Sullust as its first governor. The treasures of Juba and the estates of Roman citizens who had opposed Caesar were sold by auction, and heavy contributions in cash, wheat and olive oil were levied form the towns of the region. The area could now resume its enormous contributions of grain and oil to the annual upkeep of Rome. A century later the African provinces west of Egypt were sending enough corn to feed the city for eight months of each year.

Travelling by way of Sardinia ('the only one of his properties he had not yet visited,' said Cicero bitterly) Caesar reached the capital on 25 July 46. After the savagery which had accompanied the concluding stages of the African war, it seemed essential to re-establish his reputation for clemency. The climax of this endeavour was the pardon he extended in September to Marcus Claudius Marcellus, who as consul five years earlier had led his enemies with great gusto, and was consequently now living in exile. At the instance of the senate, Cicero delivered a speech which skilfully interlards an array of fulsome compliments with the discreet invitation to avoid autocracy and restore the Republic, under his protection, to health and renewed activity. Soon afterwards, a reference to Pharsalus in another speech of Cicero's moved Caesar so deeply that, according to onlookers, he dropped the documents he was holding onto the ground. The purpose of the speech was to secure the restoration of a certain Ligarius from banishment, and Caesar, though he felt the greatest distaste for the man, complied. In the course of a fresh crop of flatteries Cicero managed to point out in this oration that men of rank, on the whole, had regarded Pompey's as the better cause. Moreover, the essay on which he was now at work, a fine historical account of Roman oratory known as the *Brutus*, insists that the art can only flourish in a free country, and alludes repeatedly to the need not to abandon the heritages that one's ancestors had handed down.

However, Caesar made no move to restore the Republic. Instead he decided that, although Pompey's sons were still at large, the time had now come to regale the people of Rome with celebrations in honour of his achievements. Accordingly, soon after the pardon of Marcellus, there followed an orgy of Triumphs, with all the appropriate, gigantically expensive rituals, festivities and banquets. The thanksgiving was to last forty days, twice as long as ever before, and between 20 September and 1 October (July, according to the season) four Triumphs for Caesar's victories were held. Since none of these ostensibly commemorated victories over fellow-Romans, the defeated countries were listed as Gaul, Egypt, Pontus and Africa; the four ceremonies were distinguished by the use of trappings made of citrus wood, acanthus, tortoise shell and ivory respectively.

Caesar was escorted by an unprecedented array of seventy-two official attendants, the full quota for his three dictatorships. At the Gaulish Triumph which opened the proceedings, they were accompanied by men carrying vases in which perfumes were burning—a welcome thought on a hot and crowded day—and there were musicians playing oboes and zithers. One of the floats bore a golden statue symbolising the ocean in chains. But when Caesar himself appeared, with the heavy gold crown of Jupiter held over his head, the axle of his chariot snapped in two. Whereupon, since this, of all others, was an occasion to humour archaic superstitions, Rome witnessed the amazing spectacle of the general climbing up the steps of the Capitol on his knees to atone for the omen. Annoyance was again caused to Caesar when the ribald songs about his sexual prowess, which his glorious veterans were apparently licensed to sing on such occasions, included references to that ancient story of his immoral relations with the king of Bithynia; and this time he momentarily lost patience.

Pompey, after his own Triumph, had spared enemy leaders, but now it caused the Romans no distress when the heroic Vercingetorix, saved six long years for this occasion, was led off at its end to be strangled as a treacherous rebel. The second, Egyptian, procession was somewhat less successful because, although pictures of the deaths of Achillas and Pothinus were well received, the sight of an actual princess in chains, the young Arsinoe who was there to please Cleopatra, caused the usually hardhearted Romans to feel chivalrous emotions of pity. However, she escaped the fate of Vercingetorix and was allowed to live. The Pontic Triumph perpetuated on a placard Caesar's borrowed epigram 'I came, I saw, I conquered', and struck a humorous note by displaying a picture of Pharnaces running away. At the final African Triumph one of the exhibits was Juba's four-year-old son of the same name, who survived the ordeal to become an extremely learned king of Mauretania under Roman protection; and he married Cleopatra's daughter. His inclusion in the Triumph was designed to prove that the African campaign had been foreign and not civil strife. However, the effect was ruined by the display of paintings gruesomely depicting the deaths of Cato, Scipio and Petreius. For Caesar, with his usual blind spot about Cato, chose to regard these men as having lost their claim to Roman citizenship because they were dominated by a foreign king and had supposedly promised away parts of the empire. They probably had not done so, whereas Caesar had, but this was not the moment for objective facts. Nevertheless, the allusion to victories over Roman commanders caused a painful impression, at least among senators.

The Triumphs were spiced with plays, a naval action, a battle between war prisoners and criminals, and a murderous hunt not only of four hundred lions but of giraffes, a novelty provided from the new province by its governor, Sallust. This massacre took place, unfittingly enough, in commemoration of Caesar's daughter, Julia, and an added attraction was a series of gladiatorial duels enlivened by the appearance of upper class Romans of knightly rank in the ring. Another knight, Decimus Laberius, an eminent author of popular plays, was punished for a slighting reference to the autocrat by having to undergo what was regarded as the disgraceful fate of acting in one of his own productions. But he took his revenge for this humiliation by inserting in the performance a number of all-too-clear references to the present situation of Rome. 'The man whom many fear,' he declaimed, 'must also fear many himself.' Compliments to Caesar, it is true, were not lacking, but they contained barbed allusions to the fact that freedom was no more.

But see how easily an old man slips, and shows
(Moved by the complacency of this most excellent man),
Calm and complaisant, a submissive, fawning speech.[11]

The vast crowds who watched these shows were protected by awnings of the luxurious silk substitute that was now being made at Cos. The populace were also entertained to a banquet at which they sat on twenty-two thousand couches, drank Falernian wine and ate six thousand sea-eels 'lent' to Caesar by Pompey's wealthy cousin, Lucilius Hirrus, who was famous for his fish-ponds. There were also distributions of meat. Senior officers became rich men, if they had not done so already, and every centurion was handed two thousand pounds and every legionary at least a thousand—more than three times what Pompey had given. Even so, there were soldiers who complained they could have had more still if the Triumphs had not cost so much. Caesar seized one of these malcontents by the scruff of the neck and hauled him off to execution. Then, in an ominous outburst of brutality and archaic ritualism, he actually had two others of his old soldiers ceremonially served up as human sacrifices by the priest of Mars. As a conclusion to this unprecedentedly alarming display, their heads were hung up on the front of the office building he occupied as chief priest.

The loot which helped to pay for this orgy of expenditure included 2822 gold crowns presented by communities of the empire; they added up to a total weight of 20,414 pounds. Accordingly, many of the donations now distributed by the dictator took the form of, or were paid for by, gold coinage. The staple Roman coin had long been the silver *denarius*, but Caesar's gold pieces still survive in unfamiliar abundance. Another official, in north Italy, ingeniously issued base metal coinage not in the traditional bronze, discredited by light-weight issues, but in the bright yellow alloy of brass. This looked attractive and was very little known, so that it could be issued at artificial and highly token values which were no doubt extremely lucrative to the moneyer and his master. When Caesar returned to Rome, someone had asked him how his gigantic impositions of money and valuables were going to be spent. His reply was no doubt held to be reassuring. 'I shall do my best to be rich *with* you,' he said, 'rather than to rob anyone of his possessions.'

Like many autocrats, he desired at least a part of his largesse to assume the monumental, permanent form of vast buildings which would adorn his city. For the past eight years, work had been continuing on the Forum of Julius, with which Cicero had been profitably associated. This splendid annex of the Roman Forum, designed to relieve congestion in the centre of Rome, was still not complete, but its formal opening ceremony now took place as part of the victory celebrations. According to a fashion already impressively

developed at other Italian centres, the whole huge precinct was planned as
the court of a mighty shrine. It had originally been proposed that this temple
should be allocated to Venus the Victorious (Victrix), and her name was
Caesar's battle-cry at Pharsalus. But Pompey had already completed a temple
of this divinity beside his theatre, and Caesar now chose to dedicate his building instead to Venus the Mother (Genetrix), the ancestress of the Julian clan,
whose patron goddess was thus to be regarded as the provider of victory. Her
statue by a Greek sculptor, Arcesilaus, was not yet ready, and meanwhile it
was replaced by a clay model; but when the masterpiece arrived, the breast
of Venus was laden with British pearls (though so few had been obtained)
and her shrine was richly endowed with six collections of cameos and gems.
In front of the temple stood an equestrian statue of the dictator himself, riding
upon a horse sculptured by Lysippus, which had been plundered from a mon-
ument of Alexander the Great.

Other great buildings also were under construction. Across the old
Forum from the Forum of Julius, on the south side of the Sacred Way, the
Basilica Julia also was dedicated on this occasion, although it too was unfin-
ished. The Basilica, a huge rectangular chamber surrounded by porticoes,
was to house the proceedings of four law-courts, but children's games played
in the echoing hall have also left their traces on the pavement. Elsewhere,
vast libraries were projected, and Varro, who had failed to oppose Caesar on
the battlefield but was the most famous encyclopaedic scholar of his day,
obtained a commission to fill these buildings with the whole of Greek and
Latin literature. Caesar also planned to construct a new election building in
the Campus Martius, to protect the voters from the sun and distract attention
from the fact that elections had become a fraud. This construction, girdled
by a lofty portico a mile in circumference, was, in fact, built after his death.
He also intended to erect the largest temple in the world in the same area,
and the largest theatre in the world beside the Tarpeian Rock on the
Capitoline Hill. This emphasis on vast dimensions was in the tradition of
the east rather than of Greece or early Rome. But the previous century of
the Republic had already produced much architecture of a new grandeur and
freedom, and the increasing frequency with which new buildings were now
depicted on the coinage shows that the propagandist significance of this activity was recognised to be very great. A vindictive detail directed against one
of the only two men whom Caesar had ever really hated was the erasure of
Catulus' name from the reconstructed temple of Jupiter on the Capitol.
Caesar's name was inscribed in its place.

In contrast to this petty-mindedness, he also accomplished a measure
which had beneficial and lasting results. This was his reform of the calendar.
For the last few years the calendar had got increasingly out of step with the
seasonal solar year. This old calendar, which was lunar, consisted of 355 days,

a total which had been increased by the insertion of an extra (intercalary) month of twenty-two or twenty-three days in every alternate year. This brought the annual average to 366¼, which was too large, but the excess balance could be eliminated if the extra month were dispensed with about every twenty years. The responsibility for ensuring that the necessary insertions were made at the appropriate times fell upon the board of priests. But during the turbulent fifties BC, when their chairman Caesar was away, they had failed in this duty, and had omitted to arrange proper intercalations. This caused anger among ambitious young politicians, who would have liked an extra month in order to hold on to office longer and propose more laws; indeed a refusal by conservative interests to intercalate was said to be one of the reasons why Curio left their party. The priests, on the other hand, were afraid of being accused—as had happened—of intercalating months arbitrarily for their own purposes of political trickery. The calendar year had in this way drifted nearly two months ahead of the seasons.

On the advice of the astronomer Sosigenes of Alexandria, Caesar now proceeded to replace the existing calendar by a solar year of 365¼ days. That is to say, the year was normally to be of 365 days, with the intercalation of one day every fourth year (now called Leap Year) to take up the extra quarter. In order to get the new system into gear, two months of twenty-nine and twenty-eight days respectively were inserted between November and December of the year 46, so that the year in question, which had already received an intercalary month, attained a record length of 445 days. This Julian calendar, although it required minor modification by Augustus and then by Pope Gregory XIII in AD 1582, was widely adopted. It is still in force, and has therefore proved the most durable of all the changes Caesar imposed upon the world.

Cicero and other Republicans, while hoping Caesar would one day relinquish the reins, often urged him to use his great authority, while he still had it, in order to revive something of the purity of the old Republican way of life. Caesar could say he was fulfilling this demand when he now accepted for three years the special task of supervising public morals. Extravagance had reached fantastic heights, and even the cleverest Romans suffered from the delusion that it could be curbed by suitable legislation. Sulla had passed a number of ineffective laws seeking to cut down private expenditure, and Caesar, in spite of the fantastic profusion of his own Triumph, now attempted to reduce outlay on food, funeral monuments, riding in litters, and the wearing of jewels. Compliance with these price regulations was enforced by inspectors who descended upon the markets. Indeed, it was said, perhaps with exaggeration, that they also invaded private dining-rooms, sometimes accompanied by military escorts, and even whisked forbidden dishes off the tables under the very eyes of the guests.

These sumptuary measures were, of course, disregarded, and we learn from one of Cicero's correspondents that Caesar soon realised that this was so. It is doubtful whether it worried him very much. His Prefecture of Public Morals, with its rather vague old-fashioned ring, was probably welcome to him because it provided a more respectable means than the dictatorship for pushing through reforms and threatening sanctions for those who were slow to accept them. It also enabled him to assume rights which had traditionally belonged to the censors, normally appointed every five years; and in particular it was useful for controlling admissions to the senate.

But all Caesar's plans for Rome and Italy were severely delayed when it became clear that the civil war was not ended after all. Once again the Pompeian cause had vigorously revived, this time in Spain, only four years after Caesar's victorious campaign there. The revival was largely brought about by the cruelty and incompetence of the official he had left as his representative in Further Spain, Quintus Cassius Longinus, an effective tribune but a dreadful governor. When he was attempting to join Caesar for the African campaign, the Spaniards had made an unsuccessful attempt to assassinate him. This had been ferociously avenged, but two veteran legions Cassius had taken over from the Pompeians mutinied, and his capital, Corduba, likewise abandoned its allegiance to him. Caesar, on hearing disquieting news of his conduct, ordered his recall; but as he started back to Italy he was shipwrecked in the mouth of the Ebro and drowned, and the immense treasure he had collected went to the bottom of the sea. But the damage had already been done, and his successor, Trebonius, failed to re-establish Caesar's cause. For he, too, was disowned by the rebellious legions, when they heard, before the battle of Thapsus, that Pompey's elder son Cnaeus had crossed over from north Africa and occupied the Balearic Islands. He soon moved on to the Spanish mainland, where, after Thapsus, he was joined by his younger brother, Sextus, and by Labienus. Although Cnaeus was not conspicuously bright, mistaking, so it was said, cruelty for bravery, the magic of his name brought to his side almost the whole of southern Spain. He was able to raise a large army of thirteen legions, mostly consisting of native levies, though it also included the two veteran units and many retired Pompeian legionaries. He also had six thousand cavalry.

If, as seems probable, Caesar had celebrated his Triumphs in the belief that the war was virtually over, it was now apparent that he had been mistaken. Two commanders sent against this army at the end of the African campaign—one of them Caesar's own nephew—proved unable, with their much smaller force, to make any headway. Indeed it was becoming rapidly all too clear that no one except Caesar himself was capable of dealing with a general of the calibre of Labienus. Accordingly, at the beginning of November 46, for the fourth time in his career, he set out for Spain.

On the seventeenth day of his journey, he reached Saguntum, north of Valencia, and ten days later he was with his troops at Obulco (Porcuna) in the neighbourhood of the hostile city of Corduba. For a man of fifty-four the journey of fifteen hundred miles in a springless carriage, covering fifty or sixty miles a day, must have been a punishing ordeal. However, he had enough spare energy on the road to write, not this time a treatise on grammar like the study he had once composed when crossing the Alps, but a poem describing the journey upon which he was engaged.

On arrival in southern Spain he found that his problem was to bring the Pompeians to battle. For if he could do this, his four veteran and four other legions, not to speak of his eight thousand cavalry who for once gave him the superiority in this arm, would be more than a match for the enemy's less experienced troops and disunited leadership. Although seriously handicapped by the need to keep two legions in Corduba, which they dared not lose, the Pompeians persisted for two months in their refusal to be provoked into a battle. These tactics confronted Caesar with the difficulty of finding supplies and shelter for a winter campaign, but on 19 February 45 he succeeded in capturing the well-supplied town of Ategua, only one day's journey away from Corduba itself. This had a very damaging effect on the spirits of the enemy army, as well as on the morale of the local towns, which interpreted the sensible delaying tactics of Cnaeus Pompeius as an unnecessary prolongation of the war.

And so Cnaeus, as he withdrew southwards harassed by Caesar, was forced by the disaffection all round him to offer battle after all. On 17 March, at Munda, forty miles east of Hispalis (Seville), he found a favourable position and turned at bay. The engagement that followed, incompetently described by the eye-witness who wrote the *Spanish War*, was a ferocious and prolonged hand-to-hand struggle. Caesar had never before asked his men to go into battle with the ground against them, and the Pompeians fought desperately because, in a campaign already characterised by savagery, their prospects after defeat were grim. Caesar, who had felt an unusual depression before the battle, later remarked that this was the first time he had ever had to fight for his life. At one point he seized a shield from one of his soldiers and appeared in the front line himself, shouting 'aren't you ashamed to hand me over to these boys?' What seems to have finally turned the scale, however, was his decision to send his Mauretanian ally, Bogudes, across with a squadron of cavalry, to attack the enemy left wing in its flank and rear. Labienus foresaw the move, as well he might from his knowledge of Caesar, and quickly began to transfer troops from the opposite wing to protect his left flank. But this counter-move was catastrophically misinterpreted by his own side as the beginning of a retreat. The misunderstandings which had so often prevailed between Labienus and other Pompeians had reached a disastrous climax, and their line flagged and broke. The entire army turned in flight, and during the rout he himself fell. So did thirty thousand soldiers on his side—thirty times more, it was reported, than Caesar's losses, in spite of the close-fought struggle.

The short campaign was at an end. But the brutality which had characterised its earlier stages was by no means over. In overcoming the continued resistance of Corduba, Caesar killed between twenty and thirty thousand men. An enormous indemnity was extorted, and even Gades, the home of his closest associate, Balbus, suffered the confiscation of its rich temple treasure. For the ingratitude of these towns seemed inexcusable, especially in an area where Caesar, after his periods of residence in the country, had regarded himself as the accepted patron.

Once again Pompey's younger son, Sextus, got away, and he lived on to plague Caesar's successors. But his elder brother, suffering from a wound and a sprained ankle, failed to escape by sea and was betrayed, cornered and killed. His head was taken to Seville and exhibited to the crowd and to Caesar; he had now seen the severed heads of both father and son.

Then he turned to the usual problems of reorganisation, staying on several months in the country so as to settle its outstanding affairs. In mid-September he was back in Italy.

CHAPTER TEN

The Despotic Last Years

*A*fter more than four terrible years, punctuated by furious convulsions in many countries, the civil war had at last come to an end. The most urgent thing that now needed to be done was to prevent further disturbances by pensioning off as many as possible of the vast numbers of soldiers who were still under arms. There were at least thirty-five legions in existence; nothing like so many were going to be needed in future, whatever foreign adventures Caesar might have in mind. That meant that gratuities had to be found for an enormous number of men. But they wanted land, not money, which had nothing like the same reputation as a security. What was required, therefore, was a revival on a greatly expanded scale of the land distributions which had played such a part in the legislation of Caesar's first consulship fourteen years before.

And so veterans were now distributed on plots of land throughout many areas of Italy. But the Italian land with which the earlier measures had been concerned was virtually exhausted, and there was a limit to the hardships which could be imposed on local populations. Accordingly, Caesar had recourse, on a massive scale, to a device which had been started very cautiously by Rome towards the end of the previous century: the foundation of citizen communities, not only in Italy which was the home of the Roman franchise, but in the provinces of the Roman empire as well. Moreover, as in 59, this was to be a dual process: the settlers were to include not only ex-soldiers, but also many members of the workless, parasitic proletariat of Rome. Perhaps eighty thousand of these urban citizens were moved overseas. How many veterans Caesar had time to settle in the brief period of his lifetime that remained is uncertain, but the total did not fall short of twenty thousand, and may have amounted to half as many again. The number of citizen foundations in the provinces—brand new towns, and settlements incorporating native communities or added alongside them—was multiplied many times over, and rose to the total of nearly forty. These centres were to serve purposes not only of trade but of defence, seeing that the veterans formed a useful military reserve; and several became recognisable forerunners of the great cities of today.

Nowhere was this more apparent than in the Iberian peninsula where towns given new settlers included Romula (Seville, formerly Hispalis), Carthago Nova (Cartagena) and Tarraco (Tarragona). In Gaul, Arelate (Arles) obtained part of the territory of Massilia, and another settlement was the naval base of Forum Julii (Fréjus). In north Africa, the prejudice against the revival of ill-omened Carthage was overcome, and colonists were sent out in the centenary year of the city's destruction. Corinth had likewise been destroyed by the Romans in the same year of 146, and here too a settlement was planted, encouraged by a project for a canal, which remained unfulfilled until 1893. Corinth formed part of a completely novel aspect of the colonisation scheme, which envisaged the establishment of a few citizen communities, not only in the west where Latin was so much better known, but at key-points of the Greek east as well. Another such settlement was Sinope (Sinop) on the south coast of the Black Sea, and yet another was to be at Buthrotum, near the Greco-Albanian frontier opposite Corfu. But Cicero's friend Atticus, who was patron of that region, complained to Caesar about the confiscations which the scheme would necessitate. On the characteristic condition that he should receive compensation in cash from the wealthy Atticus, Caesar agreed to waive the plan. But then Cicero was much surprised to learn that the prospective settlers, starting out for their new homes, had not been told that these had vanished into thin air. Caesar, taxed with this failure to inform them, was reported to have explained 'that he did not want to upset the people, while they were still in Rome—for, as you know, he aims at popularity—but when they were across the Adriatic he would see to it that they were transferred to some other territory'.

In the east, Greek civilisation left no room for Latin, and there could be no question of Romanisation. But in the west this extension of the Roman bourgeoisie over an enormous area constituted a decisive step in that direction, and so did the hard thinking about the organisation and constitution of these communities and their councils which already started under Caesar, though its full fruits were yet to come.

The Romanising process was also advanced in a less conspicuous way by the grant to native towns of the Latin rights which meant that their principal officials and town councils became Roman citizens. This privilege was made universal in Sicily and southern France (Narbonese Gaul), so that these provinces now obtained the half-way status that the Italian cities north of the Po had possessed until their full incorporation into the peninsula four years previously. There were also extensive Latin grants in that other heavily Romanised area, southern Spain. This status was not so much a promise of full future citizenship for the entire community—which rarely followed—as an avoidance of unnecessary friction by elevating the native upper class to legal equality with the Roman colonists who lived among them. By the same token, Caesar was relatively generous in individual gifts of citizenship to provincial magnates and scholars and doctors, many of them oriental; though he put a stop to the sale of such gifts by his secretary, Faberius, who had bought a palace on the Aventine Hill from the profits.

And so Caesar, with his widely ranging brain and experience, took a broader view of the empire than any Roman before him; and he made a first breach, which others would widen two centuries later, in the barriers between Italians and provincials. Furthermore, the fact that his colonies included not only veterans but the workless poor of the capital entitles him to be called the only Roman statesman who ever dealt effectively with this problem of the surplus metropolitan proletariat. For the departure of so many of them overseas (combined with a population decline since the beginning of the civil war) enabled him to reduce the number of recipients of free corn from 320,000 to 150,000. Caesar also attended with great care to his duties of legal administration, and even planned to codify the Roman civil law, a task which was not finally undertaken for nearly six hundred years. It appears that he also returned again to the debt problem, authorising debtors to admit insolvency before a public official and cede land or goods in lieu of cash, retaining enough for their own subsistence. If, as seems likely, this measure was passed during Caesar's last months, he was attempting a further humane mitigation of the brutal old unfettered power of the money-lender, and creating the rights of a debtor upon which modern bankruptcy regulations are based.

Such measures helped Italy as well as Rome, and in the rural parts of the peninsula Caesar attempted further reforms. Steps were taken against brigandage, and an endeavour was made to reduce unemployment by stipulating that at least one-third of the labourers on large ranches should be men of free and not slave status. Seeking also to leave his mark on the physical appearance of Italy, he planned to increase arable land by draining the Fucine lake in the mountains east of Rome and forming a new waterway which would drain the Pontine marshes south-east of the city. These projects had already begun to receive attention over a hundred years earlier, and were revived by the emperors, yet not accomplished with complete success until modern times. But other schemes of Caesar's, though he did not live to carry them out, were to bear useful fruit during the century or two immediately following his death. Such, for example, was his plan to deepen the harbour of Ostia, so that Rome should have its own Piraeus and no longer be obliged to rely on distant Puteoli (Pozzuoli) as its principal port.

During his brief presences in Rome the dictator was responsible for an immense amount of valuable administrative and legislative activity. Nothing was a marked breach with tradition, and there was no great attempt to look beyond immediate needs. But in dealing with the situations of the moment, in the light of what had been achieved in the past, Caesar's flair for efficiency was swift and strong. Indeed his eye for detecting and removing abuses seemed to some people too quick by far. Laws and senatorial decrees were rushed through at such a speed that Cicero complained he was receiving thanks from foreign princes quite unknown to him for honorific measures of which he had likewise never heard. When someone remarked in the course of conversation that a certain constellation was due to rise the next night, the orator produced one of his famous spiteful jokes—'no doubt it has received orders to do so!'

The senate which was entrusted with the execution of this programme had changed considerably in composition. Its numbers were increased from five or six hundred to nine hundred, and nearly half of these came from outside Rome. Most of the new members were Italian bankers, industrialists and farmers, many of them from sections of the peninsula which civil war and obstruction had hitherto prevented from receiving their share of Roman office. It was easy but misleading for conservatives to sneer at these solid new members of what had at last become the national body it ought to be. It was easier still to make fun of the quaint exoticism of a few Gauls among their number, who were, in fact, unpicturesque, influential citizens from the Romanised Cisalpine and Narbonese regions. For Caesar brought in men who had a valuable contribution to offer; and they were also his partisans. 'Even if,' he remarked, 'in defence of my position, I had been obliged to call upon the services of bandits and cut-throats, I should have given them their rewards.'

But the consuls during the years of Caesar's dictatorship were by no means revolutionary. They included five nobles, including three of his own patrician class, and four 'new men' who had proved their worth in Gaul. The innovation lay in the fact that their election was due to Caesar and Caesar alone. His only concession to the electorate was to abolish the political guilds which, with his own connivance, had converted the elections of the fifties into bloodthirsty scuffles. But he made a mockery of the assembly itself, whose record, as he saw, was one of lamentable failure to express the will of the Roman people. Henceforward it was to be called upon only to do what he desired. To fix senior appointments was nothing new, but Caesar fixed them quite openly, and indeed legislation was finally passed conferring upon him the right to 'recommend' a large proportion of the total number of senior posts, and even to do so for a number of years ahead. Offence was also caused by election delays which sometimes meant that consuls only held office for a few months; and, when one of them died on the last day of 45, Caesar had him replaced for the few hours of the year that were left. Cicero remarked bitterly that this was a peculiar term of office in which no one had lunch and the consul himself got no sleep. The dictator's intention, however, was not to mock at the institution but to take the opportunity of bestowing consular rank on one of his loyal subordinates. With the same purpose in mind, and in the interests of efficiency, he increased the number of praetors from eight to sixteen, aediles from four to six, and quaestors from twenty to forty. As for the tribunes, one of whom had tried to keep him out of the treasury in 49, he continued to express severe exasperation at their pin-pricks. When a tribune remained seated at his Spanish Triumph, he remained furious for days, and two others who too officiously stopped a demonstration in his honour were angrily suspended for a time from their functions.

So much for the battle-cry of tribunician inviolability and democratic rights with which he had launched the civil war. But more serious still was his failure to spare the feelings of the higher officials, ex-officials and would-be officials who had hitherto been the rulers of the state. He failed to reconcile Republican forms and aristocratic pride with his own personal régime; indeed, he scarcely even tried. He had never thought much of the constitution, or of the nobles for whose supremacy it stood. 'There is nothing I like better,' he had once pronounced, 'than that I should be true to myself—and others to themselves.' Now this intellectual pride was becoming more and more apparent and impatient.

But his most dangerous critic was one who rose up from the grave. Immediately after Cato's suicide in Africa, his legend had begun to assume those massive and potent proportions which were to cause Virgil, a generation later, to represent him as the noble lawgiver in the lower world; while Lucan, at odds with Nero, saw him as the very essence of opposition to imperial tyrants.

> Justice and rigid honour—these he worshipped,
> And virtue serving the world. No act of Cato
> Was touched by pleasure and the greedy self.[12]

That was written a hundred years after his death, but eulogies about Cato were already being prepared during the very first months after he had put an end to his life. One such pamphlet was written by Cicero. Although he had found the living Cato a good deal too rigid, July 46 already found him at work compiling this obituary testimonial. A year later he wondered very much if he had been wise to attempt such a composition under the dictatorship. Caesar wrote in August 45 politely praising the essay, but, in view of the special hatred he had always felt for Cato, Cicero's effort must have infuriated him, and after Munda, with the help of a draft by Hirtius, he began to write a counterblast. The *Anticato* has not, for the most part, survived, but there is record of an elegant compliment to Cicero, whose gifted eloquence, says Caesar, his plain soldierly style cannot equal; and then the pamphlet descended to venomous abuse about Cato's avarice, incest, drunkenness, and the mercenary greed with which he sold and then repurchased his own wife. Cicero privately expressed the hope that Caesar's book would be published, partly because of the kind remarks about himself, but partly also because this coarse invective would cause a revulsion of feeling in favour of the Republic. He was even finally induced to praise Caesar's treatise as Caesar had praised his own—and with equal insincerity.

On returning from Spain, the Republic had been in Caesar's mind to the extent that the new Triumph he shared with two lieutenants (including his nephew) was given the leading theme of Liberation. The celebrations were not as popular as they might have been, because it was impossible to conceal the fact that the defeated enemies were fellow-Romans. Nevertheless, the theme was persevered with: a temple of Freedom was planned, and LIBERTAS appeared upon a coin. Yet, politically speaking, the idea was elusive and meaningless. Before Pharsalus, in the course of a peace-feeler to Metellus Scipio, Caesar had offered something like a political programme: tranquillity for Italy, peace for the provinces, security for the empire. But in that formula the ancestral constitution was conspicuous by its absence. Caesar had been away from the centre of government for eleven years, and at a time when the Republic had been reduced to appropriate subordination his mind could range over wider horizons. Meanwhile, the order to re-erect the statues of Pompey, which had been put out of the way, was perhaps a good sign, if only a trifling one.

During the early summer of 45, Cicero formed the idea of submitting a memorandum indicating how, under Caesar's guidance, the Republic could be restored. But Balbus and Oppius advised him not to include in it any recommendations which did not coincide with the dictator's actual intentions. They also expressed the view that the draft looked too much like a protest against despotism—and an expression of fear that this would be intensified if Caesar did not achieve a constitutional settlement before leaving for further campaigns. And so, towards the end of May, Cicero gave up the idea altogether. 'It is not the shame of the thing that prevents me,' he wrote to Atticus, 'though that is just what should. But I cannot think of anything to write.'

Meanwhile, however, Caesar maintained his usual courtesy. He asked Hirtius and Dolabella to collect Cicero's witticisms for him; this would serve the double purpose of enabling him to express appreciation and to see that the orator's barbed tongue did not run away with him. For Cicero's attitude to Caesar soon underwent a rapid deterioration again. Deeply gloomy about the abolition of the Republic, and shattered by the death of his beloved daughter, he wrote to Atticus, 'For heaven's sake, let us give up flattery, and be at least half free!' Brutus had expressed the view that Caesar was becoming a good conservative, but Cicero, although touched by a friendly letter of condolence, saw that this was ludicrous over-optimism. And yet the activity in which he plunged to combat his misery was of infinite importance to the world. For this was the time when he was composing his semi-philosophical treatises which gave Latin thought a whole system of moral values and helped substantially to make this dying Republic an era of magnificent literary flowering.

In this field, if in no other, he and Caesar could meet on terms of happy mutual respect, and we have from Cicero's pen a private and unique picture of the visit he received from the dictator at Puteoli during December 45.

A formidable guest, yet no regrets! For everything went very pleasantly indeed. However, when he reached Lucius Marcius Philippus on the evening of the 18th, the house was so full of soldiers that there was hardly a room free for Caesar himself to have dinner. Two thousand men! I was distinctly alarmed about what would happen the next day, but Cassius Barba came to my rescue with a loan of some guards. A camp was pitched on my land and the house was put under guard.

On the 19th he stayed with Philippus until one o'clock and let no-one in—I believe he was doing accounts with Balbus. Then he went for a walk on the shore. After two, he had a bath. Then he was told about Mamurra; but there was no change in his expression. He had an oil-massage and then sat down to dinner.

He was following a course of emetics, so he ate and drank without *arrière-pensée* and at his ease. It was a sumptuous dinner and well-served, and more than that, *well-cooked and seasoned, with good talk and in a word, agreeable*. His entourage were very lavishly provided for in three other rooms. Even the lower-ranking freedmen and the slaves lacked for nothing; the more important freedmen I myself entertained in style.

In other words, we were human beings together. Still, he was not the sort of guest to whom you would say "do please come again on your way back". Once is enough! We talked no serious politics, but a good deal about literary matters. In short, he liked it and enjoyed himself. He said he was going to spend one day at Puteoli and the next in the neighbourhood of Baiae. There you have the story of how I entertained him—or had him billeted on me; I found it a bother, as I have said, but not disagreeable.[13]

But Cicero's relatively cheerful mood about Caesar, induced by this memorable occasion and the man's formidable charm, was only a momentary ray of watery sunshine amid his despair about national affairs. Nor was he by any means alone in these feelings. Country, honour, respect and position, things as dear as one's own children, were all lost. Thus wrote privately to him the jurist Servius Sulpicius Rufus. Yet Caesar did not know, or did not care, how deeply people felt for the traditional politics of the Republic. To him, they were a sham. He said so, and was also reported as observing that people must take his word as law. His personal magic and charm, his tactful courtesy and amusing high spirits were still sometimes in evidence, but rather more fitfully than hitherto. The hand was of iron, and the velvet glove as alarmingly threadbare as Shakespeare saw.

> Why, man, he doth bestride the narrow world
> Like a Colossus; and we petty men
> Walk under his huge legs, and peep about
> To find ourselves dishonourable graves . . .
> When could they say, till now, that talked of Rome,
> That her wide walls encompassed but one man?[14]

The situation expressed itself in novel forms which were not so much constitutional as personal. For instance, Caesar had become the 'general' (*imperator*) par excellence, and the term achieved a special and semi-official significance that was to give rise, shortly after his death, to the official, autocratic development of the word which gave history the term 'emperor'. Already in his lifetime the media of publicity, such as the coinage, were insisting strongly on his lifelong possession of the office of chief priest; it reflected, for the benefit of his superstitious people, his close relation with the gods and his position as executant of their divine will. Greeks declared that he himself was a god, for they were accustomed to say this of their own monarchs, and Rome, too, by various technical *nuances* of its complicated religious procedures, moved gradually, though never quite officially or decisively, in the same direction. His statues, amid sneers from Cicero, were placed in temples. Cults were established, not exactly for his worship but in his honour. The usual sharp line between human and divine was becoming blurred. At the beginning of the year 44, when he was dictator for the fourth time, his head began to appear on the Roman coins. This would have been normal for Greek monarchs, and Caesar's likeness too had appeared on a few local coinages in the eastern provinces soon after the victory at Pharsalus, but official coin-portraits in the capital had hitherto been limited to men who were dead. The innovation of portraying the living Caesar was a visible sign, if one was still needed, that he was not as other citizens were.

A very sharp reminder of the same point appeared in February 44 when Caesar's dictatorship was converted into a lifelong office. The sinister new title DICTATOR PERPETVO appears with his portrait on a number of coins. Some of these, at least, appear to precede his death (on 9 February he was already perpetual dictator elect). But, even if they do not, he undoubtedly assumed the designation in his lifetime. This must indeed have been a shock. The whole essence of the dictatorship, according to Roman constitutional practice, was its temporary nature, which none of the previous dictators, eighty-three in number, had ever ventured to gainsay. When, towards the end of the previous year, Caesar's tenure had been extended from three to ten years, that was quite bad enough. But now, after he had continuously held the office for twenty-four months, came this appointment in perpetuity which was the very negation of the emergency purposes to which the office had always been restricted. Hitherto most of Caesar's new measures had built on the past rather than sought its abolition. The nineteenth-century version of Caesar as the superman who forged a *new* world and state cannot be substantiated: it is especially associated with the name of Theodor Mommsen, who had in mind the contemporary subordination of the Junkers, whom he hated, by the Prussian monarchy. But the germ of truth in such a view lay in this reduction of ancient constitutional forms to absurdity. When Caesar had remarked that Sulla showed he did not know his ABC when he vacated the office of dictator, he meant exactly what he said.

Perpetual dictatorship bore obvious affinities with kingship. The latter institution traditionally filled the Romans with a violent abhorrence, dating back to the legendary days, nearly half a millennium before, when they had expelled the tyrannical Tarquin. Guided by nobles and other malcontents, there was now every sort of rumour that Caesar was moving in the same sinister direction. Indeed, admirers—probably not in his confidence—had conducted demonstrations urging him to take the final step and become king. But after two of their gestures misfired owing to the offensively rapid intervention of unfriendly tribunes, he felt it desirable to stage a demonstration that he had no such designs. And so on 15 February 44 at the antique religious ceremony of the Lupercalia, Antony, now restored to favour and made consul, publicly offered Caesar a diadem, which he no less publicly and repeatedly refused, dedicating it instead to Rome's true and only monarch, Jupiter.

Cicero could privately write of Caesar as 'king'; the dictator could sit in a gilded chair; he could boast of his legendary ancestry by wearing tall red shoes like the ancient rulers of Alba Longa. But at Rome, permanent power was assured him by other means, the perpetual dictatorship. He had calculated, evidently, that this position, even if it strained the constitution, did not exactly break it. What advantage, then, could there be in seeking the status of king, which was even more unpopular and would not add to his actual power in any way whatever? Another quarter of a century of bloodshed was needed before formal monarchy would become practicable, and even then it had to be concealed, however, imperfectly, behind an elaborate and cunningly devised façade. This was to be the work of his grand-nephew Augustus who, although carefully forgetful of his predecessor's irregularities, incorporated the name 'Caesar' in his title and thus handed on the term 'Caesarism' which was bandied about as a description of the Bonapartes and Hohenzollerns.

Uninterested in kingship, Caesar was also not in the least ambitious to introduce into his Italian homeland the Greek ideas of monarchy which were applied to him, like other Romans before him, in the east and were so fascinatingly exemplified in the figure of Cleopatra. She had, it is true, pursued him to Rome. For she was understandably afraid that, unless she was able to maintain her influence upon Caesar, Rome, which was at present negotiating an alliance with her, might instead decide to annex her immensely wealthy country. The queen's charm failed to work with Cicero, who found her detestable. But Caesar had hospitably housed her and her juvenile brother-husband in a property of his own across the Tiber, and had even politely adorned his new Temple of Venus with a statue of her made from solid gold. She may, to some extent, have influenced his political thinking. But he was so busy that he cannot have found very much time for her agreeable company.

Moreover, his physical health, which had usually been good, was showing signs of giving way. Twice during the recent campaigns, at Thapsus and Corduba, he was reported to have fallen ill at critical junctures; the illness seems to have been epilepsy. We need not bother about his alleged nightmares, which are part of the equipment ancient historians traditionally allotted to the uneasy heads of tyrants. But he undoubtedly suffered, at least in these last years, from headaches and fainting fits. He had always driven himself desperately hard. Portrait-busts are not a safe guide to his appearance, since they may or may not date from his life-time. But contemporary coin-portraits, too, make him look a good deal older than his fifty-six years. Moreover, he himself had begun to speak, as early as 46, about the possibility of an early death. Whether you looked at it from the viewpoint of nature or of glory, he said, he had lived long enough.

It was only reasonable, then, that some thought should be given to the future, and as soon as Caesar came back from Spain in September 45 he had proceeded to his estate at Lavicum (Labici), south-east of Rome, in order to make his will. But this document, which was not opened or known until after he was dead, makes it clear that all he intended to provide for was the disposal of his private property—not of the Roman state. Indeed, such a thing would have been quite out of the question, since Caesar's powers were based on his position as dictator, and the idea of a succession to the dictatorship, hereditary or otherwise, just did not exist in the constitution and could not be broached at all. Nevertheless his will was of great importance, because the estate amounted to five million pounds, one-seventh as much as the total contents of the Roman treasury. Moreover, it provides insight into the workings of Caesar's mind.

He proposed to leave three-quarters of his property to a youth who was not yet eighteen. Gaius Octavius (Octavian), the future Augustus. This young man, the grandson of one of his sisters, had been with him in Spain, and, in spite of a somewhat frail physique, his altogether exceptional, somewhat cold-blooded talents could not fail to win the dictator's attention. At the end of the will, he went on to arrange that Octavius should be adopted as his son, unless his wife Calpurnia had borne him a male heir. Subject to the same proviso, which perhaps only applied to a child already conceived when the will was made, the remaining quarter of the estate was divided between the well-tried nephew who had served him in Spain (and had been given a not wholly merited Triumph) and another little known man who was either a nephew or grand-nephew. Among various persons named in default of these three heirs was Caesar's very able general and admiral, Decimus Brutus Albinus; and mentioned in the same capacity was Antony. These two men were thus passed over for first-line inheritances in favour of Caesar's own family. No mention was made of Cleopatra's son, Caesarion, who, according to quite a probable interpretation of an Egyptian document, had been born on 23rd June, B.C. The queen later claimed that Caesar was his father, and after putting an end to her young brother adopted the infant as her consort, under the name of Ptolemy xv Caesar. The dictator himself, however, remains oblivious of this situation in his will. And indeed the boy's paternity, already disputed at the time, remains doubtful, especially as Caesar, for all his sexual activity, only once in his whole life unmistakably fathered a child, namely Julia—and she had been born over thirty years previously.

In any case, his will provides not the slightest guidance as to what Caesar believed would happen to the government of the Roman empire after his death. Perhaps he hoped to give attention to this problem at a later stage. Perhaps, like many rulers, including a number in our own time, he dismissed the thought altogether, whatever the dangers this involved for his country. At all events, we have it on the authority of one of his closest friends, Gaius Matius, that he never thought of a solution; he devised no formula capable of producing political stability.

Indeed, if the Roman state had broken up at this moment, as well it might have, few tears would have been shed by other races. Except for the superb literature of these years and the political successes of the distant past, most of the worth-while achievements of the Roman world, though they owed much indirectly to the upheavals dominated by Caesar, still lay ahead, in many cases far ahead, in the future.

Meanwhile the dictator had come to rather a startling, and as it proved conclusive, decision. For he had impatiently determined to spend no longer, at this time, in sorting out the embittered, nagging, baffling situation that his autocracy had created among the frustrated nobles of Rome. Instead, he

decided to fight a new war, a more gigantic war than any that had ever been
fought before; and the foe he had chosen was Parthia, the national enemy
in the east. This was a foot-loose pugnacity,

> restless, unconfined,
> Which no success could sate, nor limits bind.[15]

According to Plutarch he felt a consuming desire for a new glory, 'as though
he had exhausted the first—a kind of rivalry with himself'. He was a not
very well-preserved man of fifty-six, and in a similar spirit Hitler decided
at fifty that world war could no longer wait. Pascal remarked that one might
forgive Alexander his world conquest as a youthful excess, but that Caesar
ought to have known better. Yet there were also profound psychological reasons for getting away. Surely the life of the camp would prove a better restor-
ative to his powers and spirits than the suffocating life of Rome, which he
had enjoyed so much when he was young but which now, with power, was
dust and ashes. Besides, the legionaries he had forged into the greatest fighting machine of ancient times must be employed again before they, too,
became too old. And their response to his orders was the most thrilling stim-
ulation and satisfaction that Caesar had ever known.

Moreover, if a more respectable pretext should be needed, it was there
for the publicists to exploit. A ruler of Rome was manifestly obliged to avenge
the humiliating defeat and death of Crassus at Parthian hands nine years earlier. A special reason why the civil war between Romans had been a cause
of reproach was because it delayed this punitive action against the alien foe:

> While slaughtered Crassus' ghost walks unrevenged,
> Will you wage war, for which you shall not Triumph?[16]

Furthermore, the Parthians had offered still further provocation in the very
recent past. After Pharsalus, a Roman knight and adventurer, dubiously
claiming to have been appointed by Metellus Scipio, had driven Caesar's kinsman and representative out of Syria, and a new governor sent out by the dictator was prevented from acting against the rebel by a Parthian raid on the
province.

And so Caesar was now amassing sixteen legions and ten thousand cavalry and archers, in order to inflict upon the Parthians a far greater invasion
than they had ever experienced before. The war was to be launched from
the north, by way of the upper Euphrates; how the operations would finally
end nobody could yet foresee, especially when one remembered how Caesar's
Gallic campaigns had expanded from their original intentions.

Meanwhile, nearer home, Vatinius, having been successful in Illyricum
four years earlier, had been given the tough job of reducing the country
completely; he complained to Cicero that his hard taskmaster expected the

impossible. But Vatinius' mission was particularly important, because on his flank a powerful barbarian kingdom had arisen under Burebistas, backed by the teetotal severity of his priestly adviser, who had every vine in the country pulled up. The centre of Burebistas' realm was Dacia (Transylvania), but he had defeated tribes in much more westerly areas bordering on the Roman province. He had also expanded in the other direction as far as the Black Sea, and although he admitted traders from the empire his suzerainty of the Greek coastal towns could well be interpreted as an encroachment upon Rome's sphere. Worst of all, before Pharsalus Burebistas had initiated negotiations with Pompey. Here, then, lay the significance of Vatinius' task. For it was rumoured that after Caesar had defeated Parthia he would strike north up through the Caucasus and then wheel inwards to the west, dealing with Burebistas on the way and following the Danube back to Gaul. No doubt even Caesar did not yet know whether the rumours of these gigantic journeys, so manifestly rivalling Alexander's, were likely to come true. But something of a thoroughly spectacular nature was certain to be attempted.

He had decided to leave Rome as early as 18 March, so as to give himself the unusual luxury of starting his campaign at the normal spring season. The last fragments of the Republican constitution were reduced to nothing by the completeness with which he fixed all appointments, at home and abroad, for two years ahead. Lepidus was to be his deputy and then take over nearer Spain and southern Gaul; Antony and Dolabella were destined for Macedonia and Syria. While Caesar had been in Spain in the previous year, the normal machinery of Roman government had been superseded by the creation of eight novel prefects of the city, with armed cohorts at their disposal. Such arrangements, manifestly representing the absent potentate, were hard enough to bear during the brief Spanish campaign, but they would be far more galling during his long absence which lay ahead. The true rulers then would be Balbus with his vast Roman parks and pleasure-gardens at Tusculum, and the financial expert Oppius. They were not even senators. Yet any senator with a request would have to queue up in their anterooms.

A perpetual dictator was frightful enough. It was strange that Caesar, for all his insight, did not trouble to discern that a perpetual dictator ruling by remote control was so frightful that he could not be endured. And as the period of remote control drew nearer, the plotting began and intensified. There had been plots against Caesar's life before—by a slave for example, acting on some unknown person's behalf, and then perhaps by someone else. And Trebonius, who failed Caesar in Spain, had hinted afterwards that a change might become necessary: Antony, to whom he was speaking, did not respond, but he did not report the remark either.

The prime mover was Gaius Cassius Longinus, who had come over to

Caesar's side after Pharsalus. In January 45 he was still able to tell Cicero that he would be less keen on a cruel new master, the young Cnaeus Pompeius, than on the old and lenient one. But when Cassius was elected praetor for 44 Caesar did not give him the top job, and when the Parthian expedition came to be planned, no important command came his way, although he had gained distinction as a soldier, and knew the country and the enemy from service with Crassus at Carrhae, when he had got away (in dubious circumstances). He was a stern man of violent temper, and the unparalleled despotism which now took ever clearer shape became too much for his pride. At the turn of the year he was of a small number of senators who abstained from a complimentary vote in honour of the dictator. He joined Antony in the curious display at the Lupercalia when Caesar refused the kingship; yet by then his motive, unlike Antony's, was evidently not to help Caesar but to drive him to public indiscretion.

The wife of Cassius, Junia Tertia, was the daughter of Servilia and sister of Brutus, who had likewise changed sides after Pharsalus, joining Cassius on Caesar's staff in Anatolia. This no doubt pleased Servilia, for whose sake the dictator showed marked favour to Brutus, making him governor of Cisalpine Gaul. No doubt she was even more satisfied when Brutus responded by hopefully expressing the inaccurate view that Caesar was now practically a Republican. But the situation of Brutus was a complicated one, because he was drawn not only to Caesar but also, even more compellingly as it turned out, to the memory of his uncle, Cato. He had been on Cato's staff in Cyprus, where he brutally persecuted his Cypriot debtors and soon after Cato's death married his daughter, Porcia. Moreover Brutus wrote a posthumous pamphlet in his honour. It was much more arid than Cicero's—Balbus said the experience of reading the essay made him feel quite eloquent in comparison—but the sentiments were a good deal more sincere.

Brutus was intense, emotional and repressed. His personal relations were in a turmoil. However much optimism he might express about Caesar, his wife, who had earlier been married to Bibulus, came from two households where the opposite sentiment must have been expressed over many years with quite exceptional virulence. Perhaps Porcia helped to change her husband's mind about Caesar, pointing out that his longstanding amour with Brutus' mother was a disgrace. But there was in fact another special reason why Brutus might be expected to turn against the dictator; and that was now exploited by Cassius who (although Caesar had promoted Brutus over his head) saw him as the leader of the conspiracy. This was because Brutus was obsessed with his ancestors. There was nothing unusual about that among Roman nobles, but the ancestors fervently honoured by Brutus included two legendary figures, Lucius Brutus and Servilius Ahala, one of whom, according to the saga, had expelled the tyrant Tarquin, while the other, not long afterwards, had killed Spurius Maelius who aimed at tyranny. As a young official of the Roman mint, Brutus had exceptionally placed the heads of both these heroes upon his coinage. Aristocratic Romans had long been brought up to regard it as their duty to kill tyrants, and Brutus' ancestry, temperament, and studies in Greek history, which abounded in glorious tyrant-slayers, all combined to make him see that this was a sacred duty, and a duty peculiarly and urgently incumbent upon himself. In current versions of the annals, Rome's founder, Romulus himself, had been put to death by senators for tyranny. Now, everyone was talking of Caesar as the second Romulus or second Tarquin, and surely on this occasion, again, the magnificent idea of tyrannicide would win support. Cassius worked on him, and he had calculated rightly; for Brutus was successfully enlisted as the figure-head and joint leader of the plot.

Under the guidance of these two men, small groups of malcontents, already provoked by the intolerable situation to discuss action in their own limited circles, coalesced quickly into a single body of sixty conspirators. We know the names of twenty of them. Nine had fought for Pompey; a stern Roman emperor, reading the story more than two hundred years later, commented that the policy of clemency had led to fatal results. But the allegiance of seven others during the civil war had been to Caesar, and before that four had been among his lieutenants in Gaul. Some of these had grudges. Trebonius felt guilty because he had done badly in Spain, though he was now to receive the lucrative province of Asia. Basilus was annoyed because he had not been allowed to become a governor—though he had received a large sum of money in compensation. Tillius Cimber was destined by Caesar for the province of Bithynia; but he may have resented the banishment of his brother. Of the two Casca brothers who both came into the plot, Publius was an impoverished follower of Cassius, whom he had supported, for the same subversive reason as his patron, in the ceremony at the Lupercalia.

But in the enlistment of another and more eminent conspirator it does not seem possible to detect any personal motive or grudge. This was Brutus' distant relative, Decimus Junius Brutus Albinus, who had served continually under Caesar, with marked distinction and success. He was named as a residuary legatee in his will, and now was earmarked for the governorship of Cisalpine Gaul, to be followed by a consulship in two years' time. And yet this man risked all his magnificent prospects by joining in the plot. Could he have been influenced by a family connection with the Claudii Marcelli, who, although subsequently pardoned, had led the anti-Caesarian movement some years earlier? Or had he hoped for a higher degree of preference in the dictator's will? More probably he was guided purely and simply by the abominable nature of Caesar's power; the old Republican system, for all its scarcely less preposterous faults, still seemed a much better alternative. To a man like

Decimus, promotion was of no value if it had to depend on the whims of a single man. In the words of William Blake:

> The strangest poison ever known
> Came from Caesar's laurel crown.

Dante saw the matter very differently. Seeing Caesar as the forerunner of his admired German or Holy Roman Empire, he places Brutus and Cassius with Judas Iscariot in Hell. However this may be, the conspirators certainly miscalculated in the most disastrous way when they supposed that, once the deed was done, the Republic would automatically resuscitate itself and renew its ancient existence. In fact, the nobles, already more than inadequate for decade after decade, had lost the threads irretrievably and could never recapture their old position. Brutus and Cassius were overwhelmed at the battle of Philippi in 42 by the Second Triumvirate of Antony, Lepidus and Octavian. Lepidus was forced into retirement in 36, and in 30 Antony and Cleopatra were defeated at Actium by Octavian, who assumed the name of Augustus three years later.

What a miscalculation it had been to suppose that killing Caesar would be effective if his supporters such as Antony were allowed to live! The murder of Antony was decided against by Brutus himself, so that the plain act of removing the tyrant should not be blurred. Later on Cicero, while applauding the assassination of the man he had so recently flattered, profoundly regretted the decision to spare Antony. But he himself had not been brought into the secret, because he was so bad at making up his mind, and so excessively good at talking—in fact, a year later, his tongue cost him his life, on the orders of Antony, or Antony's wife, Fulvia, who had once been married to Cicero's enemy, Clodius.

Caesar, for his part, knew very well that people must dislike him; he said as much when he had to keep Cicero waiting for an interview. He was also conscious of the danger he might run from provincial governors with armies (a danger suggested all too clearly by his own career), for he limited their tenures of office by law. But it is doubtful if he realised just how greatly his growing autocracy had given offence. He felt that people ought to be pleased with his clemency; if it humiliated them, he did not care. He did not appreciate the extent to which his talent for propaganda, never wholly successful with the nobles, had finally failed him, and he may also have imagined that men would not strike at him because they ought to have the sense to understand the disarray his death would cause.

He even dispensed with his Spanish bodyguard, and it was in vain that Hirtius and others counselled its revival. Instead Caesar designed a security measure on a psychological rather than a physical level. He planned that all

Roman citizens should swear personal allegiance to himself, in the same way, perhaps, as clients swore allegiance to their patrons. The patron was a father to his client; and it is no accident that at this time Caesar was hailed Father of his Country, a title which although lacking constitutional implications possessed, as Augustus was to appreciate, an intimate and powerful significance within the social context of ancient Rome. The clients must protect their patron as the son was bound to protect his father. There cannot have been time, during the few months that remained, for every ordinary citizen to take this oath, but it was administered to the senators, disquieting though they must have found the experience.

The fact that they had sworn themselves into this special relationship with their master may explain a curious incident that occurred in late January or early February of 44. The senate, bearing a list of flattering and indeed grovelling decrees, came in a mass to pay him their respects. He was working on the plans for his Forum in front of the Temple of Venus, and when they arrived he failed to rise to his feet. This produced much criticism and surprise, and was excused by his friends on grounds of ill-health. But it may have been a gesture that misfired; he may have wished to display himself as the patron receiving his clients, and perhaps this was the sort of extra-constitutional, emotional basis that the future monarchy might have been intended to possess. As clients, every senator had enrolled himself, rather more than metaphorically, as Caesar's bodyguard. He was also formally invested with the inviolability possessed by tribunes. It is quite evident that these measures on the theoretical plane were inadequate precautions against assassination. But Caesar's aristocratic pride and nonchalance could not permit him to worry on such a score. No doubt he appreciated the possibility, and regarded it with a mixture of fatalism and contempt.

On 15 March, only three days before he was due to leave for the east, the senate assembled in the hall adjoining Pompey's theatre. It would have been surprising if a plot shared by so many had remained a complete secret, and there seems to have been a leakage. As Caesar approached the meeting-place, a Greek who had once been employed as Brutus' tutor tried to speak to the dictator, and passed him a warning note. But it remained unread in his hand. The conspirators had planned that some gladiators of Decimus Brutus, who were due to fight in a show that day, should be at hand outside in case of need. It was also arranged that Antony, whose physical strength might be dangerous, should be detained in conversation at the door by Trebonius.

Approaching the dictator, Tillius Cimber fell on his knees as though to petition for the recall of his exiled brother. Caesar motioned him aside, but Tillius caught and pulled his toga. Then Casca's dagger struck him from sideways just below the throat. The blow slipped, and Caesar, pulling his toga

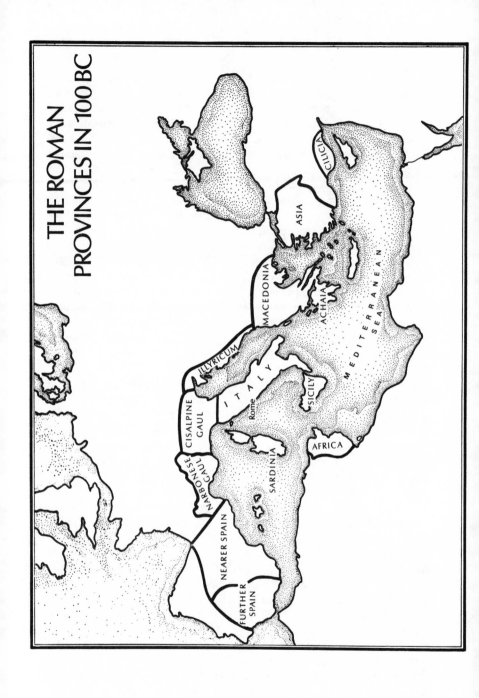

THE ROMAN
PROVINCES IN 100 BC

CILICIA

ASIA

MACEDONIA

ACHAIA

ILLYRICUM

ITALY

MEDITERRANEAN SEA

CISALPINE GAUL

Rome

SICILY

NARBONESE GAUL

AFRICA

SARDINIA

NEARER SPAIN

FURTHER SPAIN

clear, leapt up, turned and stabbed Casca in the arm with his metal pen. But at that moment another dagger pierced his unprotected flank, and now they were attacking him from every side. All, it had been agreed, must take part in the bloody sacrifice, and as Caesar, screaming, turned first one way and then another, Cassius wounded him in the face and Brutus in the groin. Riddled by twenty-three wounds of which only the second, a doctor said later, was fatal, Caesar covered his head with his robe and fell down against the pedestal of Pompey's statue. Out of all the senators who had sworn to protect him only two tried, vainly, to intervene. The rest remained frozen where they were. When the deed was done, every one of them rushed out of the building, the plotters with them, and Caesar lay where he had fallen. After a time three slaves placed his body in a litter and carried it to his home, with one arm hanging down towards the ground.

References

1. *The Poems of Catullus*, xciii (trans. P. Whigham), Penguin Books.
2. Suetonius, *The Twelve Caesars, Julius Caesar*, 51 (trans. R. Graves), Penguin Books (revised by M. Grant).
3. Shakespeare, *Julius Caesar*, ii, 2, 44–5.
4. Lucan, *Civil War*, ii, 63–4 (trans. J. Wight Duff), Ernest Benn.
5. Ibid., i, 8–9 (trans. Christopher Marlowe).
6. Ibid., vii, 504–5 (trans. E. Ridley).
7. Ibid., x, 528–9 (trans. J. Wight Duff).
8. Shakespeare, *Antony and Cleopatra*, ii, 2, 244–6.
9. Lucan, *Civil War*, x, 72–5 (trans. G. Highet), Routledge and Kegan Paul.
10. Shakespeare, *Julius Caesar*, ii, i, 19–20.
11. Decimus Laberius, O. Ribbeck, *Scaenicae Romanorum Poesis Fragmenta*, ii, 3rd ed., 1897, p. 339 (trans. J. V. Cunningham, New Mexico Quarterly Review).
12. Lucan, *Civil War*, ii, 389–91 (trans. G. Highet), Routledge and Kegan Paul.
13. Cicero, *Letters to Atticus*, xiii, 52 (trans. M. Grant), Penguin Books. Cicero's quotation, 'well cooked . . .', is from Lucilius.
14. Shakespeare, *Julius Caesar*, i, 2, 134–7, 153–4.
15. Lucan, *Civil War*, i, 160–1 (trans. N. Rowe).
16. Ibid., i, 11–12.

Sources of Information

1. Ancient Sources

There is no reliable surviving account of Caesar. To attempt to write one today means piecing together a mass of inadequate and often unreliable evidence from many sources.

(a) Latin Writers

CAESAR *Gallic War*, I–VII; *Civil War*, I–III. These masterpieces, written to justify as well as to inform, have been described in the text. Hirtius completed the *Gallic War* with an eighth book, and unknown persons completed the *Civil War* with accounts of the Alexandrian, African and Spanish Wars. The last of these works is particularly inadequate and ill-preserved.

CICERO (106–43 BC). The huge and fascinating collections of his letters, numbering over seven hundred (sixteen books to Atticus, sixteen to other friends) represent our nearest approach to a connected history of the period, and a picture of Cicero's relationship with Caesar emerges. Valuable letters from his correspondents are also included. His fifty-eight surviving speeches and his philosophical and rhetorical treatises add many features to this picture. A pamphlet known as the *Commentariolum Petitionis (Electioneering Manual)*, which is usually attributed to Cicero's brother Quintus, may be a literary exercise of imperial date.

SALLUST (86–c. 34 BC). His brilliant essay *The War of Catiline* (finished 42–1) displays a Caesar who is not reverentially treated like Cato but, like him, is depersonalised, in accordance with the writer's searching, disillusioned, rhetorical, intention of pillorying the degenerate nobles, against whom the two men are contrasted as imposing lay figures. Surviving fragments from the *Histories* (78–67), drawn from varied sources, portray Pompey as a calamitous destroyer of the Republic. Two so-called *Letters to Caesar*, attributed to Sallust, have been attributed to 51–50 and 48–6 BC but were probably composed under the empire.

VELLEJUS PATERCULUS (c. 19 BC–after AD 30) was an officer whose *Roman*

Histories include a summary of this period. Although hasty and enthusiastic rather than critical, he inserts some material of biographical interest.

LUCAN (AD 39–65). His epic poem *The Civil War*, generally known as the *Pharsalia*, tells an intensely rhetorical and melodramatic story of the war between Caesar and Pompey. Estranged from the emperor Nero, he formed an increasing hatred of Caesarism and its founder.

SUETONIUS (c. AD 69–140). His *Lives of the Caesars* start with Julius (a few chapters are lost). The biography, like his others, is full of fascinating detail, much of it scandalous but presented in an unprejudiced 'dead-pan' fashion, so that although criticism and proportion are lacking there is a welcome absence of the subjective bias and rhetorical colour which makes so much ancient historiography suspect. Suetonius is a grammarian collecting and classifying the data about his human subjects.

(b) Greek Writers

PLUTARCH of Chaeronea (c. AD 46–after 120) included among his *Parallel Lives*, which have awakened so much enthusiasm throughout the ages, a biography of Caesar, who is paired with Alexander the Great. Although based on a wide range of reading, the *Lives* are naively planned—birth, youth, character, deeds, death—and laced with many moral reflections and noble sentiments in addition to a wealth of anecdote. Plutarch is concerned not with historical relations but with the images of great men. 'The hero is there, all one piece'; and in Caesar the biographer finds ambition to be the dominant motive.

APPIAN of Alexandria (c. AD 160) wrote a history of Rome in twenty-four books. We still have the preface and eleven complete books, with considerable extracts from some of the rest. He is chiefly interested in wars, and arranges his material according to the regions successively conquered by the Romans. His approach is graphic and psychological but often muddled and over-compressed. He adds detail to the comparison between Caesar and Alexander. His sources are varied, one of them apparently being Pollio, an officer of Caesar who wrote a Latin history of the civil wars, now lost.

DIO CASSIUS of Nicaea (early third century AD) compiled a Roman history from its beginnings up to his own time. Books 36–54 (68–10 BC) are completely preserved, later sections in abbreviation or in part. Dio possesses a stronger historical sense than Appian and is capable of independent criticism, but regards detail as undignified and is by no means a vivid narrator. His main source seems to have been Livy, whose own account of the age of Caesar is lost. Dio has less knowledge of Republican than of imperial institutions, and his admiration for the autocracy of his own day has coloured his picture of Caesar.

(c) Other Ancient Sources

Inscriptions.
Papyri.

Buildings and works for art.

Coins. The coinage of the late Republic displays a vast wealth of historical allusions which are still imperfectly dated and understood and offer a fine field for the researcher. The coins of Caesar's last years are significant for our understanding of his constitutional position and aims. The first bronze issues of Roman colonies in the provinces also occur during this period, and Greek cities throughout the eastern provinces continued to produce a wide variety of little-known coinages.

2. Some Modern Writings

F.E. Adcock, *Caesar as Man of Letters*, Cambridge, 1956. *Cambridge Ancient History*, Vol. IX, Cambridge, 1932 (Chs. XV–XVII; From the Conference of Luca to the Rubicon; The Civil War; Caesar's Dictatorship.

C.M. Amici, *Il Foro di Cesare*, Rome, 1990.

E. Badian, review of M. Gelzer, *Kleine Schriften* (rev. ed.), in *Journal of Roman Studies*, 1967, pp. 216–22. *Roman Imperialism in the Late Republic*, Pretoria, 1967.

J.P.V.D. Balsdon, *Julius Caesar and Rome*, London, 1967, 1971.

M. Borda (etc.), *Gaio Giulio Cesare*, Rome, 1957.

J. Carcopino, *César*, Paris, 1965 ed.

M. Cary, *Cambridge Ancient History*, Vol. IX, Cambridge, 1932 (Chs. XI–XII: Rome in the Absence of Pompey; the First Triumvirate).

Cesare nel Bimillenario della Morte (Ed. Radio Italiana) Rome, 1956.

F.R. Cowell, *The Revolutions of Ancient Rome*, London, 1962.

J. Dickson, *Death of a Republic: Politics and Political Thought at Rome 59–44 BC*, New York, 1963.

G. Dobesch, *Caesars Apotheose zu Lebzeiten und sein Rigen um den Königstitel*, Vienna, 1966.

T.A. Dorey (ed.), *Latin Historians*, London, 1966.

A. Duggan, *Julius Caesar*, London, 1966.

J.F.C. Fuller, *Julius Caesar: Man, Soldier and Tyrant*, London, 1965.

E. Gabba, *Sull' Esercito Professionale Romano da Mario ad Augusto*, Pavia, 1951.

M. Gelzer, *Caesar: Politician and Statesman*, Oxford, 1968 (from the German of 1921, revised). *The Roman Nobility*, Oxford, 1969 (from the German of 1912).

H. Gesche, *Caesar*, Darmstadt, 1976. *Die Vergoltung Caesars*, Frankfurt, 1968.

M. Grant, *Caesar* (Great Lives), London, 1974 (especially Chapter 8, Caesar's Memory Lives On). *Cleopatra*, London, 1972, 1974.

E.S. Gruen, *The Last Generation of the Roman Republic*, Berkeley, 1974.

J. Harmand, *L'armée et le soldat à Rome de 107 à 50 avant notre ère*, Paris, 1967.

C. Hignett, *Cambridge Ancient History*, Vol. IX, Cambridge, 1932 (Ch. XIII: The Conquest of Gaul).

E. Hohl, *Caesar*, Rostock, 1930.

Julius Caesar (Greece and Rome, Bimillenary Number), Oxford, 1957.

P. Jal, *La guerre civile à Rome: étude littéraire et morale*, Paris, 1963.

A.D. Kahn, *The Education of Julius Caesar*, New York, 1986.

E.J. Kenney and W.V. Clausen (eds.), *The Cambridge History of Classical Literature*, II, 2 (*Latin Literature*), Cambridge, 1982.

P. Krarup, Analecta Romana Instituti Danici IV, 1967, pp. 7ff. (*Antichi Ritratti di Gaio Giulio Cesare*).

C. Meier, *Caesar*, Berlin, 1982.

E. Meyer, *Caesars Monarchie und Das Principät des Pompejus*, 3rd ed., Stuttgart–Berlin, 1922.

A. Momigliano, review of R. Syme, *The Roman Revolution*, in *Journal of Roman Studies*, 1940, pp. 75–80.

T. Mommsen, *Roman History*, 1911 (translated from the German of 1854–6).

F. Münzer, *Römische Adelsparteien und Adelsfamilien*, Stuttgart, 1920.

C.W.C. Oman, *Seven Roman Statesmen of the Later Republic*, London, 1902.

H. Oppermann, *Caesar: Wegbereiter Europas*, Göttingen, 1958.

D. Rasmussen, *Caesar*, Darmstadt, 1967.

T. Rice Holmes, *The Roman Republic and the Founder of the Empire*, Oxford, 1923.

W. Richter, *Caesar als Darsteller seiner Taten*, Heidelberg, 1977.

J. Sabben-Clare, *Caesar and Roman Politics 60–50 BC*, Oxford, 1971.

H.H. Scullard, *From the Gracchi to Nero*, London, 1959, 1970.

O. Seel, *Caesar-Studien*, Stuttgart, 1967.

H. Strasburger, *Realencyclopädie für Altertumswissenschaften* (Pauly–Wissowa–Kroll), Vol. XVIII (1939), columns 773–798, s.v. optimates. *Caesar im Urteil seiner Zeitgenossen*, 2nd ed., Darmstadt, 1968.

R. Syme, *A Roman Post Mortem*, Sydney, 1950. *Sallust*, Cambridge, 1964. *The Roman Revolution*, Oxford, 1939, 1971. *Caesar: Drama, Legend, History* in *Roman Papers*, V, 1988, pp. 702–707. *New York Review of Books*, XXXII, 3, 28/2/85, pp. 12ff.

L.R. Taylor, *Party Politics in the Age of Caesar*, Berkeley, 1949.

H. Volkmann, *Cleopatra*, 1958 (translated from the German).

G. Walser, *Caesar und die Germanen*, Wiesbaden, 1956.

G. Walter, *Julius Caesar*, 1953 (translated from the French) (semi-fictional).

R. Warner, *Imperial Caesar*, London, 1960 (semi-fictional). *Young Caesar*, London, 1958 (semi-fictional).

S. Weinstock, *Divus Julius*, Oxford, 1971.

H. Willrich, *Cicero und Cäsar*, Göttingen, 1944.

Z. Yavetz, *Julius Caesar and his Public Image*, Ithaca, 1983.

Genealogical Tables

THE FAMILY OF CAESAR

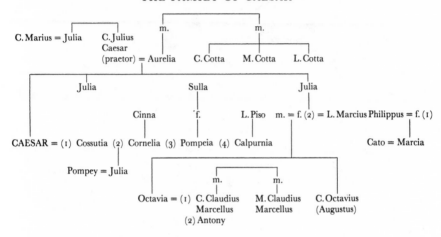

THE FAMILY OF POMPEY

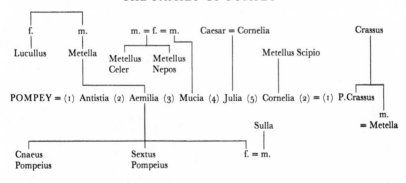

THE FAMILY OF CATO

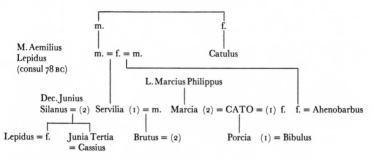

M. Aemilius
Lepidus
(consul 78 BC)

m. = f. = m.   Catulus

L. Marcius Philippus

Dec. Junius
Silanus = (2) Servilia (1) = m.   Marcia (2) = CATO = (1) f.   f. = Ahenobarbus

Lepidus = f.   Junia Tertia   Brutus = (2)   Porcia   (1) = Bibulus
               = Cassius

THE FAMILY OF CLODIUS

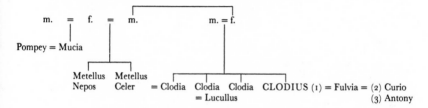

m.   =   f.   =   m.   m. = f.

Pompey = Mucia

          Metellus Metellus
          Nepos   Celer   = Clodia   Clodia   Clodia   CLODIUS (1) = Fulvia = (2) Curio
                             = Lucullus   (3) Antony

THE FAMILY OF CLEOPATRA

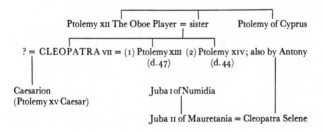

Ptolemy XII The Oboe Player = sister   Ptolemy of Cyprus

? = CLEOPATRA VII = (1) Ptolemy XIII (2) Ptolemy XIV; also by Antony
                         (d. 47)   (d. 44)

Caesarion   Juba I of Numidia
(Ptolemy XV Caesar)

                             Juba II of Mauretania = Cleopatra Selene

Index

Narbo, 78
Narbonese Gaul, 4, 40, 42f., 49f., 51, 55,
57, 61, 78f., 81, 83, 93, 94, 144, 146
Nemetacum (Arras), 83
Neapolis, 91
Nemi, L., 16
Nero, 43, 162
Nervii, 56f., 73
Nicomedes IV, 7, 9
Nicopolis, 126
Nile, R., 124
Noviodunum (Nevers), 79f.
Novum Comum, *see* Comum
Numidia, 108, 118, 131f., 134

Obulco, 141
Octavia, 76, 90
Octavian, *see* Octavius
Octavius, Gaius (Octavian, Augustus),
151ff., 158, 159
Oise, R., 89
Oppius, 68f., 100, 148, 155
Osca, 107
Ostia, 14, 145

Padus, R., *see* Po
Palaeste, 111
Parisii, 79; *see also* Lutetia
Parthia, 75f., 109, 118, 154f., 155
Paullus, Lucius Aemilius, 90
Pedius, Quintus (Caesar's nephew), 140,
153
Pelusium, 119, 122, 124
Pergamum, 123
Petreius, 25, 106f., 131f., 134, 136
Pharnaces II, 126ff.
Pharos, 123
Pharsalus, 115f., 118, 120, 121, 124, 126,
128, 129, 131, 135, 148, 150, 155, 156
Philippi, 158
Philippus, Lucius Marcius, 58, 149
Picenum, 14, 66, 97, 99, 106
Piraeus, 145
Pisae (Pisa), 5
Piso, 38, 41, 42
Pistoria, 25
Placentia, 108

Plutarch, 26, 154, 162
Po, R., 11, 40, 103, 144
Pollio, 48, 164
Pompeia, 12, 26
Pompeius, Cnaeus (jun.), 118, 121, 131,
134, 135, 140ff., 156
Pompeius Magnus, Cnaeus (Pompey), 6,
12, 14, 15–6, 20f., 23, 24, 27, 28, 32–3,
34f., 37–42, 43ff., 55, 56, 57–61, 64f.,
69f., 74–77, 83, 87, 88–92, 94, 96ff.,
99f., 102–8, 109, 111, 114ff., 117–9,
120, 121f., 124, 125–8, 129ff., 135,
136, 137, 138, 148, 155, 157, 159ff.
Pompeius, Sextus, 118, 131, 134, 135,
141, 142
Pompeius Trogus, *see* Trogus
Pontine Marshes, 145
Pontus, 7, 9, 15, 124, 126f., 135f.
Porcia, 156
Porcius, *see* Cato
Posidonius, 53
Pothinus, 119, 121, 122, 123, 136
Ptolemais Ace, 125
Ptolemy XII the Oboe-Player, 39, 61f.,
119, 120
Ptolemy XIII, 119, 120, 122, 123, 124
Ptolemy XIV, 124, 153
Ptolemy XV, Caesar, *see* Caesarion
Ptolemy of Cyprus, 45
Puteoli, 145, 149
Pyrenees Mts., 51, 59

Quiberon Bay, 59

Rabirius, Gaius, 19f., 22, 32
Rabirius Postumus, Gaius, 39, 61f.
Ravenna, 58, 92
Red Sea, 27
Remi, 55, 74, 79
Rheims, *see* Durocortorum
Rhine, R., 53, 62f., 65, 89
Rhodes, 119
Rhône, R., 52
Romula, *see* Hispalis
Romulus, 157
Rubicon, R., 94, 101
Rufio, 125
Rufus, *see* Caelius, Sulpicius, Vibullius

DATE DUE